UNREACHED PEOPLES:
CLARIFYING THE TASK

Harley Schreck and David Barrett, editors

MARC

Unreached Peoples Series

Edward R. Dayton and Samuel Wilson, editors

New Hope

GLOBAL EVANGELIZATION MOVEMENT
The AD 2000 SERIES

UNREACHED PEOPLES: Clarifying the Task, edited by Drs. Harley Schreck and David Barrett, is produced by MARC under the auspices of the Lausanne Committee on World Evangelization (LCWE). It is the seventh volume of MARC's "Unreached Peoples Series" and the third in "The AD 2000 Series," a cooperative publishing effort of New Hope and the Foreign Mission Board of the Southern Baptist Convention. The present volume is co-published and marketed jointly by MARC (see address below) and New Hope, P.O. Box 11657, Birmingham, AL 35202-1657.

Library of Congress No. 82-061991
ISBN 0-912552-58-1

ACKNOWLEDGEMENTS

UNREACHED PEOPLES: Clarifying the Task has been a team production, encompassing Christian workers from all parts of the world. They have guided us with their comments, their sound advice and their encouraging words. Fellow researchers at sister institutions have shared in the conceptual process which has led to what we offer in this book. Present colleagues and former co-workers of our own organizations have carried out solid work on which we have built. All were intimately involved in the production process of this volume.

Above all, we acknowledge with gratitude the authority and inspiration of the Holy Spirit, and trust that He has been at work in our hearts and minds as we have prepared these materials for the consideration and use of the Church.

As we think of individuals, the editors wish to acknowledge the many hours of labor given by World Vision staff in the preparation of the camera-ready text and in the close reading of manuscripts and proofs. You have kept us honest and on track. Thank you, good friends.

We thank David Fraser, an "elder of the tribe" when it comes to unreached peoples thinking, for allowing us to adapt his thoughts and words for our use. Pages 11 and 12 are largely based on his earlier work.

We especially want to thank Ed Dayton for his twenty years of visionary and faithful leadership in the whole area of world evangelization and unreached people research. May he continue to serve with his characteristic fervor and wisdom.

-- The Editors

FOREWORD TO THE UNREACHED PEOPLES SERIES

With considerable pleasure we put before you *UNREACHED PEOPLES: Clarifying the Task.* This is the seventh in a series begun in 1979. The initial volumes were co-edited by C. P. Wagner and Ed Dayton. Subsequent offerings have been overseen by the current series editors.

The **Unreached Peoples Series** found its genesis in the work of the International Congress on World Evangelization held at Lausanne, Switzerland in 1974. The Lausanne Committee for World Evangelization (LCWE) has carried forward the work begun so well by that congress. The Strategy Working Group (SWG), first chaired by Wagner and then by Dayton, felt the strong need to hold up the millions of people who have yet to hear the gospel in such a way that they would be known and reached by the Church. (See Appendix for more information about the LCWE.)

MARC and the SWG have pioneered the concept and data collection on "people groups," with a particular emphasis on unreached people groups. The idea has found wide acceptance and application, but there have been doubts in some quarters as to whether the concept is complete enough to cover the entire task of world evangelization. We are grateful to Harley Schreck and David Barrett for the work they have done to "clarify the task."

The two authors bring together here the **Unreached Peoples Series** and the **Global Evangelization Movement: The AD 2000 Series** sponsored by the Southern Baptists. It is a privilege to see these two series, both concerned with the significant task of world evangelization, converge in this volume.

Edward R. Dayton
Samuel Wilson

Series Editors

TABLE OF CONTENTS

Acknowledgements, i

Foreword to the Unreached Peoples Series, iii

Editors' Preface, vii

PART ONE   **CLARIFYING THE TASK:**
                                  Approaches and resources   **1**

CHAPTER I   **Two ways of understanding peoples and the process of reaching them, 3**

CHAPTER II   **A selective chronology, 43**

CHAPTER III   **Development of literature, 57**

CHAPTER IV   **Helpful resources, 65**

CHAPTER V   **Selected periodicals, 70**

PART TWO   **REACHING PEOPLES IN AFRICA:**
                                  13 case descriptions   **71**

CHAPTER VI   **Overview, 73**

CHAPTER VII   **Applied research and church growth: a Turkana example, by Edgar J. Elliston, 85**

CHAPTER VIII   **Kabyles of Algeria, 99**

CHAPTER IX   Tuaregs of Niger, 109

CHAPTER X   Komonos of Burkina Faso, by M. B. Vaillant, 121

CHAPTER XI   Nubians of Egypt, by Steve Chism, Fran Hart and Teresa Toms, 127

CHAPTER XII   Zanzibaris of South Africa, 137

CHAPTER XIII   Asians of Nairobi, Kenya, by Archie Hensley, 145

CHAPTER XIV   Indian Muslims in South Africa, 155

CHAPTER XV   Baraguyu of Tanzania, by Doug Priest, 167

CHAPTER XVI   Bassari of Senegal, by James Stanley, 177

CHAPTER XVII   Komas of Ghana, by Howard Brant, 185

CHAPTER XVIII   Konkombas of Ghana, by Ross F. Gaskin, 195

CHAPTER XIX   Aari of Ethiopia, by Brian Fargher, 203

PART THREE   REGISTRY OF THE UNREACHED   213

APPENDIX: Lausanne Committee for World Evangelization   297

EDITORS' PREFACE

In 1979, the Lausanne Committee for World Evangelization and MARC, the Missions Advanced Research and Communication Center, a division of World Vision International, inaugurated an annual series of publications called *Unreached Peoples.* Its object was to describe the variety of ministries and strategies needed to reach hitherto unreached peoples with the gospel.

In 1985, the Foreign Mission Board of the Southern Baptist Convention initiated an ongoing sequence of publications concerned with the burgeoning global evangelization movement of the 1980s. This was called *The AD 2000 Series*, and its object was to put in place basic background materials essential to the implementation of global evangelization. Both series were designed to appeal, essentially, to the entire spectrum of Christians and their organizations.

For the year 1986, these two series overlap in their interests, and the sponsoring bodies and authors have agreed to cooperate in producing this volume which presents fresh materials on the subject of reaching the peoples of the world with the gospel. In this volume, we are concentrating on origins, history, biblical mandates and methods of implementing ministries to reach peoples and people groups. The last topic has been the major interest and concern of the Unreached Peoples series since 1979.

In keeping with past practices, this year's Registry of Unreached Peoples is not intended to be a complete world listing of unreached peoples and people groups. Instead it is an illustrative, descriptive and selective listing which we hope will stimulate and encourage readers to work out their own effective ministries with unreached people groups among which they are present. One minor change in this year's Registry is that it is presented in a slightly different format, embodying two distinct typefaces (medium and bold) in one single alphabetical, country-by-country listing of people groups. The typefaces show ethnolinguistic peoples in medium and people groups defined on other than ethnolinguistic criteria in bold.

Later, we anticipate that an entire peoples database, compiled primarily by David Barrett of the Foreign Mission Board of the Southern Baptist Convention and designed to cover exhaustively ethnolinguistic peoples of the world, will be published in a separate, limited volume.

Both future publications in the *Unreached Peoples* series and Barrett's future publication in *The AD 2000 Series* volume will embody feedback, commentary, and discussion from those who are interested in this fascinating subject at the heart of the Christian world mission. For this reason, we invite you to set your thoughts, opinions, or questions on paper and send them to us.

The reader will find a variety of materials in this book. The volume begins with an essay which takes stock of current research efforts pertaining to people groups. This is set in an historical and scriptural framework, both in the text and in a chronology of major events related to the Church's effort in reaching peoples. Following are a bibliography of relevant works and a listing of resources of various types. The volume then includes case descriptions of evangelistic efforts among African people groups, illustrating what God has been doing through his Church. Last, is a revised and updated Registry of Unreached People Groups.

-- Harley Schreck
David Barrett

PART ONE

CLARIFYING THE TASK:
Approaches and Resources

Chapter 1

TWO WAYS OF UNDERSTANDING PEOPLES AND THEIR EVANGELIZATION

Introduction

> Go therefore and make disciples of all the nations, baptizing them in the name of the Father and of the Son and of the Holy Spirit, teaching them to observe all things that I have commanded you... (Matthew 28:18-19, the New King James Version)

With the words of the Great Commission on their lips, missionaries have plowed tossing seas and stepped unflinchingly into the martyr's fire. They have found in those words the source of their authority and power, the direction of their geographic thrust -- and, to a large extent, the dimensions of their task.

This Great Commission finds its roots in the responsibilities of the Old Testament covenants, and might be considered as much a "great reminder" as a "great commission" from a holistic viewpoint. It is nevertheless a new statement of Christ's purpose for his Church. It is God's renewed call to the Body of Christ to witness specifically, articulately and universally to his power in salvation.

The narrower task of gospel-proclamation is the basis of most missionary research. In this vein we offer the present volume. The Church has been faithful to Christ's command. Christianity is now found across the globe and amongst many of the world's peoples. It is our intent to present here the rationale for a further research effort which will allow us both to understand the degree to which this commandment has been followed and to understand how we, as the Church, should proceed.

Even the "narrow" mandate, however, leaves room for different perspectives. And this simple task -- to evangelize, to disciple and to teach obedience to "all the things I have commanded you" -- is seen in two different, but complementary ways, by the authors of this essay. This will be clarified farther along.

Found in different form in all four Gospels and in the Acts, and expressed in a variety of different words, the Great Commission has been accepted generally by Christians as a mandate for ministry. Its exegesis has a long and dynamic history in the story of Christian missions. Unfortunately, some of its key words have at various times been misunderstood, if not badly translated.

In the original New Testament Greek, for example, the verb "to disciple" (*matheteusate*) meant literally "to turn people into followers (or pupils)." Jerome, translator of the Vulgate, used in Latin the word *docete*, which means "to teach," or "to educate." We may call this one of the more serious errors in scripture translation from the standpoint of world evangelization. The misunderstanding arising from Jerome's translation has been perpetuated in many languages and translations, depriving the Great Commission of its life-changing edge and its emphasis on conversion, as opposed to education.

A second mandate is "to evangelize." This is a transliteration of the Greek word *evangelizo*. The most authoritative single-word translation is "to preach." It means more, however, than that. Kittel's *Theological Wordbook of the New Testament* (1932) says:

> *Euangelizesthai* is not just speaking and preaching: it is proclamation with full authority and power. Signs and wonders accompany the evangelical message. They belong together, for the Word is powerful and effective. *Euangelizesthai* is to offer salvation. It is the powerful proclamation of the good news, the impartation of *soteria* (salvation).

Clearly these two mandates are not identical nor exactly synonymous. They each underline different aspects of the overall Commission. We would do well to emphasize them both, along with the command to teach obedience to Christ's instructions.

These verbs -- especially "disciple" -- are linked to "the nations." They point to the importance of recognizing that human beings live in the context of society, and in interaction with one another. In order to see disciples appear, we must evangelize persons in their social and cultural matrices. In current terminology, used in many mission circles, this includes evangelizing **people groups**. We shall be looking at this concept, trying to discover to what extent it can be a helpful way of looking at the world.

Two Questions, Two Responses.

Almost two thousand years have passed since Jesus commissioned his followers. It is time to ask ourselves if we, as the Church and the heirs of this mandate, have really heard and obeyed him. Have all "nations" indeed been baptized? Have all "nations" indeed been taught to observe all Jesus commanded? We need to ask ourselves two questions: **How have we done?** and **What should we be doing?**

An emphasis upon either one of these two central questions will result in strikingly different -- but pleasingly complementary -- results in terms of the types of information we collect and how we go about the task of analyzing and utilizing the data to further the task of world evangelization.

An emphasis upon the first question, **How have we done?**, leads us to attempt to understand the world in **global** terms. We want to know, for the entire world's population and peoples, how far the gospel has traveled, what God has been doing, and where the Church is now found.

An emphasis upon the second question, however, **What should we be doing?**, leads us to an attempt to understand the world in **particularistic** terms. We want to know something about the progress and results of evangelization among specific people groups -- we need to understand people and how to reach them in the complexity of their social and cultural contexts.

Both these questions can be understood and answered in terms of people groups. This is not a new idea. The task of world evangelization has been approached before from this perspective. There is clear scriptural, as well as historical, precedent for the idea of peoples or people groups and the desire to understand them in their social and cultural contexts. But before making reference to these approaches, it may be helpful to lay down some definitions which will guide the development of this essay.

A **people** is here defined as "a human population with a common language, shared ethnicity, and significant patterns of social interaction."

A **people group** in this chapter is understood to be "a significantly large sociological grouping of individuals who perceive themselves to have a common affinity for one another. From the viewpoint of evangelization this is the largest possible group within which the gospel can spread without encountering barriers of understanding or acceptance."

By **unreached** we mean "a people or people group among which there is no indigenous community of believing Christians with adequate numbers and resources to evangelize the rest of its members without outside (cross-cultural) assistance."

The contemporary interest in unreached peoples and people groups has a long record of antecedents. The Scriptures are rich in references to peoples, nations, tribes and other types of social groupings. These are keys to understanding the way God dealt with the world in the growth of the early Christian Church.

Scriptural Precedents. There are several places in the Bible where Jesus gives the Church the imperative to evangelize the world (Mark 16:15, John 20:20, Acts 1:8). Yet, in only two of them (Matthew 28:19, Luke 24:47) is it explicitly expressed as encompassing *panta ta ethne*, i.e., all of the *ethne* (plural), peoples. In both cases, *ethnos* is used in an inclusive, non-technical way. The commission is to evangelize Israel as well as all the gentiles of the world.

Implications of the Scriptures for the people or people group approach to evangelism are found in I Corinthians 9:1-23, but especially verse 22b: "I have become all things to all men, that I might by all means save some." Paul explicitly mentions four groups for whom he deliberately adjusted his lifestyle and message presentation in order to gain a hearing and if possible their allegiance: Jews, those under the Law, those outside the Law, and the weak. This point is that winning "the more" (vs. 19) involves discovery and eliminating whatever offends or confuses (so far as lifestyle, message presentation, methodology) and enhancing what will maximize the number of those who become obedient to the gospel.

This necessarily implies a careful knowledge of the group to whom the evangelist directs his or her ministry. What are their values, beliefs, and ways of making decisions? What adjustments must be made in methods, media, or roles if there is to be a culturally authentic opportunity to respond to the gospel?

Paul is an example. He let his audience determine his mode of evangelism. He understood that evangelism would be effective only if the particular attributes of receptor groups were understood and carefully respected. What he preached was always the same: Christ crucified and Christ risen from the dead. But how he preached it, what words he chose, the approach he used, and the lifestyle he lived differed from group to group depending upon which people he sought to reach.

Thus, there is a certain scriptural precedent for evangelizing persons in terms of peoples or people groups. The Scriptures do not claim that this is the only way the task might be approached. Yet, it seems clear that Jesus himself stated our task in these terms. Paul developed his missions strategy along these lines. Seeing the world in terms of peoples or people groups is an effective approach to the basic task of world evangelization.

History of Evangelization in Terms of Peoples and People Groups. We are all familiar with the Table of the Nations given in Genesis 10. This presents a fascinating picture of the world of peoples as it existed a few thousand years ago at the beginning of recorded history. It shows us that the Hebrews' knowledge of their surrounding world was wide ranging. This Table lists 70 nations or peoples, such as the Canaanites,

Jebusites, Amorites, and so on, many of whom are known from recent archaeological investigations.

This way of looking at the populations of the world has secular precedents as well as religious. In the year 58 BC, Julius Caesar painstakingly amassed data and information on the ethnography and statistics of the peoples of Gaul. Then in ten years of the Gallic wars, he was able, based on his superior knowledge of peoples and their interrelationships, to defeat them utterly and bring his campaign to a successful conclusion.

Many church leaders and Christian strategists have also used this concept. The story is rich, but lengthy. It is reflected in the "Selective Chronology of Reaching Peoples and People Groups" in Chapter 2 of this book.

During the 20th century, interest in defining and targeting the unreached populations of the earth has often surfaced, and has led to immediate missionary action. Thus in 1929, the director of the China Inland Mission surveyed China's remaining unreached sectors and issued a call for 200 evangelists to reach the nation's unreached people "within two years!"

A decade earlier, in 1916, Christians in Britain who were concerned for world evangelization, founded the World Dominion Movement, which in 1924 was renamed "Survey Application Trust." They published a long series of missionary surveys, giving information on peoples, groups and languages in unreached countries of the world. One of the best known of these missionary authors was Kenneth G. Grubb, who 30 years later began his 1948-1967 series, the *World Christian Handbook*.

Another pioneer was Lesley Brierley of the Worldwide Evangelisation Crusade. He was one of the earlier Protestant missionary researchers of the modern era. He is known for his world surveys, called the "Black Spot" series because of his method of depicting unreached areas on maps. He popularized

C.T. Studd's "remaining unevangelized peoples" as "RUP's." Meanwhile, Pierce Beaver and the Missionary Research Library were performing similar services for the Protestant community on the American side of the Atlantic, and more recent discussions of the concept can be found in *Missiology*, the *International Bulletin of Missionary Research* and EMQ (*Evangelical Missions Quarterly*).

The emphasis on evangelizing persons in their social and cultural contexts thus is not new. Nevertheless, there has been an increasing interest in "unreached peoples" in recent years. The term "unreached," as opposed to "unevangelized," was first used in a report prepared by MARC for the International Congress on World Evangelization held at Lausanne in 1974. For a complete description of MARC's role in the development of the people group concept, see Ed Dayton's 1983 article, "*Reaching the Unreached: a Status Report*," as found in the 1983 volume of the Unreached Peoples series.

Supporting this renewed emphasis are the endeavors of a whole network of Christian research centers in a fair number of countries. These centers have collected data concerning people groups, the Church, and evangelization among populations large and small. Among other things, this effort has produced the six earlier volumes in this *Unreached Peoples* series, as well as the present volume and the large number of other publications and resources listed in Chapters 2 and 3.

A number of missions and churches have focused on unreached peoples and people groups in their planning for missions and evangelistic undertakings. This again has called for sizable research operations.

An American pentecostal denomination, the International Church of the Foursquare Gospel, set a goal in the early 1980s of beginning evangelistic work in 100 new unreached people groups by the year 1990. They have already passed that goal.

This effort has been guided by a well-grounded research program.

Youth With a Mission (YWAM) has embarked on an ambitious effort to incorporate comprehensive research in support of its ministry around the world. This includes a sizable emphasis on reaching unreached people groups.

Peoples and People Groups reached in the 1980s. The chronology demonstrates how, at a number of points throughout the 20th century, surveys of unreached peoples and people groups have been made and published. In most cases, maps and statistics were used and the unreached peoples of the world were clearly depicted. In most cases, too, they galvanized readers into some kind of new missionary initiatives. This is a long process, however, and so the original authors were seldom able to demonstrate that hitherto unreached peoples were being decisively reached as a result of the new endeavors.

We may well ask the same question in 1986. For the past 15 years, the Christian public has been informed about the situation of unreached peoples and people groups and has been urged to support their evangelization. Materials on the subject have multiplied since the International Congress on World Evangelization (1974). Inevitably, people are asking what progress has resulted in the 12 years since. The missionary public wants to know, what has happened to those peoples? Has anybody in fact undertaken their evangelization? Have any such peoples subsequently been reached?

The case descriptions in this volume illustrate stories of such achievement. Two in particular, those reporting on work among the Baraguyu and Turkana, have direct connections to the rising effort in identifying unreached peoples and people groups and developing evangelistic strategies to reach them. The Registry also reflects progress which has been made. If the reader compares it with earlier registries, changes will be noted. Some changes are surely due to evangelistic efforts. Yet, a systematic study of progress made has yet to be carried out. It is clearly a research priority.

Clarifying the Confusion: Two Ways of Understanding Groups

An honest appraisal of the research task with regard to unreached peoples and people groups and a recognition that there are two components of this task allow us to clarify the apparent confusion concerning these efforts. One component is to look at the task globally. The other is to look at its particulars. Global and particularistic ways of looking at the world of peoples result in very different definitions of basic concepts and constructions of research designs.

The **global way** of looking requires a unit of analysis which allows us to count every person in the world once and only once. This means that the groups so defined must be discrete; no person can belong to more than one group at a time (adherents of this approach, however, do recognize that individuals can be multilingual or claim identity in more than one group). These criteria are essential because they then allow us to say definitively how far the gospel has traveled throughout the world.

There are any number of ways in which this can be done. We could divide the world into males and females. This is both a scriptural statement and is supported by our observations of the world. We would define two groups and the task would be done. Yet, the level of detail would not be very helpful for our purposes. Also, we would probably agree that such a division does not make much sense in terms of Matthew 28. Male and female are significant social (as well as biological) facts, but they hardly provide the type of group upon which we could measure world evangelization.

One division of the peoples of the world which **does** make sense for this purpose in these terms is based on ethnicity, language, and political boundaries. This would give us a database which meets our criteria. Unfortunately, ethnicity is not completely tidy. Although the vast majority of the world's population claims a single ethnic identity, a smaller proportion claims multiple ethnic identities. Boundaries of ethnicity change and overlap. Again, many persons are multilingual. However, these characteristics can give us what we want if we make certain assumptions, including that there is a most central ethnicity with which each person identifies and that we can identify one specific home language (or mother-tongue) for each person. This approach then gives us the type of global partitioning we need.

With the **particularistic way** of looking at people groups we are more interested in understanding a group in the context of its social and cultural life. There is little need to concern oneself with building a data file which counts or includes every person in the world. There is no reason to attempt any discrete partitioning of the world. Individuals can be part of a number of groups at the same time. We define these as **people groups**.

What is important in this approach is to base our research on groups which are suitable for the ministry objectives with which we are concerned. The process of evangelization has many components. Proclamation and church planting are certainly at the core. Yet, works of mercy and discipling are also elements in a Christian response to the world and a sign of Christ's presence.

For example, if our ministry is meeting basic human needs, a people group of interest may be "Prostitutes in Bangkok." Given the reality of the patterns of economic and moral bondage in which these persons are trapped, a church made up of prostitutes is a contradiction in terms. Yet, if we can address the financial, social, and spiritual bondage of these persons, we will prepare the way for them to see Christ. We will build bridges out of this lifestyle and into the Church or establish new churches with different and redeeming social and financial structures for all those related to the trade in prostitution.

Thus, the particularistic approach requires a quite different research design from the global approach. We repeat: both are essential for the overall task of world evangelization. Let us now consider these in more depth by examining in detail the contents of our Registry of Unreached Peoples and People Groups.

Two Kinds of Peoples

Looking at the Registry, we should first remind ourselves that it is illustrative and is not intended to be comprehensive or all-encompassing. The goal of the Unreached Peoples Program of MARC since its inception has been to work toward the development of strategies for ministry along the lines of the particularistic approach. On the other hand, Dr. Barrett, one of the authors, will soon produce a comprehensive listing of ethnolinguistic peoples, to the extent that it is possible in fulfillment of the global research design.

The present Registry illustrates a twofold division of peoples and people groups into:

(1)   ethnolinguistic **peoples,** and

(2)   sociologically defined **people groups.**

If we examine the Registry we find it reflects the patterns of interest in the subject on the part of Church workers and missionaries in the various countries of the world over the last

14 years. Note that it only lists 116 of the total 243 countries in the whole world. No unreached people groups have been reported from the remaining 127 countries. Many of the latter are very small territories, or perhaps there are no unreached people groups. Yet, it may well be that Christians in these countries have not yet caught the vision of evangelistic strategies tuned to cultural and social settings, and so have not responded to requests for people group information.

Let us have a closer look at the two types of peoples and people groups in the Registry.

1.   **Ethnolinguistic Peoples**

The first category of peoples refers to ethnic and ethnolinguistic peoples found within the countries. An example is: Moroccan Arabs in France. All peoples in this category are shown in the Registry in medium type, that is, the lighter of the two typefaces we employ. They are unreached peoples in the sense that they have no indigenous evangelizing church, or at any rate none strong enough to continue the evangelization of their own people without outside aid. To give our Registry some degree of objectivity, we have included only peoples among whom church members number less than 20 percent of the population. In this way, we hope to identify those peoples which present the greatest priority in terms of evangelism - we are not claiming a new definition of unreached.

The reader will immediately notice that in 35 of the countries listed, all the people groups listed are ethnolinguistic, with no sociologically defined people groups shown. These are: Angola, Benin, Bhutan, Burkina Faso, Burundi, Chad, Comoros, Fiji, Gambia, Ghana, Greece, Guinea, Guinea Bissau, Kampuchea, Kuwait, Liberia, Libya, Malawi, Maldives, Mali, Mauritania, Mongolia, Morocco, Namibia, Niger, Oman, Paraguay, Reunion, Sierra Leone, Sikkim, Surinam, Togo, USSR, Venezuela, and South Yemen.

This does not mean, however, that these countries contain no unreached persons which might make up sociologically defined people groups, but only that none have been reported. One reason for this omission is as follows. The researchers and observers in those countries who have assisted this inquiry over the last 14 years have reported only ethnolinguistic groups to us. In some of these countries, ethnic diversity is marked, and the ethnolinguistic way of seeing peoples is often regarded by those reporting as most significant.

A second reason for the omission of non-ethnic groups in these 35 countries is the lack of detailed data. For example, the USSR certainly needs to be understood both in terms of ethnicity and other factors--even if only in its urban areas. The fact that no sociologically defined groups are listed reflects a current gap in our knowledge for the USSR. This is true for a number of other countries.

In the other 81 countries listed in the Registry, however, researchers and observers have seen and described large numbers of sociologically defined people groups, and certain countries, notably Canada and the USA, have reported almost exclusively in terms of these groups. In many of these countries, with their high degrees of industrialization and urbanization, the ethnolinguistic way of seeing peoples has become less significant. In general, the social forces of urbanization and industrialization add social and cultural factors to ethnicity in the structuring of interaction and the formation of social groups.

2. Sociologically Defined People Groups

Our second category embraces a whole series of social groupings which we characterize by such terminology as socioeconomic, sociopolitical, sociogeographical, and socioreligious. It includes groupings based on residence, class, caste, career, nationality, leisure, travel, clubs, societies, industrialization, and so on. We can divide this broad category into ten major subdivisions. Obviously, these groupings are not mutually exclusive; there are instead many overlapping categories. Not only does this mean that numbers of people groups could well be classified under more than one of our ten subdivisions--it also means that large numbers of individuals can belong at the same time to two, three, four, or even more of these groups at the same time.

In the Registry, all of these social groupings are shown in **boldface** type to help the reader recognize them.

By contrast with ethnolinguistic peoples, we need to note that these types of social groups have an unreached status which must often be thought of in a somewhat different way than the presence of an indigenous evangelizing church made up exclusively of members of one particular group. Sociologically defined groups are often "unreached" in the sense that they are made up of individuals who have not yet been evangelized. There exist social, political and cultural factors which impede the effective communication of the gospel to members of these groups by those with a desire to reach them. The goal may be the establishment of a church in their midst. Yet, often it may be to evangelize the members of the group with the goal of drawing them into pre-existing churches. The crucial task is to develop effective evangelistic strategies which surmount social, political and cultural barriers to hearing the gospel. Which goal is chosen will depend upon results of further research into the particular case.

The ten subdivisions will now be described. As in the Registry itself, names of specific people groups whom we list here by way of description will be shown in **boldface** type. We add in parentheses after each (or in an adjacent column) the country under which each is classified.

(1)   **Sociolinguistic groups.**

Some groups are broader than simply ethnolinguistic, in that they cover a variety of second- and third-language speakers and might, in fact, subsume a number of ethnicities. An example would be:

English-speakers in Guadalajara   (Mexico)

(2)   **Sociogeographical groups.**

By this term we mean groups which may be either ethnolinguistic or some form of social grouping such as socioeconomic, but which are restricted geographically to areas or regions smaller than their country as a whole. This is usually a city, town, major civil division, e.g. province or lesser area. Examples in the Registry are:

Aborigines in Brisbane	(Australia)
Americans in Geneva	(Switzerland)
Bengalis in London	(UK)
Chicanos in Denver	(USA)
Coloureds in Eersterust	(South Africa)
Expatriates in Riyadh	(Saudi Arabia)
Hazara in Kabul	(Afghanistan)
Indo-Canadians in Vancouver	(Canada)
Japanese in Sydney	(Australia)
Metis settlements	(Canada)
Rural Javanese	(Indonesia)

(3)   **Sociopolitical groups.**

Next are groups which are defined politically in that they have collectively suffered adverse political circumstances. This includes people groups who have been forcibly repatriated against their will:

Sudanese repatriates	(Sudan)
Zimbabwean repatriates	(Zimbabwe)

By far the major kind of such groups are refugees. These are peoples who have been forced out of their homes and territories, or have fled from political repression or chaos. They have had to flee either externally to other countries or internally elsewhere within their own countries. Examples:

Hmong refugee women	(Thailand)
Refugee doctors	(Hong Kong)
USSR Kirghiz refugee shepherds	(Pakistan)

Once again, the Registry is merely illustrative, since the world's 20 million refugees can certainly be classified into several thousand more people groups than we list here.

(4)　**Socioreligious groups.**

We refer here to people groups whose identity is best defined by either religion, religion plus ethnolinguistic terminology, or by religion plus geographical area. These are so interesting that we list here a large selection from our Registry:

Ahmadis in Lahore	(Pakistan)
Alawites	(Syria)
Baha'is in Teheran	(Iran)
Bengali Sufis	(Bangladesh)
Brahmins in Tirunelveli	(India)
Dawoodi Muslims	(India)
Druzes	(Israel)
Hindus in Andhra Pradesh	(India)
Jains	(India)
Jews in Winnipeg	(Canada)
Khojas (Aga Khan)	(India)
Muslims	(Albania)

Parsis	(India)
Rajneeshees of Oregon	(USA)
Rastafarians in Edmonton	(Canada)
Rural Vodun believers	(Haiti)
Secret society members	(Singapore)
Sikhs in Toronto	(Canada)
Soka Gakkai believers	(Japan)
Targumic-speaking Jews	(Israel)
Yezidis	(Iraq)

Although it might seem that these groups are permanently unreached, religious identification can be, and often is, a cultural fact as much as a personal belief and practice. It is debatable whether, in many senses, a Jewish person ceases to be Jewish upon conversion to Christianity. Or does a Muslim in the Zanzibari people group lose all ties to his or her former community members? A person may be a Christian and yet continue to identify and participate with his or her religiously defined community. Thus, we have evangelists in Islamic groups working toward the establishment of Christian mosques and groups like Jews for Jesus attempting to form messianic synagogues. Whether or not a socioreligious group is unreached depends upon the meaning of religious identification and how that changes upon conversion, and on the ability of converts from the group to reach them. Essentially, this is a research question and will vary from situation to situation.

(5) **Socioeducational groups.**

By this subdivision we refer to school children, pupils, college students, and university students who live in a community that is so tightly knit that it can be considered to be a "real" group. Because of the age segregation implied here we also include groups defined by age alone. These include youth groups, and a whole variety of other age groups including old age pensioners, senior citizens, and so on. In the Registry, we note particularly:

Chinese students	(Australia)
High school students	(Hong Kong)
Pension students in Madrid	(Spain)
Tertiary level youth	(Iran)
University students	(China)
Youth in Toronto Peanut District	(Canada)

(6) Socioeconomic groups: the poor.

There are many poor people in the world. Relatively speaking the large majority are financially deprived. However, in some situations the results of poverty have special significance for political disenfranchisment or loss of privilege. Thus, we have chosen to create two categories of socioeconomic groups, one for poor and one for elites.

Favelados in Rio de Janeiro	(Brazil)
Harijans (Scheduled Castes)	(India)
Metro Manila poor	(Philippines)
Shopping bag women in Toronto	(Canada)
Slum dwellers in Madras	(India)
Squatters in Manila	(Philippines)
Street people in Victoria	(Canada)
Tramps in Malang	(Indonesia)
Wandering homeless	(USA)

(7) Socioeconomic groups: elites.

Even though enmeshed in a common socioeconomic system with the poor, the rich and privileged demand special ministry approaches and are distinct enough to be categorized as a type of people group. It is no surprise that Jesus specifically identified the rich as those with the greatest difficulty in following him. Indeed, this might be one of the greatest resistant "peoples" of the earth! In this category, the Registry notes:

Cebu middle class	(Philippines)
Copacabana apartment dwellers	(Brazil)
Middle class in Mexico City	(Mexico)
Patels (a commercial caste)	(India)
Upper class of Lima	(Peru)
Urban elite Haitians	(Haiti)
Urban elites in Bogota	(Colombia)
Urban Mestizos	(Ecuador)

(8)   Sociomedical groups.

In this subdivision are listed people groups comprising the handicapped, sick, mentally ill, hospitalized, blind, lepers, and deaf. These all deserve special approaches. Examples are:

Blind	(Philippines)
Deaf Japanese	(Japan)
Ex-mental patients in Hamilton	(Canada)
Handicapped	(Singapore)
Lepers of central Thailand	(Thailand)

(i)   Sociodeviant groups.

This includes those persons practicing behaviors far enough outside the norms of mainstream society to be considered deviant. By this we are not, of course, condemning or passing ethical judgments--it is simply an aid to our thinking and therefore our planning to assist such persons. Indeed, there might be cases, like Urban Street Women in the United States, where the social and cultural system is "deviant", in a moral sense, in that it fails to prescribe the adequate care and housing needed to help these women live in a humane way. In our Registry they include:

Dead end kids in Amsterdam	(Netherlands)
Deviant youth in Taipei	(Taiwan)
Drug addicts in Sao Paulo	(Brazil)
Gays in San Francisco	(USA)
Homosexuals	(Canada)
Prisoners	(Korea)
Prostitutes in Abidjan	(Ivory Coast)
Urban street women	(USA)
Western alienated youth	(India)

The potential list is endless.

(10)   **Socio-occupational groups.**

We should not be surprised to find that our final subdivision is by far the largest of all. Each of these groups, we remind ourselves, are identity groups in which members have an affinity for each other and are characterized by significant patterns of social interaction such that ministry is most effective when directed to them as specific people groups. To demonstrate the rich proliferation and diversity of approaches which are possible when we direct ministry toward occupational or professional groups.

Baguio area miners	(Philippines)
Barbers in Tokyo	(Japan)
Becak drivers in Bandung	(Indonesia)
Bus drivers in South Korea	(Korea)
Bus girls in Seoul	(Korea)
Casual laborers	(USA)
Chinese businessmen	(Hong Kong)
Chinese restaurant workers	(France)
Chinese students	(Australia)
Civil servants	(Mozambique)
Dentists in Fukuoka	(Japan)
Factory workers in Manila	(Philippines)
Farmers of the Tsugaru	(Japan)

Fishing village people	(Taiwan)
Fur trappers	(Canada)
Geishas in Osaka	(Japan)
Government officials	(Thailand)
Hotel workers in Manila	(Philippines)
Industrial workers in Yongdungpo	(Korea)
Jeepney drivers in Manila	(Philippines)
Korean Army personnel	(Korea)
Laborers	(India)
Malay construction workers	(Malaysia)
Military officers	(Ecuador)
Military personnel	(Ecuador)
Moroccan peddlers in Naples	(Italy)
Nurses in St. Louis	(USA)
Oil executives in Calgary	(Canada)
Police	(Hong Kong)
Professionals in La Paz	(Bolivia)
Pro hockey players	(USA)
Sekah Laut fishermen	(Indonesia)
Tamil plantation workers	(Malaysia)
Tea garden workers	(India)
Theater arts performers	(Canada)
Turkana fishing community	(Kenya)
Turkish workers	(Belgium)
Vietnamese fishermen	(USA)
West Indian migrant workers	(Canada)
Women laborers	(Taiwan)

This final listing concludes our analysis of the rich human mosaic described in the Registry. As stated earlier, we could, almost without limit, add further such groups. Consider taxi drivers, for example. Many of the world's 3,000 plus metropolises with over 100,000 in population have at least one community of taxi or cab drivers. The larger megacities may each have several hundred such groupings - often in Two-Thirds World cities, taxi drivers are clearly further subdivided into distinct rival ethnolinguistic groups. Thus, there could well be over 10,000 people groups in these cities consisting entirely of taxi drivers, cab drivers, operators of pedicabs and rickshaws. Whether each of these groups would be significant in terms of ministry would depend on the specific situations. Indeed, in some cities there may be very little sense of common identity amongst taxi drivers and marginal degrees of social interaction. Thus, no real groups and no significant barriers to the communication of the gospel would be found. In these cases, there would be little justification for defining people groups made up of taxi drivers.

Within each city there are hundreds of additional major occupational or professional groupings, and no doubt hundreds of groups in our other nine subdivisions listed above from (1) to (10). Furthermore, many such groups can be variously defined or delimited. The definition of people groups depends on one's ministry purposes and foci.

The net worldwide total of all such sociologically defined people groups in existence today is probably huge. This presents a massive challenge to the churches to adjust their thinking to minister effectively to these types of people groups. It goes without saying, that one should not attempt to total such groupings per country on a worldwide scale to list exhaustively all unreached people groups, since the resulting totals will mean little or nothing. As a method of ministry it may be regarded as a major breakthrough which, though certainly present in many and diverse ways in the earlier centuries of Christian mission, does not appear to have had such clear articulation until the second half of the 20th century.

A Problem Area: Homogenous Groups.

Both the global and particularistic approaches are subject to criticism due to their insistence upon people groups as units of analysis. This comes from the perception that the people group approach shares close historical and conceptual affinity with the Church Growth Movement as developed by the School of World Mission at Fuller Theological Seminary, Pasadena, California. The Church Growth Movement's central assumption is that churches should be planted in homogeneous units--defined by ethnicity, class and so forth. The intent of this is to allow persons to become Christians without crossing racial, linguistic, or class barriers.

The assumption is based upon the simple observation that people prefer to have the gospel communicated to them in a way that respects their cultural and social contexts.

A number of objections have been raised concerning this homogeneous unit principle and applied by extension to the unreached peoples group approach. The homogeneous unit principle has been challenged as racist and divisive to the true or universal Body of Christ, which welcomes into its fellowship all peoples, races and classes without distinction. Rene Padilla, in one of the most articulate critiques of the homogeneous unit principle (1982), claims that there is no biblical justification for its use in church growth. He argues that it allows a missiology based upon the social sciences, not upon Scripture. The Church should be the "new humanity" created by Christ--not the broken humanity cowed and fractured by racism or division into class or caste.

When written from a South African perspective, the critique becomes even sharper. David Bosch, et al., argue that the Church Growth Movement bases its theology on the same German school of theology as that which formed the rationale for the racially segregated churches in South Africa (1985).

These objections alert us to possible dangers in advocating the evangelization of people in groups. Yet, the objections seem to be based upon questionable social science and unconvincing reading of Scripture. They form an inadequate basis for effective evangelization, ministry, or development. It is clear that

Christ calls us all to him, in the process ideally erasing any barriers or fractures which divide and keep us from knowing each other as brothers and sisters. There can be no doubt that Christ's ultimate purpose is to have us become one in him, even as he is one with God.

Unity is Christ's ultimate purpose. This is the eschatological reality of the Church. How is this to be realized? It is to be realized by peoples being impacted by the gospel. How are they impacted by the gospel? They are impacted in their social and cultural contexts. This brings us to a great mystery traceable back to God. He created us in his image--a thinking, sensing, perceiving image. Furthermore, he created us to live in community as social beings. Community can take the form of people groups, cultures, nations--*panta ta ethne*, in fact.

So then, what have we said? God created humans as cultural beings--beings in community and people in relationships. Cultures are gifts from God in that he created us as cultural beings. It is with the cultural lens that we understand the gospel and each other. The Church is formed with cultural tongs and hammers. It is to the person in community, in culture, that we must speak if we are to communicate the gospel.

The problem comes when cultural, racial, ethnic or class divisions are the bases of injustices perpetrated upon humans by other humans. What has gone wrong? Sin can taint even God-given gifts. Sex is an example of that. What does this say about ethnic, cultural, or other so-called "homogeneous" churches? What it says is that such churches can be sinful. They can be racist. They can be supportive of unjust power inequalities.

This brings us to a difficult but vital distinction. People groups are not necessarily homogeneous units. To evangelize, to bring the good news of Jesus Christ to all, might mean that the people group most appropriately defined for the purposes of evangelism would include class divisions or other forms of divisions due to structural injustices. It might be multiethnic. It might be multilingual (a trade language could be the most appropriate linguistic medium of the Church). The definition of a people group appropriate to one's ministry must be considered prayerfully and carefully with full knowledge of the local situation. Fast changing realignments of ethnicity or institutionalized patterns of injustices might require non-homogeneous peoples to be our concern for ministry. In the former case, effective evangelization would be to an audience which is multiethnic. In the latter, the need to confront injustice and evangelize in a way that allows people to see Jesus Christ in his full truth would require ministering to a people group fractured by class or other types of division. The most appropriate people groups for the purposes of evangelism are often, but not always, "homogeneous."

Thus, it must be admitted that the homogeneous unit principle can lead to ungodly patterns of Church planting and growth. Yet, outright rejection of the "principle" does not bear witness to either God's creation and gift of culture or the realities one faces in social and cultural life.

In sum, objections to the central assumption of the homogeneous unit principle have not harmed the people group approach. For one, people groups are not always homogeneous units. Furthermore, if it is the whole gospel which is being communicated, an unjust or racist status quo will be challenged by it. Even as Christ freely gives us his presence, his presence calls us to change. The people group approach is not a rationale for racist and unjust churches. It is an agenda for bringing to a people group the good news of Jesus Christ--all of the good news with all of its implications. For years, proponents of the homogeneous unit principle have made a similar defense.

Let us now consider the two ways of understanding people groups and their implications in more depth.

Global Research Design

The global approach to reaching peoples derives from the need to know the overall status of mission in every part of the world. It has parallels in government, industry, commerce, economics, finance, military circles, and just about every sphere concerned in one way or another with the entire world and its populations. Thus, the United Nations organization has some 43 major global agencies, each of which compiles and keeps up-to-date a computerized database detailing the status of its concerns across the globe.

For our purposes, the global approach is exemplified by the Global Mission Database being developed by the Foreign Mission Board, Southern Baptist Convention (later to be shared with all other concerned Christian organizations). It starts with data from secular databases. Then religious and Christian data is added so as to understand the global situation with regard to Christianity and the Christian mission.

The world is first divided by listing and describing the world's 243 countries. These are the continental areas standardized by the U.N.

Next, a whole variety of national variables, in particular demographic ones, are added. These are derived from sources such as the U.N.'s published database which gives populations and projections for the years AD 1950-2025 for every country on earth--population, annual increase, fertility, mortality, life expectancy and so on. Other sources specialize in economic data, health, literacy, food, agriculture, communications, broadcasting and the like.

The next step is to subdivide the continental areas. One way is into MCDs (major civil divisions)--the USA with its 50 States, the USSR its 15 Republics, China its 22 Provinces, and so on. Each MCD has its own area, population and demographics projected to AD 2025.

A second division of the world's population is into rural dwellers and urban dwellers, and within the latter, metropolis dwellers (persons living in the world's 3,000 plus metropolises of over 100,000 population, each of which is named and described in the database). Again, these city populations are projected to AD 2025.

Then the world is segmented into its 100 or so component religions, and Christianity into its 21,000 component denominations.

The next stage is the significant one for our subject in this book. Constituent ethnolinguistic groups--a world total of 14,000 ethnic groups (peoples) speaking 7,000 different mother tongues are identified within each country. The variables for each people are population and related demographic factors, autoglossonym (people's own language name) and related linguistic factors, scripture translation and distribution, Christian broadcasting, and a whole range of variables measuring Church membership, churches, denominations, Christian institutions, service agencies, full-time workers, ministries of all kinds, evangelistic endeavors, and various measures of the status of evangelization.

Graphic and geographic dimensions are necessary.

A final dimension is time, enabling us to study the development of any of these variables over time.

These variables can be analyzed comparatively in ways likely to yield insights into the past and present status of world evangelization, as well as a series of alternate futures (possible scenarios) concerning how global evangelization might proceed. Every year an updated report concerning a selection of 70 or so of these global variables is published in the January issue of the *International Bulletin of Missionary Research.*

In the near future, results from this global analysis will be presented as it relates to reaching unreached peoples.

Particularistic Research Design

The *Unreached Peoples* series, 1979-1984, generated as part of the Unreached Peoples Program, a ministry of MARC, and sponsored by the Lausanne Committee for World Evangelization, has been an example of the particularistic approach to people groups.

This approach argues that to evangelize effectively we must think in terms of the people groups which are appropriately defined for particular forms of ministry. That is, we need to consider (1) patterns of interaction and communication, (2) shared values and understanding of proper behavior, (3) and the way in which individuals see their social world in terms of people groups. This approach is thoroughly grounded in scriptural principles, the insights of sociology and anthropology, and the practice of missionaries, communicators, development workers, and others involved in identifying and responding to the needs of human populations.

There has been a significant amount of controversy and confusion associated with this approach over the last ten years. Although a fair number of missiologists and mission executives have assisted in its development, others still hold major reservations about this approach. The primary area of difficulty centers on the definition of people group.

If one accepts the central argument of the people group approach which states that evangelizing the world in people groups is not only expedient but biblical, then the question of what is a "people group" must be carefully addressed. The answer is not obvious.

In the Unreached Peoples Program a "people group" has been defined as:

> ". . . a significantly large sociological grouping of individuals who perceive themselves to have a common affinity for one another. From the viewpoint of evangelization this is the largest possible group within which the gospel can spread without encountering barriers to understanding or acceptance."

Note the emphasis on the spread of the gospel. Ultimately, the definition depends on the development of strategy for evangelism.

A Problem Area: Sociologically Defined People Groups. Nothing has occasioned more comment or criticism in recent years than the insistence of the Unreached Peoples Program upon including groups other than ethnolinguistic as people groups. There are a number of reasons for this reaction. For one, the concept of culture or ethnicity has already found a permanent home in the worldview of many missiologists and church executives. Other legitimate ways in which people groups are formed have not been understood to the same degree.

There seems to be an implicit belief that only ethnicity defines meaningful or scripturally relevant groups among humans. We maintain that this is not the nature of social life. Ethnicity is not the only basis upon which social life is constructed. It is certainly very important, but anthropological and sociological literature give abundant illustrations of the salience of other social and cultural factors in terms of social interaction and group formation. Especially in the city, with its high levels of heterogeneity and social complexity, there are multiple ways in which persons sort themselves into groups:

> The urban system is really a series of subsystems which at various times are discrete and localized entities and at other times widely distributed and overlapping. . . . These sub-systems are often made up of ethnic units (or parts thereof), occupational, class or political groupings. . . . Individuals and groups are simultaneously involved in the structures, activities, and objectives of many different kinds of groupings which, on the surface, may appear contradictory. . . . Thus ethnicity may conflict with class and occupational groupings, political sub-systems may clash, trade union membership may accommodate itself to government demands to the disadvantage of the rank and file. . . . Each of these sub-systems, therefore overlap. (P. Gutkind, *Urban Anthropology: Perspectives on "Third World" Urbanization and Evangelism*, 1974: 65-67).

Ethnicity is only one of many forces which shape human social life. Increasingly, it is being replaced in terms of primacy by class, residence, and occupation in the shaping of human social life. Jules-Rossette, in the 1984 monograph *Symbols of Change*, looked at two Christian sects in urban Zambia. Jules-Rossette found that although both of these sects arose in a homogeneous ethnic context, in the urban situation they had become the center of a multiethnic community of recent migrants into the city. The communities of which they were centers were defined more clearly in terms of ethnicity interacting with deliberate affiliation, shared economic and political position within the greater society, and the shared experience of recent migration, than by ethnicity alone.

The Unreached Peoples Program has documented a number of such people groups in urban situations. For example, racetrack residents on American horse racetracks made up a multiethnic people group with the clear status of being unreached prior to the formation of the Race Track Chaplaincy, Inc. These people were separated from the greater community in terms of their work schedules, characteristics perceived by the larger population, and physical isolation. Churches had not been able to minister in any effective way to these racetrack workers. A chaplaincy program and the development of effective ministry with racetrack workers changed this. This is clearly a people group defined in other than ethnic terms.

A second objection to the inclusion of non-ethnic groups in the Unreached Peoples Program has to do with whether it is appropriate to plant churches in such groups. That is, we may agree that groups defined by other than ethnicity exist and are salient in terms of interaction and communication, but still have strong reservations about using this insight as a guide for evangelization or church-planting. Warren Webster, a former missionary and chairman of the Evangelical Foreign Missions Association, states:

> Special evangelistic thrusts and even Christian fellowship groups may prove useful among taxi drivers, barbers, apartment house residents and nurses, but it is very doubtful that separate churches are either necessary or desirable for such affinity groups. In any event they do not seem to be the kind of people groups our Lord had in mind when he gave the command to disciple all nations (*panta ta ethne*) (1985:9).

Is there justification or clear scriptural support for these comments? No, not really. In the New Testament, *ethne* refers to a number of types of people groupings, even including tribes. The concept of an ethnic group is a model of a social fact. It is one of many models developed in social science for the explanation of social organization and human life. Other models include social classes and kinship groups. They explain how people interact and see each other. All would seem to have equal application for church planting in ways which are socially and culturally relevant. Scripture tells us that we are to take the gospel to all peoples--in a way that all persons can hear and respond to the message of hope. This must be done in a way that is culturally appropriate and should be done in the context of the people group. Anthropological and sociological wisdom tells us that there are many times when reliance upon ethnicity will not allow this to happen. In many situations, ethnicity is not the primary shaping force for people groups. It may be most appropriate to plant churches in other types of groups.

In addition, remembering our concern with the "whole gospel of Jesus Christ," it can be suggested that church planting is not the only form of ministry which is of relevance here. If our concern is evangelization and if the good news we bring is the total good news of the Scriptures, then we will often have to think in terms of ministry which is preliminary or supportive to church planting or incorporation in a church.

For example, there are 80,000 taxi drivers in Taiwan. These persons face significant problems and situations which have created a sense of common identity. Christian outreach to them is limited to a large degree by their work habits and by the reputation they have in the city. Is this a people group? Yes, it certainly is. The shared sense of identity and patterns of social interaction act to create a social grouping of persons with significant ties to one another. Would it be possible or even desirable to plant a church among this group? Perhaps.

A cell group within the people group itself in which we would find an emphasis on evangelism and nurturing, could certainly become a church, as has so often happened. An example would be the Church of the Lepers in Taiwan. Eventually, they could certainly become members of churches within the wider community. This indeed has been the approach of the Taxi Drivers Evangelical Fellowship in Taiwan.

A last reason for criticism of the inclusion of non-ethnic groups is the feeling that this approach does not assist us in measuring the progress made in world evangelization. There are two issues here. First, we recognize that there is great satisfaction in seeing researchers exhaustively describing the status of world evangelization. People feel that the result might well be powerful statistical analyses. In fact, we might even have in front of us some kind of final or universal solution! This provides a basis for a very strong research design. Second, a desire for research power is often combined with the theologically-based conviction which looks to the completion of the task of world evangelization as a precondition of the Lord's return. Clearly the particularistic research design does not meet these needs.

This has caused much of the concern over a perceived contradiction between the global (people) approach and the particularistic (people group) approach. It is true that the particularistic approach cannot fully address this need; this is not the intent of the approach. But, it should be clear that there is no contradiction at all. Instead, there is a difference in the foci of the research efforts, and this difference is best described in terms of complementarity. Ethnicity is a suitable unit of analysis for peoples, allowing the formation of a global research design, but it is not suitable for a particularistic research design which aims at developing ministry strategies for specific people groups. Both research designs, however, have a place in the overall effort of world evangelization.

Defining People Groups   If we take the particularistic approach to this task, what are people groups and how can we define them in operational terms?   The Unreached Peoples Program's definition captures two essential properties of people groups: (1) Members of a people group recognize one another in the sense that they are . . . "a significantly large sociological grouping of individuals who perceive themselves to have a common affinity for one another," . . . and (2) people groups are bounded in space or distinguished from the surrounding social matrix, in that . . . "from the viewpoint of evangelization this is the largest possible group within which the gospel can spread without encountering barriers to understanding or acceptance."

The first characteristic leads to an awareness of the importance of being culturally and socially sensitive as we attempt to minister to a group, i.e., the primary issue is contextualization of the gospel. A people group is a collection of persons who sense a common identity. Among those in the group there is a shared understanding about how the world is constituted, how people behave, and which things are inordinately important.

Individuals in a people group can state who is a member of the group and who is not. Outsiders can only sense this indirectly. Recognition of the fact that members of people groups share a sense of identity is essential for evangelization, as is an understanding of the social and cultural contexts of the people group, their core values and worldview.

The second characteristic of people groups leads to a concern with the recognition of group boundaries and how to minister effectively across such boundaries, i.e., it leads us to a concern for cross-cultural communication. Boundaries are germane in the discussion of cross-cultural communication. They restrict communication.

Boundaries distinguish members of a people group from surrounding peoples and groups. For example, Black Carib Indians of Central America share the same language, Garifuna, and many other cultural and social characteristics. As such, one mission strategy would seem to be appropriate for all of them. Yet, these people live in several separate nations, including Belize, Guatemala, and Honduras. Political boundaries thus separate the Black Carib Indians into a number of separate groupings. Because of the difficulty of transmission of goods or ideas among the groupings, there are actually several separate people groups. This is an important consideration for ministry. One ministry strategy will not reach all groups.

The above discussion calls us to recognize that to define people groups adequately, in the most useful sense, we must include characteristics which speak both to the identities and to the boundaries of people groups.

Measuring reached or unreached. Assuming we are able to identify our unit of analysis, people groups, what are the key variables we want to measure? The basic measure is whether or not the people group is "reached" or "unreached." This would include the degree to which its members have been made disciples, baptized, and taught to observe all of the commandments of Jesus (Matthew 28:19-20).

The way to construct a definition based upon this passage is not readily apparent. In fact, we again are confronted with the two different research tasks--one global and the other particularistic. For the global approach, a measure of reachedness which is applicable to all of the data is essential. It must be constructed once and for all to allow us to see the extent to which the gospel has traveled to all peoples.

The particularistic approach, on the other hand, needs a different method of defining reached or unreached. Our task is to suggest variables which will indicate where a people group is on the path away from or toward Christ. Variables needed to do this are of a number of different types. Variables must measure whether the Christian community in the people group is of a sufficient size relative to the size of the group to communicate the elements of the gospel effectively to the rest of the group, whether the resources of the Christian community are sufficient to allow it to evangelize effectively (this could include financial, personnel, and material resources), whether the structural position of the Christian community is such that it is effectively listened to by the rest of the people group, whether the Christian community adheres to biblical and theologically sound principles and beliefs, and last, whether the church and its practices and doctrines are truly contextualized in terms of the culture of the people itself.

These variables could then be used to **construct** measures of "reached" and "unreached." The actual construction of these measures is not necessarily or always the role of any particular research agency. Instead, if our goal is to empower the Church to do ministry, we need to provide the appropriate data needed for the Church to decide if a group is actually in need of its particular ministry. It should be clear that the determinants of reached/unreached will vary greatly from church to church.

Operation of the Particularistic Design. The Unreached Peoples Program, with its particularistic approach, is guided by the assumption that its role is to empower the Church to do the work of evangelism. That is, the ownership of the whole process of evangelism belongs in the hands of the church or mission. This means that church and mission should participate in the gathering of research data and deciding upon its use and thereby "own it."

A second assumption is that data is valuable only if it is available. That means that data should be circulated early in the research process. This may mean foregoing some of the rigor which would ensure the highest quality of data. Built into this assumption is the realization that research is an interactive process. As data is gathered and circulated, it is intended that the audience will respond with more accurate data or questions concerning the data, which will lead to better data which then can again be republished and responded to by the audience.

Essential to the research design of the Unreached Peoples Program is the continuing process of creating working partnerships between persons in the field, and researchers in home offices. The process of collecting data for the Unreached Peoples Program is essentially one of developing networks of persons who are concerned with people groups in need of the gospel. These networks are best defined by the type of people group which we are considering. For example, we try to interact with networks of persons who are interested in evangelizing Fulbe people in West Africa or an overseas Chinese people group. By interacting with these persons, we develop and maintain current data on unreached people groups.

An area of high priority is the encouragement of, and involvement in, the establishment of research centers in different parts of the world. A powerful research design would rely upon a center for research located, for example, in West Africa to cover West Africa. It makes more sense to develop the skills and to provide the training for local researchers to study the status of Christianity among people groups in West Africa than it does to develop that same facility in the United States of America.

Thus, the process employed by the Unreached Peoples Program is one of partnership. The process of collecting data aims to empower or train persons to collect data from the field. It involves centralizing the results of these efforts and then redistributing data to persons in need of it both for use and for verification. This is mainly a communications exercise. The data belong to the field, and the entire process involves the persons in the field working with the people group in question, researchers in research centers, and the Church at large in need of such information. The purpose of all this is to empower the Church to recognize the need for evangelism and to be able to develop strategies for evangelism. Such strategies would be effective and would respect the place of each element of the Church in God's overall design for reaching people groups with his message of salvation.

Summary

Thus, there is a steadily growing interest in the evangelization of peoples and people groups. Research centers around the world have collected large amounts of information toward this end. Missions and churches have announced priorities for their missionary outreach along these lines. Books and articles on the subject abound. Most importantly, the Kingdom of God has been expanded with new believers and households of faith.

There has been a general failure to recognize that we are dealing with two different ways of looking at this entire scene. These are motivated by different but complementary purposes. On the one hand there is the widespread desire and need to document, on a global scale, the status of the unfinished task of worldwide evangelization. This requires adherence to a clear definition of peoples and an adequately thought-out, accompanying research design. On the other hand there is the widespread desire and need to develop strategies to evangelize specific people groups in their cultural and social contexts. This has required a somewhat different approach to defining people groups and a quite different type of research design.

Both approaches are valid. Both approaches are needed for the task of world evangelization. The former speaks most clearly to the question, "How have we done?" The second speaks most clearly to the question, "What should we be doing?"

It should be clear that they stand in complementary relationship to one another. With these two approaches we will be in a better position to know how we have done and what we should be doing to be faithful to our Lord's Great Commission.

Chapter 2

A SELECTIVE CHRONOLOGY OF REACHING PEOPLES AND PEOPLE GROUPS

This chronology gives a small selection of dates and events on the subject of how the Church has seen, for the purposes of evangelization, the human race in terms of constituent peoples and groups. It describes in outline how the Christian approach to peoples and special populations has developed over the last two millennia up through 1986.

The selection is decidely not exhaustive and clearly reflects the backgrounds of the authors: one a British missiologist and the other an American anthropologist. It does, however, serve to reflect the fact that the Church has long used the people group approach to evangelization.

Readers are encouraged to add their own "critical events" and then to consider their roles in the ongoing task of world evangelization over the next 14 years and pray about how they might become involved.

GOD'S PLAN OF GLOBAL REDEMPTION BEGINS
(1950 BC - AD 32)

BC
1950   Beginning of divine election of a chosen People of God to be repository of ethical monotheism; call of Abraham, first Hebrew patriarch, who migrates (at age 75) from Ur of the Chaldees to Palestine ("Go: in you all the families of the Earth will be blessed," Genesis 12:1&3), dies 100 years later; son Isaac has son Jacob who has 12 sons, ancestors of Twelve Tribes of Israel.

c1270   Bible (beginning with five Books of Moses, Pentateuch) enumerates, in order to match up, two distinct entities: (1) the world of Gentile nations as harvest field (numbered at 70, in Genesis 10), and (2) the People of God as harvesters, or harvest force, or people concerned with God's harvest plans--e.g. 70 descendants of Israel (Exodus 1:5), 70 elders (Exodus 24:1), censuses in Numbers, later Jesus' Mission of the 70 (Luke 10:1), etc.

550   Israel begins to transcend its nationalistic exclusivism; aided by apocalypticism and increased contacts with other people, arrives at sense of God's mission to all peoples of the whole world; then progressively compromises its mission in the world through disobedience and unbelief.

MISSION OF JESUS SON OF GOD TO
SAVE THE WORLD'S PEOPLES (AD 33 - 497)

AD 33   Jesus' Great Commission as spiritual counterpart of Genesis 1:28 with two components of evangelizing and discipling: "Go forth to every part of the world (in Greek *cosmos*), and proclaim the Good News to the whole creation" (Mark 16:15, NEB); "Go to all peoples everywhere and make them my disciples" (Matthew 28:19, GNB); Jesus' presence from now on is the ever-present Shekinah glory.

Day of Pentecost in Jerusalem: 3,000 converted among Diaspora Jews and Gentiles from "every nation under heaven," from North Africa to Persia.

Large-scale people movement of families into the church: "More than ever believers were added to the Lord, multitudes both of men and women" (Acts 5:14).

38   After five-year period of hesitation and partial obedience to Christ's Great Commission, first Gentiles are deliberately evangelized by the Twelve Apostles.

Influx of Italians (Cohors II Italica Civium Romanorum) converted through ministry of Apostle Peter at Caesarea (Acts 10:48).

65   Prophecies of John the Divine: "I saw another angel flying high in the air, with an eternal message of Good News to announce to the peoples of the earth, to every race, tribe, language and nation" (Revelation 14:6, GNB).

66   Evangelist Luke concludes his two-volume narrative (Luke-Acts): The worlds of the Roman Empire and Judaism have now been evangelized and the gospel is now known throughout them.

c150   Justin Martyr (c100-165) founds disciple-training school over a house in Rome, and writes: "The first Apostles, twelve in number, in the power of God went out and proclaimed Christ to every race of men"; and "There is not one single race of men (probably referring to the then known world), whether barbarians, or Greeks, or whatever they may be called, nomads, or vagrants, or herdsmen dwelling in tents, among whom prayers and giving of thanks are not offered through the name of the Crucified Jesus."

c170   Portions of Scriptures translated into Coptic.

197   Tertullian (c160-222) writes: "Christ commanded them to go and teach all nations. . . . Immediately, therefore, so did the apostles;" "There is no nation indeed which is not Christian."

c220   Origen (c185-254) writes: "The gospel of Jesus Christ has been preached in all creation under heaven, to Greeks and barbarians, to wise and foolish. . . . It is impossible to see any race of men which has avoided accepting the teaching of Jesus;" "The divine goodness of Our Lord and Savior is equally diffused among the Britons, the Africans, and other nations of the world;" but also "Many people, not only barbarians, but even in the Empire, have not yet heard the word of Christ;" and "The gospel has not yet been preached to all nations, since it has not reached the Chinese or the Ethiopians beyond the river, and only small parts of the more remote and barbarous tribes."

249   Seven missionary bishops sent to peoples of Gaul by Cornelius of Rome: Gatien (Tours), Trophime (Arles), Paul (Narbonne), Saturnin (Toulouse), Denis (Paris), Martial (Limoges), Austremoine (Clermont).

287   Mass conversion of the Armenian people begins under Gregory the Illuminator (c240-332), provoking violent persecution from pagan king Tiridates II; 295, king baptized, Christianity declared state religion.

378   Jerome (c345-419) writes: "From India to Britain, all nations resound with the death and resurrection of Christ."

398   John Chrysostom (c344-407) appointed patriarch of Constantinople, founds training school for native Gothic evangelists; writes "'Go and make disciples of all nations' was not said for the Apostles only, but for us also."

c400   Scriptures being translated into Ethiopic by monks
       from Egypt.
420   An Arab tribe in Arabia is converted to Christianity
       under sheikh Aspebet.
425   Nubia: Olympiodorus of Thebes observes that the
       Bejas and Blemmyes peoples (south of first cata-
       ract) are still pagans.
c450   Conversion to Christianity becomes mainly by com-
       munities, led by their kings or princes.

CHRISTIAN FAITH REACHES PEOPLE GROUPS
THROUGHOUT ASIA AND EUROPE (AD 498 - 1500)

498   Christianity spreading widely in Central Asia, with
       whole tribes converted; Nestorians active in
       Turkestan until eliminated c1350.
520   Nestorians (Syriac evangelists) reported on island of
       Ceylon, with many converts, also in Malabar
       under a Persian bishop, in Ganges region, among
       Huns, Turks and Uighurs, in Tibet and Sumatra.
523   Massacre of 14,000 Arab Christians in Najran and
       Himyar (Arabia) by Jewish Arab king Dhu-Nuwas
       Masruq.
c540   Emperor Justinian orders that all pagan tribes on
       periphery of Byzantine empire be converted to
       Christianity; 70,000 persons forcibly baptized in
       Asia Minor.
549   Nestorian patriarch sends a bishop to Hephthalites
       (White Huns) north of Great Wall of China.
c640   Eighty percent of 6.5 million Berbers across North
       Africa (2.6 million urbanized) now Christians; but
       by 950 all become converted to Islam.
730   *Church History of the English People* compiled by
       Bede, describing conversion of Anglo-Saxon race.
c780   Forced baptism of Saxon race by Charlemagne;
       4,500 executed in one day for resisting, thousands
       more deported.

864   Baptism of Boris king of the Bulgars; 870, conversion of Bulgars, with a Bulgar consecrated as archbishop; Basil I, emperor 866-886, forces baptism on Serbs of Narenta Valley; 874, conversion of Serbs to Orthodoxy.

c900   Magyars of present day Hungary now evangelized.

c949   Fifty percent of all former Christendom now captured by Islam, including nomadic Berbers of Mauritania.

1009   Northern Mongolia: Nestorians convert and baptize prince and 200,000 Keraits (a Turkish tribe) in capital Karakorum; also Namians and Merkites.

1124   Several Cumans (Kipchak Turks) received by Stephen II of Hungary and come into contact with Christianity.

c1150 Onguts (Tartars) become Christians in central Asia.

1200   Europe entirely christianized except for Wends, Prussians, Lithuanians and other Baltic races.

c1250 Central Asia: Uighurs, Keraits, Mongols and all other major peoples partially christianized.

c1365 Komi-Perm peoples of Russia evangelized by bishop Stephen of Perm (1335-1396).

c1450 Trifo and Theodorit evangelize Kola Lapps.

1500   Newly-organized Protestant churches make little effort to contact unevangelized peoples of the world for nearly 150-200 years.

LARGE-SCALE ATTEMPTS BEGIN TO REACH OTHER NON-EUROPEAN PEOPLES (AD 1503 - 1702)

1503   Gold Coast: baptism of chief of Efutu with 1,300 subjects.

1529   Luis Bolanos, OFM works among Tucuman Indians of Argentina, converting 20,000.

1530   Many reformers, including Luther, teach that Great Commission to disciple all peoples (Matthew 28) was given to first century Apostles only and expired with them.

1536 10,000-strong Bharatha (Paraa) fishing caste of Coromandal coast (Kerala) baptized en masse by Portuguese.

1544 Xavier begins mission in Travancore, baptizes 10,000 Mukuvas in one month.

1556 Ceylon: conversion to Catholicism of 70,000 fisher-caste Careas (Karawa, Karawola) on coast near Colombo; by 1583, 43,000 Christians on Manar island among pearl-fisher Paravas and Careas.

c1580 Jesuit theologian in Peru, Jose de Acosta (1539-1600), writes *De Procuranda Indorum Salute* (*On the Preaching of the Gospel Among the Savages*), dealing with problems of reaching Amerindian peoples.

1588 Anglican parish priest Hadrian Saravia (1531-1613), at later Dean of St. Paul's, becomes one of the first non-Roman advocates of foreign missions, stressing binding validity of Matthew 28:19: "The command to preach the gospel to the Gentiles pertained not only to the age of the apostles, but to all future times to the end of the world."

1602 Dutch government sends missionaries to convert Malays in East Indies domains.

1622 Sacred Congregation for the Propagation of the Faith (Propagation, meaning progressive plantation among world's peoples) founded by pope Gregory XV (1554-1623).

1629 Matthew's Gospel printed in Malay; first evangelistic scripture portion in a non-European language.

1649 Society for the Propagation of the Gospel in New England founded, to reach Amerindians, with first missionary John Eliot; oldest Anglican missionary society.

c1650 Russian Orthodoxy reaches across Siberia to Bering Strait peoples.

1663   Justinian von Weltz (1621-1668) writes treatises to
        challenge German churches and students to mis-
        sionary work among unevangelized peoples.

1667   English poet John Milton (1608-1674) uses phrase "to
        Evangelize the Nations" in his *Paradise Lost*.

1668   Spain establishes a military garrison and Roman
        Catholic mission on Guam; most Chamorro
        people succumb to forces of disease and con-
        quest; remaining population becomes Roman
        Catholic.

1670   Bengal: 20,000 Namasudra Bengalis (outcast Hindus)
        in Dacca converted to Catholicism in two years;
        by 1677, total 30,000.

1673   First Kalmyks converted to Orthodoxy in Russia.

1701   Russia: in Middle Volga, 3,638 pagan Cheremis
        (Mari) baptized by 1705, after large-scale distribu-
        tion of gifts, tax exemption and other incentives.

1702   Filofey bishop of Tobolsk increases churches from
        160 to 448 and baptizes 40,000 Ostyaks, Voguls,
        Zyrians and Yakuts by 1721.

REACHING PEOPLES BY ORGANIZED MASS SCRIPTURE DISTRIBUTION BEGINS (AD 1710 - 1870)

1710   Canstein House printing press, Halle (Germany) with
        first Bible society (Cansteinische Bibelanstalt)
        founded by count Karl von Canstein: three
        million Bibles and New Testaments printed in 80
        years.

1736   Moravian missionaries at work among Samoyeds of
        Archangelsk.

1740   Office for Newly-Baptized opened in Svijazsk
        (Russia); from 1741-1762, mass baptisms of Volga
        pagans: 430,550 Chuvash, Cheremis, Ostyaks, et
        alii baptized; no pagans left in Middle Volga;
        1764, Office dissolved.

1743   Organized evangelization of Kamchatka begins
        under Josef Chotunceviski, including among
        Tunguz and Lamuts; most peoples soon reached
        and christianized.
1751   Ostyaks reached and evangelized up to Arctic coasts
        in region of Obdorsk.
1787   Moravian foreign mission formed: Society for
        Propagating the Gospel among the Heathen (the
        latter word meaning Gentiles, or peoples).
1792   Eight Russian Orthodox missionary monks arrive on
        island of Kodiak (Alaska), baptize 2,500 shamanist
        Eskimos in following two years, and 10,000 in
        1795.
        William Carey (1761-1834) publishes first statistical
        global survey of Christian world mission: *An
        Enquiry Into the Obligations of Christians to Use
        Means for the Conversion of the Heathens.*
1797   London Missionary Society lands first missionaries
        on Tahiti: beginning of rapid growth of church
        in Oceania characterized by Pacific Islanders and
        Euroamericans carrying the gospel from island to
        island as missionaries.
1802   USA: Massachusetts Baptist Missionary Society
        formed for "the evangelization of frontier
        communities."
1826   Massive apostasies from Russian Orthodox missions
        in Volga region: 299,300 in Kazan, 95 percent of
        14,800 new Tartar converts, 233,500 Chuvash, et
        alii.
1828   Rhenish Missionary Society (RMG) formed (Ger-
        many); begins work among Dayaks of Borneo;
        1839, first Dayak baptism.
1847   Private missionary work among Koriak and Chukchi
        in Anadyr district of Siberia by Orthodox priests.
1849   Moravian work among Miskitos of Nicaragua
        begun.

1862   Orthodox mission begun around Amur river (Siberia) among Gold and Gilyak peoples.
1870   South India: mass movement brings one million Telugu outcastes into Baptist, Lutheran and Methodist churches in 30 years.

CLIMAX OF ORGANIZED ATTEMPTS TO OBEY THE GREAT COMMISSION (AD 1897 - 1931)

1897   Fourth Lambeth Conferences: 194 Anglican bishops present; first of 14 resolutions on foreign missions passed: "We recommend that prompt and continuous efforts be made to arouse the Church to... the fulfillment of our Lord's great commission to evangelize all nations."
1903   Evangelization of Munduruccu Indians in Brazil begun by German Franciscans.
1910   World Missionary Conference, Edinburgh, in its report *Carrying the Gospel to All the Non-Christian World*, speaks of the task of reaching "peoples" and "non-Christian peoples."
1913   English missionary C. T. Studd (1862-1931), deeply impressed by *Carrying the Gospel*, founds Worldwide Evangelization Crusade to focus on evangelizing "the remaining unevangelized peoples of the earth" (RUPs).
1916   World Dominion Movement founded in Britain (1924, Survey Application Trust), publishes long series of detailed surveys of missions by countries, peoples, people groups and languages, under Anglican missionary statesman K. G. Grubb (1900-1980) and others.
1920   Philippines: Catechism of Pius X translated into Jolo-Moro (Tausug) for Muslim population of 200,000 (1.9 percent of country).
1926   Unevangelized Tribes Mission of Borneo formed (USA).

Jesuits begin work among Japanese of Brazil; first
14 Japanese baptisms, in Sao Paulo; by 1978, of
one million Japanese there, 630,000 are Catholics.

1928   Unevangelized Africa Mission founded (1947,
merged in CBFMS), also Unevangelized Tribes
Mission of Africa, both in USA.

1929   China: CIM director D. E. Hoste (1861-1946) issues
call to Europe and America for "Two Hundred
Evangelists" to China's remaining unreached
peoples, with a goal "to reach China within two
years" including seven evangelists for Sinkiang;
over a dozen martyred.

Congregationalist missionary Frank C. Laubach
(1884-1970) begins "each one teach one" method
in Philippines, develops literacy primers for
reaching 300 languages worldwide with the gospel; 1950 publishes *Literacy as Evangelism.*

1930   Japan: Kingdom of God Movement begun under
evangelist Toyohiko Kagawa (1888-1960),
reaching over one million (75 percent non-
Christian) with 35,000 inquirers in two years.

1931   Unevangelized Fields Mission (UFM) founded in
London, UK.

CONTEMPORARY GLOBAL SURVEYS OF
UNREACHED PEOPLES BEGIN (AD 1936 - 1972)

1936   WEC missionary L. G. Brierley begins long career as
first full-time Protestant missionary researcher;
1941, begins world survey research with WEC,
resulting in surveys of "remaining unevangelized
peoples (RUPs)."

1950   Black Africa: Christians number about 44 million,
increasing rapidly by 1.8 million a year among
500 tribes; African indigenous churches (AICs)
mushroom to 1,700 separate denominations with
3,500,000 adherents among 100 separate tribes.

1955   Concept of group ingatherings (people movements, christianization within castes and tribes) brought to fore by USA missiologist D. A. McGavran.

1956   200,000 Hindu Untouchables (Outcasts) convert to Buddhism in Nagpur under B. R. Ambedkar.

Ecuador: five Protestant missionaries killed in jungle attempting to reach Auca Indians.

1965   DWME consultation in Yaounde, Cameroon: "The Evangelisation of West Africa Today," preceded by four-month survey under J. S. Lawson, D. B. Barrett, B. B. Ayam, which lists and describes 132 African peoples at various stages of being reached for Christ.

1966   MARC founded to provide technological and research support to the Church as momentum for world evangelization begins to build in conjunction with the Berlin Congress on World Evangelization. The modern idea of people groups is born.

1967   SC Propaganda (Rome) renamed Sacred Congregation for the Evangelization of Peoples, working among 9,500 ethnolinguistic peoples and 15,000 other people groups.

1969   African indigenous churches (AICs) now number over 5,800 denominations with 17 million adherents from 300 different tribes, growing by 960,000 each year.

1970   United Bible Societies' outreach: total languages with printed Scriptures--Bible 249, NT 578, portions 1,431; covering 97 percent of world's population; annual world distribution of subsidized Scriptures doubles from 80 million in 1966 to 173 million in 1970, then to 549 million in 1985.

Worldwide trend of ethnic reaffirmation gathers momentum, resulting in minority peoples in major states disaffiliating themselves from transethnic ideals (e.g. Blacks and Amerindians in USA; Ukrainians, Central Asian Muslim peoples, in USSR).

1972   Survey report "Frontier Situations for Evangelization in Africa" by D. B. Barrett, M. L. Hronek, G. K. Mambo, J. S. Mbiti and M. J. McVeigh (Nairobi) tabulates data, documents and maps situation of 213 Muslim peoples, 411 peoples responsive to Christianity, and 236 unevangelized peoples.

Consultation on the Gospel and Frontier Peoples, Chicago (December).

STRATEGIES FOR REACHING PEOPLE GROUPS WIDELY DEVELOPED (AD 1974 - 1986)

1974   International Congress on World Evangelization (ICOWE), Lausanne, Switzerland, on "Let the Earth Hear His Voice"; 2,700 delegates from 150 countries; soon after, announces that there are 16,750 unreached people groups in world.

MARC produces listing of 424 specific unreached people groups and publishes its first *Unreached Peoples Directory*.

1975   Kenya Unreached Peoples Conference, Lenana, Nairobi.

1976   Bible translators at work in over 300 of world's remaining 5,200 languages as yet with no portion of Bible (four percent of world's population); Bible revisions and new translations underway in 500 languages (representing 80 percent of world's population).

1978   7th General Chapter, Catholic Foreign Mission Society of America (Maryknoll) issues, "Statement of Mission Vision: Our particular task gives special emphasis to the evangelization of the poor, of cultures and of structures."

1979   West Germany: Conference on Unreached Peoples, sponsored by World Evangelical Fellowship, at Bad Liebenzell (January).

1980   World Consultation on Frontier Missions, Edinburgh: "A Church for Every People by the Year 2000"; 270 delegates (October).

LCWE convenes the Consultation on World Evangelization at Pattaya, Thailand.

1981   German Association of Evangelical Missions meets on theme "Hidden Peoples" (February).

UK: Evangelical Missionary Alliance sponsors conference on "Reaching Unreached Peoples: Breaking New Ground in Areas of Neglect," at High Leigh, Hertford (November).

1984   Ethnic Chinese Congress on World Evangelization (ECCOWE), in Honolulu, with 144 delegates (July).

1985   National Convocation on Evangelizing Ethnic America, Houston; over 700 attenders (April).

Zaire National Congress on Evangelism; leaders from 64 denominations plan to plant churches in 10,000 unreached villages and thousands of city neighborhoods by 1990 (April).

Nigeria Evangelical Missions Association commences survey of unreached peoples in Nigeria with "Project Searchlight" effort.

"Mission 2000" scheme proposed by missiologist D. A. McGavran, aiming to plant a church in each of world's unreached peoples by AD 2000 through formation of 100,000 local church mission fellowships in Western countries.

1986   India Missions Association commences large scale survey of unreached peoples in India.

Chapter 3

DEVELOPMENT OF LITERATURE ON PEOPLES AND WAYS OF REACHING THEM

This listing below describes, in chronological sequence, a selection of Christian materials relevant to mission and ministry among unreached peoples.

Year

1910   *Carrying the Gospel to All the Non-Christian World.* World Missionary Conference, Report of Commission I. Edinburgh, Oliphant.

1925   *World Missionary Atlas.* Ed. H. P. Beach. New York: Institute of Social and Religious Research. Includes maps of races, peoples, languages being reached by missions.

1930   *The Evangelisation of Pagan Africa: a History of Christian Missions to the Pagan Tribes of Central Africa.* J. Du Plessis, Cape Town: Juta. Contains a tribal map and index of Africa's peoples. Describes in detail how 151 African peoples hitherto unreached were first contacted, reached, evangelized and discipled.

1939   *The Book of a Thousand Tongues.* Ed. E. M. North, New York: American Bible Society.

1956 "The People Movement Point of View," in J. W. Pickett, A. L. Warnshuis, G. H. Singh and D. A. McGavran, *Church Growth and Group Conversion*, Lucknow, India: Lucknow Publishing House, pages 1-7.

1959 *Two Thousand Tongues to Go: The Story of the Wycliffe Bible Translators.* E. E. Wallis and M. A. Bennett, New York: Harper.

1961 *Second World Survey of the Areas of the World Unreached by the Gospel.* L. Brierley, London: Worldwide Evangelisation Crusade. Six volumes. Calls for action to reach "the Unreached Peoples of the Earth." Describes a "19-point programme to reach the unreached." Maps include "Reaching the Unreached."

1965 *The Evangelisation of West Africa Today: a Survey Across 21 Nations and 150 Tribes.* J. S. Lawson, B. B. Ayam and D. B. Barrett, Nairobi: Unit of Research. Based on six months of field work from Senegal to Zaire.

1965 *Scriptures of the World.* London, New York, Stuttgart: United Bible Societies. Listings and maps of all languages with Scripture translated, ranked chronologically and geographically as well as alphabetically. Published every two years; latest edition 1984, being "A compilation of the 1,808 languages in which at least one Book of the Bible has been published since the Bible was first printed by Johannes Gutenberg."

1972 *Frontier Situations for Evangelization in Africa, 1972: a Survey Report.* D. B. Barrett, M. L. Hronek, G. K. Mambo, J. S. Mbiti, and M. J. McVeigh, Nairobi: Unit of Research. Color map of 1,045 tribes or peoples (263 being unevangelized or resistant or unreached).

1972 *The Book of a Thousand Tongues.* Revised edition, Ed. E. A. Nida, United Bible Societies.

1973   "Church Planters and Ethnolinguistics," C. H. Kraft in A. R. Tippett, ed. *God, Man and Church Growth*, Grand Rapids, MI: Eerdmans, pp. 226-249.

1973   *The Gospel and Frontier Peoples: a Report of a Consultation, December 1972.* Ed. R. P. Beaver, South Pasadena, CA: William Carey Library.

1974   *Reaching the Unreached: an Introductory Study on Developing an Overall Strategy for World Evangelization.* E. C. Pentecost. South Pasadena, CA: William Carey Library.

1974   *Unreached Peoples Directory 1974.* Monrovia, CA: MARC. First edition of a long series.

1974   *Reaching All: Six Studies on Evangelizing the World for Christ.* Minneapolis, MN: World Wide Publications.

c1975   *Apostolate to Nomads.* Nairobi and Vatican City. A 12-year series of papers and reports about missions among nomadic peoples across the world.

1977   *Frontier Peoples of Central Nigeria, and a Strategy for Outreach.* G. O. Swank, South Pasadena, CA: William Carey Library. Systematic study of unreached ethnic groups in central Nigerai.

1978   *Operation World.* P. J. Johnstone, Bromley, Kent: STL Publications (new edition in 1986). Call for prayer and action based upon evangelistic survey of all the world's countries.

1978   *Unreached Peoples '79: the Challenge of the Church's Unfinished Business.* Eds. E. R. Dayton and C. P. Wagner, Elgin, IL: David C. Cook.

1979   *Bibliography of the Summer Institute of Linguistics.* Vol. 1: 1935-1975, Ed. A. C. Wares, Dallas, TX: SIL. Lists 5,924 items on reaching peoples in 638 distinct languages and cultures through Scripture translation. Volume II (1976-1982) adds 4,000 more entries.

1979   *Ethnic Realities and the Church: Lessons from India.* D. A. McGavran. South Pasadena, CA: William Carey Library.

1979   *The Native American Christian Community: a Directory of Indian, Aleut, and Eskimo Churches.* Ed. R. P. Beaver, Monrovia, CA: MARC.

1980   *New Paths in Muslim Evangelism: Evangelical Approaches to Contextualization.* P. Parshall, Grand Rapids, MI: Baker.

1980   *Planting Churches Cross-culturally: a Guide to Home and Foreign Missions.* D. J. Heselgrave, Grand Rapids, MI: Baker.

1980   *Planning Strategies for World Evangelization.* E. R. Dayton and D. A. Fraser, Grand Rapids, MI: Eerdmans.

1980   *Unreached Peoples '80.* Eds. C. P. Wagner and E. R. Dayton, Elgin, IL: David C. Cook.

1980   *That Everyone May Hear: Reaching the Unreached.* (3rd edition, 1983). E. R. Dayton, Monrovia, CA: MARC.

1981   *Unreached Peoples '81: Special Section on the Peoples of Asia.* Eds. E. R. Dayton and C. P. Wagner, Elgin, IL: David C. Cook.

1982   *The Challenge of the Unreached Peoples.* D. A. McGavran, South Pasadena, CA: William Carey Library.

1982   "Reaching Unreached Peoples: Guidelines and Definitions for Those Concerned with World Evangelization." Evangelical Foreign Missions Association, unpublished draft.

1982   *Reaching our Generation.* W. T. Coggins and E. L. Frizen, Jr., South Pasadena, CA: William Carey Library.

1982   "The Unity of the Church and the Homogeneous Unit Principle." R. Padilla, *International Bulletin of Missionary Research*, January: 23-30. Powerful critique of the homogeneous unit principle.

1982   *Unreached Peoples '82: Focus on Urban Peoples.* Eds. E. R. Dayton and S. Wilson, Elgin, IL: David C. Cook.

1983 *The Church in New Frontiers for Mission.* Ed. D. A. Fraser, Monrovia, CA: MARC.

1983 "The People Group Approach to World Evangelization." The Wheaton '83 Papers, C. P. Wagner and E. R. Dayton.

1983 *The Refugees Among Us: Unreached Peoples '83.* Eds. E. R. Dayton and S. Wilson, Monrovia, CA: MARC.

1983 *The Church in Response to New Frontiers.* Ed. D. A. Fraser, Monrovia, CA: MARC

1983 "Looking at the Task Six Ways." J. R. McQuilkin, *Evangelical Missions Quarterly*, 15(4): 4-12. Discussion of approaches to evangelization of a population.

1983 "Penetrating the Last Frontiers," S. Hawthorne, *World Christian*, March-April: 10-18. Each issue of *World Christian* deals with one unreached people (in this issue, the Wolofs of Senegal).

1983 *That Everyone May Hear: Workbook.* E. R. Dayton, Monrovia, CA: MARC.

1983 "The People of God and the Peoples." J. S. Pobee in W. R. Shenk, ed., *Exploring Church Growth*, pages 181-190.

1983 "Taiwan: Church Growth, Ethnicity, and Politics," H. M. Conn, in Shenk *op. cit.*

1984 *Beyond the Churches: Focusing on a Task Unfinished.* Ed. P. Brierley, London: Evangelical Alliance and MARC Europe.

1984 *Ethnologue.* 10th edition, Ed. B. F. Grimes, Dallas, TX: Wycliffe Bible Translators. 5,445 languages listed.

1984 *Index to the 10th Edition of the Ethnologue.* Ed. B. F. Grimes, Dallas, TX: WBT. 26,000 names listed from *Ethnologue* and identified.

1984 "Momentous Decisions About the Human Mosaic." Part 2 in D. A. McGavran, *Momentous Decisions in Missions Today*, Grand Rapids, MI: Baker, pages 87-127. Five chapters on the people group approach.

1984   "People Groups: Beyond the Push to Reach Them Lie Some Contrary Opinions." J. Reapsome, *Evangelical Missions Quarterly*, 20(1): 6-19, critique of the previous efforts regarding unreached peoples research.

1984   *Reaching the Unreached: the Old-New Challenge.* Ed. H. M. Conn, Phillipsburg, NJ: Presbyterian and Reformed Publishing.

1984   *The Future of World Evangelization: Unreached Peoples '84.* Eds. E. R. Dayton and S. Wilson, Monrovia, CA: MARC.

1984   *Studies in the International Apostolate of Jesuits*, 1, VIII, June, 1984. Issue devoted to refugees.

1984   *Heirs of the Same Promise: Using Acts as a Study Guide for Evangelizing Ethnic America.* Ed. W. D. Balda, Arcadia, CA: National Convocation on Evangelizing Ethnic America.

1984   *The Hidden Half: Discovering the World of Unreached Peoples.* S. Wilson and G. Aeschliman, Monrovia, CA: MARC. Views the biblical nations as people groups.

1985/6 Series of letters responding to McGavran's 1984 article. Ed. R. Fung, *Monthly Newsletter on Evangelism*, WCC. Provides substantial Third World and non-evangelical insights into possible weaknesses of the people group approach (including a South African perspective in a letter by Bosch, D., J. Kritizinger, P. Meiring, and W. Saayman).

1985   "1.3 Billion 'Unevangelized' or 2.4 Billion 'Unreached'?" J. A. Holzmann, *Mission Frontiers*, August-September: 20-21.

1985   "Understanding the task." W. Webster, *Impact*, 42(4): 6-11.

1986   *S.I.L. Publications Catalog 1986-87.* Dallas, TX: Summer Institute of Linguistics. Details of some 2,500 publications on reaching peoples through scripture translation.

1986   *List of Recorded Languages.* Los Angeles, CA: Gospel Recordings, Inc.

1986   *World Translations Progress Report, 1986.* Stuttgart: United Bible Societies. Lists and describes scripture translation projects currently underway around the world in 555 languages.

Chapter 4

RESOURCES FOR REACHING PEOPLES
AND PEOPLE GROUPS

Cultures and Social Groups

Akademia.
   1964   *Atlas Naradov Mira* (*Atlas of the Peoples of the World*). Moscow: Akademia.

Arco.
   1978   *Peoples of Africa.* New York: Arco.

Blunden, C. and M. Elvin
   1983   *Cultural Atlas of China.* New York: Facts on File, Inc.

Breeden, R. L.
   1971   *Nomads of the World.* Washington, DC: National Geographic.

LeBar, F.
   1964   *Ethnic Groups of Insular Southeast Asia.* New Haven: Human Relations Area Files.
   1964   *Ethnic Groups of Mainland Southeast Asia.* New Haven: Human Relations Area Files.

Fedders, A.
   1979   *Peoples and Cultures of Kenya.* Nairobi: Transafrica.

Gaisford, J.
   1978   *Atlas of Man.* London: Marshall Cavendish.

Gutkind, P.
1974   *Urban Anthropology: Perspectives on "Third World" Urbanization and Urbanism.* New York: Harper and Row.

Jules-Rosette, B.
1984   *Symbols of Change.* Norwood, NJ: Aldex Publishing Corp.

Marshall Cavendish.
1974   *The Family of Man.* London: Marshall Cavendish. Seven volumes, 52 parts.

Minority Rights Group.
1973   Minority Rights Group reports (36 Craven Street, London WC2N 5NG, England). 70 professional studies since 1973 on minority people groups, such as No. 49, *The Tibetans* (1981, 16 pages).

Murdock, G. P.
1954   *Outline of World Cultures.* (1963, 3rd edition, revised). New Haven, CT: Human Relations Area Files.
1967   *Ethnographic Atlas.* Pittsburgh, PA: University of Pittsburgh.

Murray, J. M., ed.
1981   *Cultural Atlas of Africa.* Oxford: Phaidon.

Rand McNally.
1982   *The Atlas of Mankind.* London: Mitchell Beazley & Rand McNally.

Stacey, T., ed.
1973   *Peoples of the Earth.* Danbury/Grolier/Europa Verlag. 20 volumes.

Thernstrom, S., eds.
1980   *Harvard Encyclopedia of American Ethnic Groups.* Cambridge, MA: Harvard University Press.

Vayda, A. P., ed.
1968   *Peoples and Cultures of the Pacific: an Anthropological Reader.* Garden City, NY: Natural History Press.

Weekes, R. V., ed.
1984   *Muslim Peoples: a World Ethnographic Survey.*
2nd edition, revised and expanded (1st edition 1978).
Westport, CT: Greenwood. Two volumes. Covers
190 ethnic and/or linguistic groups mostly totally
Muslim.
Yale University.
----   Human Relations Area Files (HRAF). Yale University, New Haven, CT. A bibliographically-oriented
abstracting service collating anthropological data on
a large number of specific peoples. Begun 1949.

Languages

Breton, R. J.-L.
1976   *Atlas Geographique des Langues et des Ethnies de
l'Inde et du Subcontinent.* Quebec: Laval University
(CIRB).
Centre National de la Recherche Scientifique.
1981   *Les Langues dans le Monde Ancien et Moderne.*
Paris: Centre National de la Recherche Scientifique.
A multivolume series of very detailed works
describing the world's languages, their location,
history, and the like. Maps, tables.
Gunnemark, E., and D. Kenrick.
1983   *What Language Do they Speak? A Geolinguistic
Handbook Covering Languages, Countries, and
Peoples in the Whole World.* Privately printed.
Kloss, H., and G. D. McConnell.
1974   *Linguistic Composition of the Nations of the World.*
Quebec: Laval University (CIRB). A six volume
series of census data on all languages including
peoples and variant names.
Malherbe, M.
1983   *Les Langages de L'humanite: une Encyclopedie des
3000 Langues Parlees dans le Monde.* Paris:
Seghers.

Voegelin, G. F., and F. M. Voegelin.
1977   *Classification and Index of the World's Languages.*
Oxford: Elsevier, 1977. Includes index of 272 pages
(22,000 language names).

Other Resources

Barrett, D. B., ed.
1982   *World Christian Encyclopedia.* London, Nairobi:
Oxford University Press.
Dayton, E. R.
1985   *That Everyone May Hear: Planning to Reach the
Unreached* (Audiovisual). Monrovia, CA: MARC.
Johnstone, P. J.
1984   *World Evangelization 1985: WEC Transparencies.*
Bromley, Kent: WEC.
Lausanne Committee for World Evangelization.
1975-   *Lausanne Occasional Papers.* Wheaton: Lausanne
Committee for World Evangelization. A continuing
series of booklets devoted to various topics and
issues in world evangelization. The series now con-
tains 24 volumes. Represents the theory and prac-
tice of the Lausanne movement since its inception.
MARC
1986   *Unreached Peoples Prayer Cards.* Monrovia, CA:
MARC.
----   *World Christianity Series.* Monrovia, CA: MARC.
Siewert, J and S. Wilson, eds.
1986   *Mission Handbook: North American Protestant
Ministries Overseas* (12th edition). Monrovia, CA:
Missions Advanced Research and Communication
Center.

TWENTYONEHUNDRED Productions.

1981 *To Every People.* A series of four films (Tribal World, Muslim World, Hindu World, Chinese World) from TWENTYONEHUNDRED Productions (233 Langdon, Madison, WI 53703). Originally produced for IVCF's Urbana '81 student missions convention.

Chapter 5

SELECTED PERIODICALS

City Watch. Institute of Global Urban Studies, 1605 Elizabeth St., Pasadena, CA 91104, USA.

Frontier Fellowship. P.O. Box 90970, Pasadena, CA 91104, U.S.A.

The Frontiersman. WEC, 24 Nutley Crescent, Goring-by-Sea, Worthing, Sussex, BN12 4LA, England.

International Journal of Frontier Missions. P. O. Box 40638, Pasadena, CA 91104 U.S.A.

Lausanne Communique. Strategy Working Group, World Vision International, 919 W. Huntington Drive, Monrovia, CA 91016, U.S.A.

MARC Newsletter. MARC, World Vision International, 919 W. Huntington Drive, Monrovia, CA 91016, U.S.A.

Mission Frontiers. U.S. Center for World Mission, 1605 Elizabeth St., Pasadena, CA 91104, USA.

Panta ta Ethni. Apostolic Diakonia, 14 Io Gennadiou Street 115, 21 Athens, Greece.

Regions Beyond. Regions Beyond Missionary Union, 8102 Elberon Avenue, Philadelphia, PA 19111, USA.

United Bible Societies Bulletin. P. O. Box 810340, 7000 Stuttgart 80, F.R. Germany.

World Christian. P. O. Box 5199, Chatsworth, CA 91311, USA.

PART TWO

REACHING PEOPLES
IN AFRICA:
13 case descriptions

AFRICA

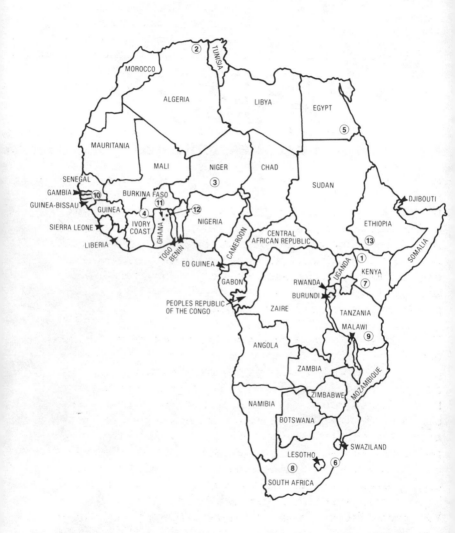

①	Turkana	⑤	Nubian	⑨	Baraguyu
②	Kabyle	⑥	Zanzibari	⑩	Bassari
③	Tuareg	⑦	Asians in Nairobi	⑪	Koma
④	Komono	⑧	Indian Muslims	⑫	Konkomba
				⑬	Aari

(Map locates people groups examined in this section)

Chapter 6

INTRODUCTION AND OVERVIEW

Africa has been much on the minds and the hearts of the world in the 1970s and 1980s, as it has been a continent of travail and suffering with droughts, wars, and widespread hunger and dislocation of whole peoples. In the midst of Africa's pain, God has been at work through his servants, both African and non-African, drawing non-believers into his kingdom, ministering to the countless needs of the African people and offering the path of reconciliation between African peoples and himself and between each other.

We need to understand what God has done and how he has been working. Earlier in this volume, the task of world evangelizing the world's people groups was described from two different research perspectives. In this section, the evangelization of people groups is further illustrated by looking at actual examples of work being done, which are described in narratives, most of which are told by the persons who have experienced them. As narratives, they are rich in detail. Naturally, they do not have the conceptual rigor of the more systematized, abstract listings and descriptions of people groups found in research reports of research centers and mission agencies. Yet, stories are an age-old form of explaining our human experience, understanding the mysteries of life, and sharing the presence of God in our midst. For this reason, they are valuable.

An Intensive Survey of Receptivity

The first essay in this section illustrates how a mission organization surveyed a people group to determine receptivity to the gospel and to identify promising areas for ministry. This survey was commissioned based upon the need to develop a sound missions strategy for working with the Turkana of Kenya. This need generated several research questions, "To what extent has the gospel impacted the Turkana; are there remaining pockets of Turkana who have not yet responded to the gospel; and where are the pockets of receptive peoples among the latter?"

Once the need for research was identified and a research question had been formulated, the research effort began. It had a purpose and its results were immediately useful. This case description illustrates many elements needed for successful research: an awareness of previous work and existing literature; basing one's investigation on sound insights gained from biblical and anthropological/sociological study (receptivity being understood as a combination of factors, including rate of social change, communication processes and styles, and barriers to communication of the gospel, both spiritual and otherwise); a systematic method of data collection; and, most importantly, a concern for discovering the perspectives and concerns of the people themselves.

Although not every church has the resources or trained personnel to carry out research at this level of rigor, we can all learn from a study like this. It demonstrates the essential role of intensive, detailed research when developing an evangelistic strategy for a people group. It is important to note that the process began with understanding the larger picture of unreached peoples in Kenya. This pointed to the need for further evangelistic efforts among the Turkana. The value of such research is amply illustrated by the results: 245 Turkana had been baptized by 1986 in the work of the missionaries who were placed based upon the recommendations of this research.

African Muslims

Reaching the 800 million Muslims of our world is probably the greatest challenge we face in missions today. The next five case descriptions feature African Muslim people groups in varying stages of being touched with the gospel. What are some of the implications for missionary strategy that arise from these diverse cases?

First, we see a need to focus upon strategic people groups. It is easy for us as missionaries and evangelists to dilute the depth and effectiveness of our ministries by failing to concentrate our efforts on that one particular people group which is most strategic for us to reach. For example, in trying to reach a large people group, we often fail to discern the rich multiplicity of its various sub-groups. A large people group might encompass a number of smaller people groups, each of which has its own needs and distinct ways of looking at themselves and the world. How much more potent our impact would be if we chose to focus our work on a smaller, more well-defined group, investing all our resources until it is reached--until an indigenous community of believers arises that is capable of evangelizing the rest of the group.

The 200,000 Kabyle immigrants in France and other countries are likely to be easier to reach and more responsive to the gospel than their fellow Kabyles in Algeria. The male migrant workers among this larger group are particularly strategic in terms of ministry. Uprooted from their culture with its overwhelming Islamic pressure, they are likely to be more willing to consider other faith alternatives. The fact that their families back home continue to be financially dependent upon them will place these migrants in an influential position in defending their newfound allegiance to Christ when, or if, they return home for good.

Tuaregs, especially from lower-class backgrounds, are migrating into West African cities to escape the harsh conditions of famine and drought in their tribal homelands. Uprooted and in desperate physical need, they are likely to be open to a sensitive, compassionate Christian ministry. In their new situation, they have little status or prestige to forfeit through commitment to Christ. While the drought continues in Africa, the window of opportunity is open for reaching these nomadic urban migrants in the cities of West Africa. In this situation, urban Tuareg migrants make up a strategic people group. Similarly, Nubian migrants to Egyptian cities are uniquely available to Christian witness.

The Komonos represent another type of strategic group. Throughout the world, tribal peoples are under great pressure to forgo their tribal identity and religions. One force in this process is Islamization. Particularly in Africa and Asia, Islam is making rapid inroads among tribal peoples. The Komono are now Muslim. Yet, 50 years ago they were not. This illustrates the urgency of mission work among tribals in this time of rapid change.

Another issue is the need to determine the most suitable force for evangelization. Due to political restrictions placed upon foreign missionaries since Algeria's war of independence and the entrenched prejudice against Western, colonial Christianity, it is critical to communicate the missionary vision to those who are believers among the Kabyle immigrants outside Algeria. They can go back as low-key witnesses and disciple makers among their own people.

The same kind of approach would be provident for Tuareg and Nubian urban migrants who convert to Christ. They could be trained and equipped to return to act as salt and leaven within their closed societies.

These case descriptions also encourage us to take a truly incarnational approach to missions. The missionaries to the Kabyle people overcame suspicion by gradually developing close relationships, freely accepting the hospitality that was offered them. They also saw the absolute priority of thoroughly mastering the Kabyle language, rather than relying on trade languages like French or Arabic. This was the key factor in coming to an understanding of the culture. It opened the door for an effective entry into their thought forms and ways of life.

The missionary to the Tuareg went further. As he put it: "I just could not stand up there and proclaim the gospel. I had to live the gospel." He and his family were willing to pay the price of cultural identification by adapting to the nomadic lifestyle of their adopted people. In addition, they made use of the Tuareg script and learned to compose music in indigenous forms that would appeal to Tuaregs.

Last, these case descriptions touch upon a key issue in evangelization of Muslims--the danger in extracting new believers out of their cultural and social contexts. When the first believers among the Kabyles returned to their villages and openly shared their faith, they were met with savage persecution. If they were not beaten or killed, they were ostracized as traitors to their society. Subsequently, most of those Kabyles who have become believers have left the country. Tragically, these first Christians have been lost as a force for evangelizing their own people. Similarly, a decision of missionaries operating in South Africa in the early 1900's called for settling the Zanzibari converts among the Zulus, which had the effect of removing them as an instrument in God's hands for garnering a wider harvest among the rest of their people.

The missionaries to the Tuareg wisely avoided extracting converts from their people. They have taught believers to quietly link themselves together in low-key support relationships, waiting patiently for discreet opportunities to bear witness by life and word. This practice is recommended by the authors of the case description on the Nubians. Only as new converts remain in close contact with their relatives and friends does the gospel have a ready conduit through which to flow to others in that people group. For many unreached Muslims, it is only as they see and hear of Jesus through their own intimates that following him will become a realistic possibility.

Asians in Africa

There are large numbers of persons of South Asian ancestry throughout Africa, especially in those nations with British colonial backgrounds. They are generally called Asians and have taken the positions of traders or merchants in African society. In these positions, they are found interspersed among African populations in almost every African nation. Yet, mission efforts have focused more on African peoples than on the Asian population. This is due both to a perception of greater need and a perceived hostility of Asians to the gospel.

The next two case descriptions report on work being carried out among the Asian populations in Nairobi, Kenya and in South Africa. The two share similarities but differ in significant ways. In both cases Asians have remained a distinct community in African society. The dynamics of this differ greatly. In Nairobi, the community is tied together by common background, similar positions in African society, and cross-linking networks of family ties and mercantile relationships. In South Africa, these forces are important, but of great effect have been the governmental policies and regulations of apartheid. This has reinforced the sense of community due to common residence, legal definition, and enforced social interaction among themselves. One result is that in Nairobi the possibilities for non-Asians of developing significant relationships with those in the Asian community are greater than in South Africa. There is more interchange between Africans, Asians, and others.

This difference is reflected in the approaches to identifying the people group of interest in these two case descriptions. In Nairobi, the Asian community was well-defined and interconnected. It included both Muslims and Hindus. In South Africa, on the other hand, the Indian Muslim population is seen as a people group distinct from Indian Hindus.

It can be argued that these definitions came about partly as a result of the ministry strategy which was employed. The Nairobi example is based upon friendship evangelism. It recognizes the nature of urban life and how urban peoples are tied together by cross-cutting networks as much as by formally constituted groups or institutions. It also recognized that there was a more permeable boundary around Asians which might be penetrated by those interested in interacting with Asians. In addition, the many religious sects and cultures represented in the Asian population were not seen as important in terms of the evangelistic effort. Networking cut across these groups. It will be interesting to see if these cultural groupings begin to be separately distinguished as an Asian Christian community forms as a result of this ministry.

In South Africa, the ministry is built upon equipping church persons to effectively witness to Muslims. There is little emphasis upon understanding the nature of the Asian community and its social organization. Indeed, given the types of ministry strategy being employed, there is no real need to do this. The "Life Challenge" campaign is basically a communications strategy designed to confront Muslims with the gospel. This is not based upon capitalizing upon those "natural" relationships developed between Asians and surrounding Christians. Thus, it can be seen that one's mission strategy has a great effect upon how one defines the people group with whom one is working.

These case descriptions point to problems cited earlier regarding the homogeneous unit principle. In South Africa is found the apartheid system with its well-known injustices and need for change. For the purposes of proclamation of the gospel and initial exposure to Jesus Christ, one might recognize this system and work within it to develop a communication strategy. Here one would see that there are boundaries between Asians and Africans or Whites. Thus one would need to rely on a mission strategy that was designed to get past these barriers and not rely upon natural relationships crossing such barriers. Yet, if the Christian church is to come to maturity, it surely would need to recognize the injustices and inequalities built into the system of apartheid. The church would need to challenge this in sensitive and loving ways so that as Christians mature they can interact freely with their brothers and sisters in different ethnic and racial groups within South Africa. Thus, as the church comes to maturity and adheres to the whole gospel of Jesus Christ, it also challenges the system dividing peoples in such ways.

Lastly, both of these case descriptions point to the challenges and promises of working in the urban environment. In both cases Asians are urban. In urban situations, social organization is characterized by complexity and choice. Complexity is highlighted as people are faced with a myriad of others who share with them some similarities and some differences. In addition, there are a host of institutions, lifestyles, and challenges of many types in urban situations. Choice is built into this system, in that people may choose, to a great extent, persons with whom they will inter-relate. Yet, these case descriptions point to the fact that this is not a free-for-all. There are structural constraints on whom one might relate with. Clearly, ethnicity is important in this situation. Yet, ethnicity is defined differently in the urban situation for Asians. The ethnic boundaries found in South Asia have not been transmitted intact to the African context. We see a merging of formerly distinct South Asian ethnic groups in the African context. In African cities, ethnicity, residence, and class all interact to create the complex social organizations shown in these two case descriptions.

Tribalists in a Changing World

Africa is changing in many ways, but an important type of change is the fast decline in the independence and autonomy of "tribal peoples." Indeed, the stereotype of Africa held by most non-Africans is that of countless tribes made up of people with exotic customs, living fairly isolated lives in small villages or as nomads crossing deserts or savannahs in search of game animals. Today, there are fewer and fewer such peoples. They are being overwhelmed by the processes of nationalism, modernization, and Islamization. Most governments are concerned with building a sense of national identity. There is increasingly no room left for tribal peoples.

The last five case descriptions deal with these types of people groups. Here we see a number of people groups which can be best described as marginal. They are at the outskirts of other more powerful people groups. Marginality may be based upon physical separation. The Koma live in an inhospitable, unattractive forest region. Over time, less powerful peoples have been pushed out to these regions by more powerful peoples coming into their traditional areas. They are often seen as "wild" and inferior by the more powerful neighbors.

Marginality may also be seen in terms of economic or political terms. The Baraguyu are a good example of this, as are Bassari and Koma peoples. It is interesting to note that the Konkomba were economically marginal, but have moved up within the social and economic system in Ghana.

Last, the Aari of Ethiopia are marginal to Ethiopian society in the sense that their physical isolation and small numbers with regard to the more dominant Amharic peoples have kept them on the outskirts of society. Marginality actually contributed to the fact that these peoples were still followers of their own tribal religious system when many of the surrounding peoples were Christian or Islamic. Marginal people such as these are under tremendous pressure by more powerful peoples and national governments concerned with national unity and efficient use of land as a resource. Their way of life is threatened as they are brought into the mainstream of national culture. There is an incredible pressure to give up their traditional religious beliefs and practices. Islam and Christianity are the two primary alternatives in Africa. Which one will it be? We have examples of groups which have gone one of both ways--the Komonos are now Muslims and the Aari are Christians. These are strategic peoples.

Summary

Many of these case descriptions point to the difficult task of defining reached or unreached. A number of these people groups which are reported on have had Christian witness and churches in their midst. Yet, for various reasons the persons reporting upon their work with these people groups argue that these groups are still unreached. This might be because of perceived nominality or lack of practice in the church. It might be because of perceived theological problems or because of syncretism. Or, it might be because the person providing the case description does not feel that the existing church presents a clear enough picture of Jesus Christ and a true enough presentation of the gospel. These are problems. They create problems for researchers and those trying to understand the distribution of reached or unreached peoples across a nation or across the world. Yet, the exact determination of reached or unreached must be made by those actually engaged in the work. As these cases illustrate, this will vary.

Enjoy the following case descriptions. Realize they are a person's perception of what has happened. Thus, they might not tell "all" the truth. They might not completely analyze what has happened. Yet, as narratives they allow us to understand how God has worked in a people group and how the people group has changed in response.

Chapter 7

APPLIED RESEARCH AND CHURCH GROWTH:
A TURKANA CASE DESCRIPTION

by Edgar J. Elliston

Given an interest in unreached peoples and a commitment to evangelization, how does one discover the information necessary to develop a ministry strategy? This task can be done in a number of ways, including library research, interviews with experienced workers, systematic surveys, participant observations, and the use of extensive questionnaires. In this case description, we see the collection and analysis of data has led to development of a successful mission strategy.

The Turkana of Kenya

Over 200,000 Turkana live in the desert-like northwest area of Kenya. Although most are pastoral people dependent upon more highly valued cattle, many others raise goats and camels. Also, along the Turkwel and Kerio Rivers there are Turkana who engage in subsistence farming to supplement their food supply, and, those close to Lake Turkana add to their diet and income by fishing.

The region is generally at a relatively low elevation, ranging from 1,200 feet at the surface of Lake Turkana to 6,000 feet in the mountains. The average daytime high temperature is about 95 degrees, with many days reaching as high as 115 degrees. Rainfall averages about ten inches per year.

The Turkana live in extended family homesteads or *manyattas*. It is at this local level that decisions affecting most areas of life are discussed and made and new ideas are considered and adopted or rejected.

The Turkana are animistic, and to date, only a small percentage have become Christian. This is now changing. One force for change is the fact that an increasing number of children are now going to school and bringing home a world of new ideas, ways of relating to one another, and hopes for the future. This has brought pressure for change upon traditional beliefs and ways of understanding the great mysteries of life.

The Need for Research: A Survey of Receptivity Among the Turkana

The Christian Missionary Fellowship (CMF) entered Kenya in 1978 to evangelize unreached, responsive peoples and establish reproducing churches among them. Several unreached people groups were identified, including the Turkana people of northwest Kenya, although several other missions or churches had been working among these people: the Africa Inland Church, the Salvation Army, the Reformed Church of East Africa, the Roman Catholic Church, the Pentecostal Assemblies of Canada, and the Glad Tidings Crusade (cf. Davis 1978 and Elliston 1979).

Development of a Research Question At CMF we asked whether the Turkana were receptive or would likely be receptive to the gospel in the next five years. CMF authorized a research project to answer that question. The purpose was to provide a basis for making recommendations to CMF about the assignment of personnel to work among the Turkana, both in evangelism and integrated development efforts. Specific goals of the research included:

1. An assessment of the relative receptivity of the Turkana people to the Christian gospel.

2. A brief description of the current status of the church and missions among the Turkana.

3. A listing of the more pressing development needs of the traditional Turkana people.

Prior Research   Gulliver's study of the Turkana (1951) provided a useful baseline description of the traditional, nomadic Turkana. Anthony Barrett's study of the traditional Turkana provided insights into the contextualization and communication of the gospel among the Turkana, based upon his investigation of Turkana rites of passage and parallel functions in Christian growth. While he acknowledged the risks of syncretism in striving for a contextualized gospel, he also noted the risks of "imported syncretism" were great (1977). Last, Mbugua (1977) suggested effective communication processes for use with traditional Turkana, such as the use of "friendship" ties, utilizing the communication networks of diviners and other influence leaders who have converted to Christianity, and focusing on centers of communication, such as local water holes.

In 1978, Davis surveyed the growth of the church in Kenya and identified a low level of receptivity among the pastoral Turkana. Since, however, nearly all of the evangelistic work previously done was carried out in small towns, it was difficult to assess the level of receptivity among the more traditional pastoral population. We suspected that the pastoral Turkana were reacting negatively to an evangelistic message developed in the urban or small town situation and shaped by prevalent values in that setting.

Research Methodology   Two data gathering techniques were used in this survey:

1.   Observations were made of the physical conditions, terrain, climate, population density and attitudes of those who were interviewed.

2.   Informal interviews were conducted with four different groups of people:

    a.   Kenyan government officials involved in planning and development activities in this area,

    b.   Church and mission leaders in the Turkana area,

    c.   Others from development agencies who had been involved with development projects in the Turkana district, and

    d.   The traditional Turkana themselves.

Informal interviews with the Turkana were conducted in a variety of contexts:

1.   Through participation in "friendship" networks.

2.   Sitting and conversing with the Turkana gathered around waterholes.

3.   Offering water and/or food to travelers and visiting with them as they enjoyed these gifts.

4.   Interviewing relatives of medical patients at clinics or hospitals.

It can be seen that most of these interviews were conducted in the context of existing patterns of interpersonal communication among the Turkana. Interview sessions were not "set up" or based upon appointments.

Interviews with missionaries, church leaders, staff of development agencies, and government officials focused on the particular interests and activities of the individual and his or her agency.

Initial Findings

On the basis of our research, we found that no evangelical church was experiencing significant growth among the traditional, pastoral Turkana. We suspected the following findings were part of the problem:

1. Evangelical churches generally followed urban or Western forms in their programs. These included formal preaching to mixed groups, highly trained ministers who came from out of the area, use of translated hymns and songs, restricting the conducting of baptismal services or serving communion to licensed/ordained men, and individualistic decision-making. In sum, the churches were western-oriented, urban institutions.

2. With the exception of the Glad Tidings Crusade, evangelical churches and missions did not indicate any forthcoming change of strategy or outreach among the traditional Turkana. The Glad Tidings Crusade had recently established one small congregation which did not yet have trained leadership, either national or expatriate.

3. Evangelical churches or missions did not appear to be using many of the indigenous communication channels of the Turkana. They did not follow natural relational ties based on reciprocal begging and special friendships

or capitalize on the influence of "natural leaders," such as initiation set leaders and diviners. The traditional centers for communication were generally ignored.

4. The Turkana often understood the gospel in negative and legalistic terms. One should not use tobacco, drink blood, have more than one wife, go to the diviner, live a nomadic lifestyle, wear beads, get married in traditional ways, or participate in initiation ceremonies.

5. With the exception of the Roman Catholic missionaries, very few missionaries or church workers were able to speak the Turkana language fluently. Missionaries and church workers frequently depended upon either Swahili or English or worked through a translator.

6. Several missionaries and church leaders stressed the importance of evangelism in the villages or *manyattas*, yet little was in fact being done in this regard.

An Analysis of the Factors Affecting Receptivity

One intent of this research was to construct and use a measure of receptivity to the gospel. From previous study of the missiology literature, the rate of social change and attitudes and methods of the evangelist were seen as key factors in shaping receptivity.

It is often noted that there is an association between the rate of social change and receptivity to the gospel. If people are experiencing widespread social change touching their central values, worldview, lifestyle, economic situation, and social organization, one may expect, in general, that they will be more open to the gospel.

Thus, when considering receptivity, the relevant question is, "What are the trends with regard to the rate of social change?"

Are they accelerating, stable, declining, uneven, or unpredictable? One should also look at factors affecting these trends and whether or not they are likely to continue.

At the time of the survey several factors were accelerating the rate of social change among the Turkana. These factors included introduced educational programs, which were increasingly affecting the Turkana with the inception of universal enrollment of children. Authority, decision making, and marriage and settlement patterns were all expected to change as a result. Another source of change was the establishment of fishing cooperatives. Although they were not traditionally fishermen, the Turkana began to be interested in fishing following the severe drought in 1960-1961. The increased availability of sheep and goats also introduced a measure of change. A fourth source of change was the establishment of irrigation projects, which brought in a whole new value system for land. Fifth, Western technology offered changes in terms of medical treatment systems, roads and other communication links, and increased cultural contact with outsiders. Last, there was increased "urbanization" of this area as small towns continued to grow, partially in response to encouragement from the central government of Kenya which wanted the Turkana to settle in villages or towns.

The second factor which affected the receptivity of the Turkana, was the attitudes or methods of those involved in evangelism. Many missionaries expected initial resistance, which conditioned their methods and attitudes and, in turn, may have further hampered the outcomes of their evangelistic efforts. Yet, resistance is often linked to the use of western methods of evangelization, which were not only irrelevant to the Turkana but, in many cases, socially offensive. For example, women and children were often approached first with the gospel, while older men were left out. This violated Turkana notions of age and gender relationships.

Basic principles of effective communication have not been followed in the past. For example, most evangelical missionaries have had virtually no direct contact with the local Turkana communities. Again, the use of the Turkana language was very limited, and existing communication channels (e.g., friendship, initiation sets, diviners, ties with medical patients' families, and so forth) were not used.

The Turkana worldview, religion, use of magic, rites of passage were often not only misunderstood, but it was often assumed that the Turkana should think and act in western philosophical terms.

Last, dramatic power encounters have been downplayed, and opportunities for using such encounters to give creditability to the gospel have not been recognized.

Given the methods and attitudes of the evangelical missionaries and church workers, combined with the rapid rate of the social change, we suspected that the assumption that the Turkana were resistant to Christianity was false. On the contrary, it appeared that the Turkana would become increasingly responsive to religious change over the next five years, if the gospel were presented in contextually appropriate ways. Provided this happened, it could be reasonably expected that many would respond positively to the good news of Jesus Christ.

A higher degree of receptivity to the gospel would likely be experienced if the methods of presenting the message were more contextualized. For example, the Turkana symbols of light and life might be used in communicating key gospel concepts. Also, Hebrew ways of referring to God and prayer are close to Turkana ways of thinking, so if the form of referring to God and the forms of prayer were altered to recognize and build on these similarities, they might be more meaningful and accepted. The gospel also provides a liberation from the pervasive fear of witchcraft, an area of great anxiety for the Turkana. Again, rites of passage among the Turkana not only provide important teaching opportunities, but need to have "functional substitutes." Barrett (1977) suggested that these rites of passage might be used to illustrate and illuminate key concepts in Christianity. Last, the Turkana rites of reconciliation provide useful "redemptive analogies" for those who would communicate the gospel. All of these areas could be productively explored in the interests of contextualization of and more effective evangelism.

Considering the real or perceived sociological barriers to the acceptance of the gospel, we can say that the fewer the barriers, the more receptive a people may be expected to be. Thus, in addition to contextualization of the gospel message, we could work at removing barriers/constraints with the expectation that receptivity would increase. Constraints which were holding the Turkana back from being responsive could be removed by changing the attitudes and methods of those working in evangelism.

Recommendations from the Survey

Following this survey, the following recommendations were presented to the Christian Missionary Fellowship:

1. The following elements should be considered in formulating an evangelistic strategy:

    a. Emphasize work in the villages.

    b. Selectively establish and follow "special friendship" ties.

    c. Emphasize the positive "good news" elements of the gospel for the Turkana (e.g., freedom from the fear of witchcraft and curses, emphasize symbols of light and life, and refer to reconciliation we have in Christ).

d. Learn and use the Turkana language in media and other channels of communication.

e. Maintain a simple lifestyle among the Turkana to reduce some of the more obvious material differences and associated tensions.

f. Train the new converts to evangelize "friends," relatives, and those of their initiation set.

g. Train leaders in biblically and culturally appropriate ways. Initially, non-formal ways (planned, but out of school) should be considered.

h. Strive to reduce the level of dependence of the Turkana church on outside sources. For example, resist paying church leaders from outside sources.

Response to the Survey

The research report, with its findings and recommendations, was submitted to the Kenya Field Mission of the CMF, approved, and then forwarded to the United States to the CMF Board, where it was also approved. Missionaries began working among the Turkana in early 1980, using the plan outlined in the recommendations.

By the beginning of 1986, seven churches had been established. A total of 245 pastoral Turkana had been baptized in the area between Kangatosa, Kerio and Lorengalup (Chapman 1986). Clearly, there have been substantial successes in this work.

Several key factors have combined to create a growing receptivity to the gospel. These include the establishment of traditionally defined friendships, participation in local development efforts, such as water, famine relief, small scale income-producing projects, and learning to function in the local language.

The importance of relying upon existing relational ties and key opinion leaders is underscored by the effect that a conversion of an influential leader, Nangodia, had on our work. Through Nangodia's influence and by virtue of his extensive contacts, a wide network of relationships, churches and preaching points have been developed among the Turkana.

Nangodia became even more effective in aiding the growth of Christianity when, a year after his conversion and at a time when local pressure to revert was very strong, he contracted tuberculosis. The treatment required frequent attention, and he stayed at Ile Springs, where Dr. Bob Chapman of CMF was able not only to treat him, but also to shepherd his spiritual growth on a daily basis. Nangodia developed into a trained, committed man of God. Upon his recovery, his influence for the gospel proved to be a major factor in the establishment of new congregations in the area.

Essential to the success of this work has been an insistence on following Turkana models of leadership. A major problem for other missions has been the relative lack of involvement of older men in the leadership of the church. Unlike many churches in this area, the age/gender distribution in our newly established seven churches parallels that of the wider society. This has allowed traditional patterns of interaction between men and women and between the generations. For example, an early emphasis on evangelizing and discipling men has raised them to more culturally relevant positions of leadership in these new churches.

Leaders are now being trained in a variety of nonformal education programs which are aimed at keeping them active in both their churches and communities. Literacy is very low, and to compensate, a set of culturally appropriate symbols for communicating gospel truths has been developed. These are drawn in the sand and then discussed, not only to teach the gospel to the leaders but also to help them demonstrate a tool which will allow them to better communicate the gospel to others.

As a result, the church is not only growing in numbers, but also growing in a truly contextualized fashion. The survey pointed to barriers and opportunities for growth. By following the recommended strategies, we have had success in our work for God.

Conclusion

In 1979, the consensus among the missionaries and church leaders who were familiar with the pastoral Turkana was that they were resistant to the gospel.

The research which was conducted in 1979-80 indicated the resistance was actually to some of the evangelistic methods which had been used. It also showed that there were a number of social changes underway and many others which should be expected because of governmental development plans, trends in local economic development, and increasing ease of communication in the area.

The intent of the research was to discover the level of receptivity of the Turkana to the gospel. Essentially, this entailed discovering how God had been working to prepare the Turkana for the acceptance of the gospel.

The research did not replace prayer in planning -- it gave focus to prayer. This research did not supplant evangelism -- it suggested appropriate methods for evangelism. The research did not change the gospel message -- it provided clues about the parts of the message which are truly good news to the Turkana and suggested ways in which the message could be formulated. The research proved to be a useful planning tool which aided evangelism and church planting among the Turkana.

On the basis of the research, several strategic recommendations, related to evangelism, church planting and development, were made. These recommendations were implemented, and the Lord has blessed us with a growing church which is now moving among the widely scattered Turkana with confidence and power.

Bibliography

Barrett, Anthony.
   1977   *Incarnating the Church in Turkana.* Eldoret, Kenya:
           Gaba Publications, Spearhead Series No. 52.
Davis, Ray.
   1978   *Church Growth and Culture Change in Turkana.*
           Unpublished M.A. Thesis, School of World Mission,
           Fuller Theological Seminary, Pasadena, California.
Elliston, Edgar J. et al.
   1979   "CMF-Daystar Turkana Survey Report." (Duplicated
           Report).
Giles, Ray.
   1985   "Feathers, Sand and the Gospel," *Impact.* January-
           March.
Gulliver, P. H.
   1951   "A Preliminary Survey of the Turkana." (Mimeo-
           graphed edition).
Mbugua, Bedan.
   1977   *Factors in a Strategy for Turkana.* Nairobi: Daystar
           Communications.

Chapter 8

THE KABYLES OF ALGERIA

Which would you regard as the most difficult mission field: (1) Urban ghettos with high rates of crime, confused family structures, and chaotic social conditions? Or (2) Communist lands with severe restrictions on open evangelism and religious freedoms? Or (3) The affluent, secular West with fast decaying morals and rampant materialism? Surely, you would put a fourth, North African Muslims, high on the list. Solid commitment to Islam, supreme regard and respect for ancient cultural traditions, and rejection of the "Western Christianity" of European colonizers all combine to increase the difficulty of sharing the gospel with North African Muslims. Yet, the gospel has been and is currently being brought to this area and to these peoples. This case description reports on over 100 years of faithful and courageous witness to the Islamic Kabyles of Algeria. It documents lives of heroism and the faithfulness of God in one of the most difficult mission fields in the world.

The Kabyles as a People Group

In the rugged mountain environment of the Atlas Range of North Africa live some two million Kabyles, scattered in numerous small villages situated along ridge lines and hilltops. This area of Algeria is well-watered with most of the rain falling during the cooler winter months and dry conditions existing throughout the hot summers. Kabyles are peasants who till the soil to grow olives and figs, various types of fruit trees such as pomegranates, peaches, apricots, pears and plums, and vegetable crops of many kinds. They produce primarily for their own subsistence but market excess agricultural products in area markets, which also serve as centers of information and communication.

The Kabyle language is in the Berber family and is totally different from the Arabic used by most of the population of Algeria. Prior to translation of the Christian Scriptures, Kabyle was an unwritten language. Although Arabic is the state language of Algeria, it is resisted by the Kabyles, who fiercely guard their independence. Kabyle is the language of the home and marketplace. Most Kabyle men also speak French, which is used widely in trade and correspondence.

Traditionally, Kabyles have lived in small villages which were largely independent of one another. At the local level, decisions are democratically made by an assembly of male heads of the extended families. This assembly, *djemaa* or *thadjmarth*, makes decisions, which are then executed by an agent of the assembly, and administers justice according to customary laws of the village.

At the present time there are two parallel structures of leadership. In addition to the local assembly, the whole area, as part of Algeria, is administered by officers of the single national, political party, "Front de Liberation Nationale," through its prefects, mayors, and counselors. Increasingly, decisions made by the national council of the party, passed down through purely administrative channels, are becoming more important and pervasive in the life of the Kabyles.

Kabyles are staunchly patrilineal and patrilocal. Women have few rights and are subject to the rule of brothers, fathers, or husbands throughout their entire life. Their authority is confined to the domestic sphere. Senior men of the extended families exercise control over family resources and decisions affecting the family and members of the family.

Central to the life of the Kabyles is Islam. Some 98 percent are practicing Muslims, while 2 percent have rejected Islam and are essentially secularists. Those who have accepted Christianity have tended to migrate out of Algeria to France and other lands. This includes as many as 30,000 persons, or 15 percent of all Kabyle emigrants.

The practice of Islam is tempered by animistic beliefs and dealings with the occult. These include non-Islamic taboos and practices which involve rituals centered on natural phenomena such as springs, grottoes, and sacred trees. Although Islam as practiced is not a pure form, it provides a strong cultural and religious focus for the Kabyles. Islamic feasts, fasts, and pilgrimages to tombs of local saints are important events and demand celebrations with much feasting, music, and dancing. In addition, religious leaders, or Imams, are influential in the communities. They lead prayers at the local mosques, teach at Koranic schools and *the zaouias*, institutions for further religious education, conduct burial ceremonies, lead evening prayers, supervise vigils in the homes of the deceased, write Koranic amulets and charms, give guidance in special situations, and, in return, receive tithes of corn, olives, dried figs, and other types of goods.

The world view of the Kabyle centers upon factors related to Islam. The five pillars of Islam are staunchly observed. In addition, the honor of the family and tribe is highly regarded. The preservation of their cultural distinctiveness and language is important to them as a people.

The Kabyles are said to have been driven into their mountain homeland from coastal lands by Arab peoples. This is supported to some degree by their mode of subsistence, which is not well-adapted to the mountainous region in which they live. It is striking that, outside of small gardens, cultivated terraces are absent in this area although they are widely used in other mountainous regions of North Africa. Some authors have suggested that the Kabyles might, in fact, be refugees from the plains who have tried to adapt a lowland, agricultural economy to a harsher mountain environment.

There have been drastic changes in recent years. The Kabyles were among the first to join in the revolution against the French after World War II. They continue to remain staunchly independent of all centralized governments, including the national Algerian government.

Economically, this has always been a rather poor area. A common method of survival is to depend upon income sent from male migrant workers who work outside the area. There continues to be out-migration of men to France and oil fields in the Middle East, who send money back to their relatives in Kabylia.

Recently, the Algerian government has poured vast sums of money into the area, bringing the beginnings of an economic boom. Development projects have included textile mills, roads, bridges, schools, hospitals, and improved agricultural techniques and projects, resulting in the creation of thousands of new opportunities for Kabyle workers. As a consequence, they have now begun to occupy a more favorable economic position within the greater Algerian society. However, it remains to be seen whether this will break down their independence.

The Kabyles are clearly a separate people group. Their cultural identity has been maintained throughout history and distinguishes them from the larger Arab population in North Africa.

Unreached Status of the Kabyles

In the first centuries after the death and resurrection of Christ, Christianity flourished in North Africa. Little of this Christian presence remains today, and North Africa has been an Islamic stronghold for at least 12 centuries.

Islam has penetrated the warp and woof of the fabric of the Kabyle society so thoroughly that all else is wrapped in an Islamic cloth. Existing knowledge of Christianity has come mainly through the teaching of Islamic teachers, much of which is distorted and blatantly hostile to Christianity.

A different picture of Christianity was presented throughout the French occupation of Algeria from 1830 through 1962. During this time, churches of European origin and predominantly Roman Catholic, were present, but they focused upon the needs of the one million French settlers. In urban areas and those agricultural areas with a large French presence, Algerian peoples received some exposure to Christianity as it was practiced by the European church. But in the rural areas, in which most Kabyles lived, there was much less contact with the French and their Church. Hardly any knowledge of Christianity was actually transmitted to the Kabyles.

More direct exposure to the gospel of Jesus came from valiant Christian workers who worked among Kabyles throughout this period. In 1880, an early Protestant worker, George Pearse, encountered four starving Kabyles during a visit to Algiers. He was told of their mountain homeland and convicted of their need to hear the gospel. Upon returning to Britain for furlough, he shared his call with Christians there. This led to the founding of the Mission to the Kabyles in 1881, which was later renamed the North African Mission.

These early missionaries discovered that the Kabyles were a proud people, practicing a form of Islam adapted to their animistic background. The work of these early witnesses was concentrated mainly in cities and towns tangential to the Kabyle homelands. Their efforts met with minimal success.

Several factors presented hindrances to the gospel. First, there was a strong identification of Christianity with the West and western influences were ardently resisted. Second, the concordat between France and Algeria stipulated that religious beliefs be respected under the French colonial administration. Thus, during this period evangelism was seen as illegal proselytism and discouraged. Third, there was a complete absence of believers in neighboring people groups, such as the Chouia and Tuaregs, and no existing forces for evangelism in the area of the Kabyles. Fourth, few evangelists were able to witness to Kabyles in their own language.

The Kabyles today remain an unreached people group. Yet, in the years prior to the independence of Algeria in 1962, there was a dynamic and effective ministry in their homeland.

Evangelism Among the Kabyles

After Pearse's work, evangelical witnesses continued to share the gospel among the Kabyles, primarily in the major villages or towns. There was little Christian witness in the more distant villages of their homeland. In the 1920s, a Protestant missionary couple, Charles and Pearl Marsh, caught the vision of working among Muslims in North Africa. They eventually became part of a small group of courageous witnesses in the area including the Griffiths, Youngs, Rollands, Arthurs, Wilsons, and others.

The first years were difficult. Both Charles and Pearl Marsh understood French and Arabic, but they found that the

Kabyles actually saw this as a barrier to effective communication and sharing of the gospel. These were "foreign languages." Pearl knew Kabyle, having grown up in a Kabyle village, but Charles had to learn the difficult language. Months were spent studying the Kabyle language before he knew the language well enough to work in it or to begin the translation of the Scriptures. Miles of steep, rocky mountain roads and footpaths were covered as they visited hundreds of Kabyle villages.

The Kabyles distrusted foreigners, and each village was a fortress unto itself. The missionaries worked at establishing rapport by developing personal relationships.

This outreach began to bear fruit as the Marshs established a reputation for integrity and openness to Kabyle culture and society. They began to be allowed into villages and Kabyle homes. They were respectfully listened to as they shared the gospel, yet the response of the Kabyles, although respectful, was seldom open and at times turned hostile.

In 1926, the Marsh family established a home in Lafayette, a French village. It was planned as a center from which the gospel could spread to the surrounding Kabyle villages. Soon they began gospel meetings in their home. These were attended by many French residents, of whom some came to faith in Christ. The success of their witness worried the Roman Catholic landlord, who forced them to move. A new home was found in a small Arab village eight miles away, and here their ministry grew.

Charles and Pearl established a biweekly dispensary, where they treated the many illnesses of the Kabyle people, while at the same time, continuing their visitation of remote Kabyle villages and hamlets. Eventually, they established an outpost in a Kabyle village where they constructed a building. Every Friday they traveled to the village to be at the strategic, busy weekly market. Classes were held in the morning and the afternoons were spent visiting and witnessing in local villages of the area. Saturday was a day for ministering to the sick and ailing.

Eventually, further trips to share the gospel were made from the Kabyle village into surrounding areas. The sick were tended, conversations were held with those present in mosques, classes were given for schoolboys, and messages were delivered to men who gathered to hear the gospel.

This ministry respected the many needs of the Kabyles and attempted to heal both their spiritual and their physical ailments. It allowed Charles and Pearl Marsh to develop their reputation as people who cared, were willing to listen, and to meet needs as best they could. The work went on for a long period and resulted in a number of new Kabyle Christians.

Great persecution met converts as they returned to their families and villages to share their good news. There are many stories of Kabyles who were ostracized, beaten, and even killed for their faith in Jesus Christ. Perhaps the women suffered the most. Being under the complete control of their husbands, fathers, or brothers, they were often abused and made to suffer severely for their faith without any support or companionship. Many became martyrs to the persecution of their countrymen and kinsmen.

Overall, reaction to this ministry ranged from tolerance to overt resistance. Factors which hindered the work included the high rate of illiteracy; 60 percent of the adult population was totally illiterate in 1950. Also, there was a long-standing, entrenched prejudice against Christianity, which was seen as the religion of Europeans.

Work was furthered hindered in 1954 when the war of independence against France began. Curfews, travel restrictions, and dangers of many types restricted the missionaries. Charles continued to visit even the most remote villages. Gradually the ferociousness of the conflict reduced the extent of his travels, and even their home base became dangerous. Yet, their witness continued as God protected them with his loving hand. In 1962, an invitation came from brethren in Chad to come and help evangelize Muslims, and the Marsh family moved to Chad, remaining there a few years.

On their return to Algeria, following independence in 1962, they found numerous restrictions on their work by the new national government. Gradually, all medical work came under national control, and open evangelism by expatriates or others was outlawed. Low key evangelism by national believers continued, but it faced increasing restriction.

Eventually, open evangelistic and mission work in Algeria became impossible, and foreign missionaires were forced out of Algeria. Continuing outreach had to be low key and carried out by tentmakers or the few Kabyle Christians that were left.

Christian outreach to Kabyles in Algeria has continued through the use of Christian radio programs, which started in 1973. Literature programs have also continued, as increased literacy among the Kabyles has opened up opportunities.

The result has been a growth in the number of conversions. In 1950, there were only ten identifiable Protestant converts among the Kabyles in Algeria, but by 1986, this had increased to over 150. The actual rate of conversion is much higher than this, but many Kabyle converts choose to leave Algeria because of persecution.

Increasing tolerance toward Christianity has been noted among the Kabyles in Algeria. Now there are even a number of small groups of Protestant believers meeting in low key, barely visible "worshiping groups." It is reported that greater openness exists among the Kabyle youth, who are beginning to see that Islam is also a foreign influence.

Present Situation

The results of the work carried out by Charles and Pearl Marsh, the people who preceded them, and those continuing to work with the Kabyles are increasingly evident. Of the 200,000 Kabyle emmigrants, many are Christians and are praying for the spread of the gospel in their homeland.

Kabyles and other North African Christians living in France meet regularly to pray, study, and plan for greater witness to their relatives still in Algeria. Others visit their homeland to share Christ with family or friends. Still others are involved in radio ministry, beaming gospel messages in Kabyle to Algeria. In addition, Kabyle believers in Algeria continue to share their faith through personal evangelism, encouraged by the periodic journeys of concerned Christian friends who bring news of the support of their brothers and sisters elsewhere. The gospel is continuing to be shared with the Kabyles of Algeria.

Based upon interviews, secondary research and, to a large degree, Charles Marsh's 1975 book, Too Hard For God, Chicago: Moody Press.

Chapter 9

TUAREGS OF NIGER

The scene is dramatic. Camels slowly moving across desert sands. Men in flowing robes, veiled in dark blue cloth from head to foot. Swords at their sides. Who are these people?

They are Tuaregs or "Warriors of the Blue Veil" and have long been known as warriors, traders, and travelers of the Sahara-- people of grace and nobility and fighters of fierce reputation. A nomadic people considered to be part of the Berber race, no one really knows when the Tuaregs first entered the desert area of North Africa. It appears that they came from the north as early as the seventh century A.D., and that certainly by the end of the fourteenth century, Tuaregs had reached as far as present day Nigeria.

Today, the Tuaregs are found in an area of North and West Africa covering Algeria, Libya, Niger, Mali, and parts of Nigeria and Burkina Faso. They are believed to number about 1.4 million, although it is difficult to state an exact figure. As with many nomadic peoples, the Tuaregs are suspicious of census takers and reluctant to give exact population figures. The Tuaregs have long been known to be fiercely Islamic and closed to Christian witness. This is beginning to change and the following is part of the story of this new beginning.

Definition of the Tuaregs as a People Group

Today, the Tuaregs can be divided into two major groupings. The Northern Tuareg are found in the Sahara itself. The Southern Tuareg live further south in the Sahel on the fringes of the true desert. Although the stereotype of the Tuareg places them in the shifting sands of the Sahara, in truth the vast majority, some 95 percent, live in the Sahel, which has a more grassland environment.

There are essentially four different Tuareg people groups. Probably the largest and most coherent single people group is the one speaking Tamashek. There are over 100,000 in this people group found in Niger around Tahoua. A second group is found further northeast in Niger. They speak Tamastariat and are centered around Agadez. A break-off of this group is found in the Hausa tribal area of Southern Niger. They are known as the Kel Gress. A third group is centered around Tamanrasset in Algeria and speak Tamahaq. There is a fourth group centered around Timbuktu in Mali. Each of these people groups needs a specific evangelistic strategy and outreach.

The Tamashek-speaking group is largely nomadic. They cover a range measuring 400 miles north to south and 300 miles east to west. In their nomadic travels they generally stay within Niger but will occasionally cross the northern or the southern border as they follow their herds, a practice that is becoming more difficult with the firmness of political boundaries increasing in this area. To meet this new constraint, they sometimes consign part of their herd to other nomads with whom they have had long-term relationships.

Tuareg society is built on herding and, to a lesser extent, farming. Yet, there has long been a tiny trickle of people to towns and villages in the area and to cities on the west coast of Africa, where they work for wages. When working outside of their home areas, the Tuaregs use the language most appropriate to the area. For example, if they move north they utilize Arabic, if they go west they use French, and if they go south they use Hausa.

The Tuaregs have a hierarchical society, which is divided into nobles, vassals or free men, priests, and servants. In the past, the nobles were engaged in warfare, raiding and long-distance caravan trade. The vassals were occupied with herding and short-distance caravans, which traded in cereals and dates. The priests formed an Islamic religious class. Their traditional roles were those of teachers, counselors, and judges in all matters concerning Islamic law and traditions. The servants were from other African tribes and performed many of the duties needed to sustain Tuareg ways of life. Even today, they are found intermingled with Tuaregs and working as herdsmen and blacksmiths.

Although the Tuaregs are considered Muslims, the religion they practice has an Islamic superstructure on top of earlier animistic practices and beliefs. Surprisingly, there is also a subterranean Christian context to their religion. Up until 1,100 years ago the Tuaregs were animists, but in contact with the Christian church in North Africa. There are many traits of the Tuareg culture that evidence this earlier Christian contact. For example, the Tuaregs use a Greek word for angel rather than the Arabic word. Also, they are one of the few people groups in this area which prefer monogamous rather than polygamous marriage patterns, even though there are strong forces for polygamy.

Within their religion, animistic practices and beliefs are powerfully entwined with Islam to the point that it is hard to see where animism leaves off and Islam takes over. Animistic practices include heavy use of charms and non-Islamic healing practices.

Full-time Islamic priests exist among the Tuareg. These positions are hereditary, yet only a few are practicing and teaching priests. These guard the orthodoxy of Islamic faith and practice among Tuaregs, while non-teaching priests live much like the rest of the Tuaregs.

The Tuareg world view is based upon the key values of courage and intellect. Tuaregs are warriors and men of the desert who pride themselves on courage. But courage is not enough, and there is a saying in the Tuareg language, "Thinking is better than strength." The Tuaregs do not define intellect in terms of scholarly achievement--knowledge of Islam is not necessarily an area of pride. Instead, they think of intellectual prowess as the use of cunning to succeed in hard situations. The two key Tuareg values are expressed in gait, gestures, postures, and various forms of behavior and can be seen in the importance they place on elegance, arrogance, refinement and strength.

Prestige built upon intellect and strength is a paramount concern. The Tuaregs are surrounded by groups which are of lower status. Traditionally, Tuaregs were the conquerors from the north. Their position of superiority only changed when the French defeated them through trickery after a long series of battles and stand-offs. Despite this, Tuaregs see themselves as superior to surrounding groups.

Tuareg society is presently threatened by great change and stress. Political boundaries have divided their territory and created obstacles to traditional forms of trade and nomadic movement. New vaccines and other benefits of modernization have increased longevity and reduced mortality, thereby leading to fast growing populations. Development efforts have led to larger herds and increased use of land for cultivation, resulting in increased pressure on land and resources. Droughts in 1973 and, more recently, 1983-85, have put tremendous pressure on the Tuaregs as they have attempted to continue a traditional form of life in an increasingly difficult situation.

Migration is beginning to be significant as thousands of Tuaregs have moved to West African cities. Two forms of urban migration exist. Within a nation, on a yearly cycle entire families move to the cities during the periods when farming is nonproductive. There they find work for four to seven months. Migration to cities in other countries is more often long term, noncyclical, and is mostly done by unmarried men.

These migration patterns can be explained partly by class. Those in the lower classes, who work as servants, are more accustomed to hard work and easily find menial or manual labor in cities. Other classes want administrative jobs and seek comparable work in towns. These are more difficult to find. Thus, there is more opportunity for lower class migrants in cities than there is for the upper classes. Although some nobles, vassals, and priests have migrated to cities and taken positions of power and prestige as merchants, guards, or Islamic teachers; the lower classes have generally been more successful.

The Tuaregs are a significant, unreached people in West Africa. In this case description, we focus more narrowly on one of the constituent, defined people groups, the Tamashek-speaking Tuaregs of Niger.

Unreached Status of the Tuaregs

As Muslims, Tuaregs have long been known for their hostility toward Christian outreach of any kind. Tuareg knowledge of Christianity is often indirect and filtered through the Islamic teaching of Christianity which results in a distorted understanding.

There has been a history of Christian activity among Tuaregs. Roman Catholics have been present in the area for many years but, until recently, had little overt outreach to the Tuaregs. Recently, however, a Roman Catholic mission station has been established in the area inhabited by those speaking Tamashek.

Protestant evangelical mission activity began in earnest in this area in the 1950s, when a missionary who had worked among the Hausa moved into the Tamashek area and began working with Tuaregs. He did not learn the Tuareg language nor attempt to contextualize the gospel in terms of the Tuareg culture. He was able to establish a Christian presence and reduce the level of hostility toward Christians, through the development of rapport among the Tuaregs. This was a significant contribution to the evangelization of the Tuaregs.

Other work that has been done among the Tuaregs include translation of the Gospel of Mark using Roman characters in 1934, and in Tifinagh (Tuareg) characters in 1936. Old Testament books in Tifinagh followed: in 1948, Ruth, and in 1954, Daniel, Obadiah, Jonah and Habbakuk.

Reaching the Tuaregs

In the 1960s a new mission work began among Tuaregs. Straight out of missionary training, a young missionary couple arrived in Niger to work with the Tuaregs. They had been praying for this opportunity after hearing an experienced missionary challenge them to this work at a missions course in their Bible college.

They saw the need for a number of preparatory steps. The language had to be learned well enough to speak about spiritual matters. Not only were language skills necessary necessary, but the culture had to be understood. It would also be essential to live a Tuareg-style nomadic life to build friendships, contextualize the gospel, and gain credibility among the

Tuaregs. Another requirement was the need to master the unusual Tuareg script, Shifinar or Tifinagh, in order to produce written materials. Last, they felt that by using traditional forms of Tuareg music there would be significant response to the gospel message on the part of the Tuaregs.

The husband states that he saw the need to build friendships with the Tuaregs by gaining credibility through their lifetyle, "I just could not stand out there proclaiming the gospel. I had to live the gospel." The missionary family began to understand the culture and develop intimate contacts with the people. They learned the Tuareg language and participated at every possible opportunity in Tuareg culture. They traveled as a family with Tuaregs, using a camel, a horse, and a wagon instead of motorized vehicles to avoid giving the impression of being wealthy. Their house in town was available to Tuaregs at all times. They provided hospitality in a traditional manner, with skins on the floor for seating and a teapot ready for tea and conversation. Frequently, Tuaregs spent the night with them as they came through the area.

The Tuaregs were made to feel comfortable with the missionary family. Their participation in nomadic travels made sense to Tuaregs. Relationships became easy to establish, both on the trail and in town. The hospitable nature of the Tuaregs and the people-oriented personalities of the missionaries and their children were a perfect fit. Many personal friendships were established, based upon hours of conversation and interaction.

These friendships opened up opportunities to share about Jesus Christ. The Tuaregs invited them to explain their beliefs, asking questions such as, "What do you believe about the prophet? What do you know about heaven?"

In the missionaries' home it was more appropriate for them to actively witness to the Tuaregs. Tracts, records and conversation were all used. Warm friendships were kept up over time, but the goal was always to share Christ.

Success has been achieved. There are now Tuareg Christians. A number of factors influenced the success of this work. The missionaries came to this work with the belief that one should share the gospel at the point of need. They looked for these points of need and found two. The first was that of forgiveness. There was a strong desire among Tuaregs to be forgiven by their God. The Islamic emphasis upon works and the fact that surrounding Islamic peoples saw the Tuaregs as bad Muslims have both worked to create a sense of spiritual unworthiness among Tuaregs. The missionary states, "Christ shines brightly in this area."

The second point of need was that of answers to prayer. The missionaries and their children prayed about everything: transportation, animals, sickness, and other needs of the Tuaregs. The power of prayer was evident as God answered these prayers.

The presence of the entire family was also significant to the success of the work. Their commitment to the Tuaregs was evidenced by the fact that the entire family lived among them.

The use of the Tuareg language was also key to the success of the work. The missionaries sought to understand the language to the extent that they could talk about spiritual matters. They demonstrated their commitment by translating materials into the Tuareg language using Tuareg script. They were able to enlist the help of a linguist who analyzed the language and helped the translation work to proceed. After five years, a translation of the Gospel of Mark was published--a major breakthrough. Because it was in their own script, it was accepted with great enthusiasm, setting the tone for early success in this work.

The use of Tuareg music also opened many doors. The missionaries were the first outsiders to use the actual musical patterns of Tuaregs for hymns, although it took 12 years to develop the facility for this. The missionaries have composed music using Tuareg patterns and given concerts, which were attended by many Tuaregs. Overall, the response has been tremendous.

Above all else, the success of this work has depended upon the commitment of the missionaries and their children to long-term work with Tuaregs. The missionaries stated it took five years to arrive at the "starting point" in their work. Perseverance was the key. Their mission was willing to commit itself to long-term development and support. It was willing to be flexible enough to allow frequent furloughs in times of family need. It kept the missionaries in the field through its flexibility and willingness to be committed to this ministry.

Present Situation

At the present time, the missionaries describes their work as "barely on the map." They have established credibility for their existence and work among the Tuaregs. They travel to other areas where they have never been before and find their reputations have preceded them. They are accepted as people of integrity. This creates an opening for sharing the gospel before they ever make contact with Tuaregs for the first time.

The Christian church among the Tuaregs is in its initial stages. Because Tuaregs are nomadic, it is hard to describe it as a community of believers. There are believers, but they are scattered throughout Tuareg country. Miles separate them, and these dispersed Christians often do not know one another.

The missionaries and their children are the links that tie Tuareg Christians together.

A present emphasis is to develop an identity for Christians and to link them in low key, low visibility ways so that they can build up and support one another. This is important because overt Christian witness would be greatly opposed, placing Christians in great danger of being persecuted or even killed if their commitment were publicized. Although, the missionaries do not demand that converts become publicly known, Tuareg Christians are beginning to stand up for the gospel in their own communities even though there has not been a corporate form of witness as yet.

The missionaries have identified their ministry priorities for the future. They will continue to evangelize among the thousands who know nothing of Christ. They plan to use widespread evangelism, personal witnessing, translation of the scripture into Tuareg script, and concerts using Tuareg musical patterns.

A second area of ministry will be discipling and building an identity for the known believers. There are believers now who are beginning to win others to Christ. A contextualized church is beginning to develop, which is already a bridgehead to the rest of the Tuareg population, but more discipleship, nurturing, and training are needed.

The third area is to work with the leaders who are emerging from among this growing community of believers. The church has not formally singled out leaders. God himself is raising leaders, who need training and encouragement.

The "Warriors of the Blue Veil" are beginning to see Jesus Christ as their personal Savior. The church among the Tuaregs is at the point where things can accelerate. With God's help, the church will take off through the work of the missionaries and the efforts of Tuareg Christians. There are Tuareg believers who are actively witnessing. The church will continue to stand. God will be glorified in Tuareg land!

Based upon interviews and secondary research.

Chapter 10

KOMONOS OF BURKINA FASO

by M. B. Vaillant

In West Africa many of the agrarian peoples belong to a group collectively referred to as the Senufo. They number almost three million and are found in the Ivory Coast, Mali, and Burkina Faso, in a less fertile area generally referred to as the Middle Volta, lying between major traditional trade routes. Islamization in this area is a fairly recent phenomenon, but it has occurred at such an increasingly rapid rate that approximately one-third of the Senufo peoples are now Muslim.

This case description deals with the Komono people of Burkina Faso, one of the various small people groups which make up the Senufo people of West Africa.

Description of the Komono as a People Group

Approximately 8,000 Komono people live in an area of southwest Burkina Faso centered around the town of Mangodara. They are also found in the Ivory Coast in an area bordering Burkina Faso.

The Komono are agrarian, cultivating millet, maize and yams. Because they have long been cultivators, much of their mythology and many of their core values are associated with the earth. Agricultural production, as with most areas of life, is organized along communal lines. No individual stands alone within Komono society; he or she is always a member of a group such as an extended family, hamlet or village. One eats in a group, produces as a group, makes decisions as a group, owns and has access to land as a group, and, from birth, is socialized to lower his or her own individual desires in deference to those of the group.

Political and social organization is primarily at a village level. Village chiefs are chosen in terms of seniority within the kinship group. This is changing. Since the August 1983 revolution, Committees for the Defense of the Revolution have been set up in each village. These committees now exert the authority of the national government in decisions regarding village economic, social, and political life.

Although, the Komono people are now Muslims, Islam came to the Komonos only 50 years ago through the preaching of Yaya, an Islamic prophet from Guinea. Before that, they were animists. There are still signs of the vitality and importance of animism, although these are hidden from public view.

As did other Senufo peoples, the Komono had long resisted the influence of Islam, although it was introduced to the area by Dyoula traders around the eleventh century. A number of factors accounted for their resistance. First, the Komonos were cultivators with strong ties to the earth, signified by rituals and beliefs which refer to nature spirits. Second, deceased ancestors are an important focus of veneration and worship. This discouraged acceptance of Islam, which would have removed the dead from direct participation with the living. A third factor was the communal nature of Komono society. An individual would not likely convert to a new religion unless the entire group converts with him or her.

Yet, the Komonos converted to Islam, and part of the cause must be found in the rapid changes coming with colonialization, encroachment of outside forces, and independence. Tribal religions, with their localized duties and particularistic beliefs, do not satisfactorily explain change. Islam, as a major world religion, offered coherent explanations for recent events and changes.

The worldview of the Komono centers around their relationship to the land. Agricultural work is highly valued. During times of heavy agricultural demands the Komono sleep in the fields instead of returning to villages. Their children are often kept from school so that they can continue traditional cultivation practices. Today, however, the traditional values associated with the land are tempered somewhat by the growing importance of Islam.

The Komono are immersed in a complex social system. They are surrounded by numerous other people groups such as the Selengele and the Banbadjon Dogosie, small tribes which are often considered to be the same people group as the Komono. Yet, each tribe has a distinct language and is best understood as a different people. Among the three, Komonos feel superior, although all three groups intermarry and communicate with one another in Dyoula. Other people groups such as the Mossi, Dyoula, and Lobi have recently come to live in the Komono area. Although they live in the same villages, they are considered strangers by the Komonos.

The Komono are clearly a separate people group in Burkina Faso. Strong core values centered on cultivation of the land, linguistic separation, and a sense of history all contribute to the making of a distinct people group.

Unreached Status of the Komonos

The Komonos are Muslims and have an Islamic interpretation of the world, including Christianity. A small minority of Komono have been taught in Koranic schools, where they have acquired some knowledge of Old Testament stories and familiarity with Christianity, albeit in a negative light. A few other Komono have gone to French schools, where they were exposed to the teachings of Roman Catholicism. This has generally been on a superficial level and was not a well worked out presentation of the gospel. Thus, the average Komono has little idea of Christianity and Christian practices. In general, what is known is not favorable, yet there has been growing respect for evangelical Christians due to their strict standards of morality, including abstention from alcohol.

Christians have been in this area for some time. The Roman Catholic church was present in the French colonial era and is still active. The Assemblies of God have now established a work in this area and have attracted four Christians from among the Banbadjon Dogosie. On the Ivory Coast side of the border, the New Tribes Mission plans to start work among the Komonos.

Communication of the gospel has been hampered among the Komono for a number of reasons. First, there are a great many people groups in southwest Burkina Faso, and the Komono, being few in number, have not been given a high priority by missions and churches. Second, the Komonos live far away from areas in which missionaries are working, and the roads into their area are in bad condition, making travel difficult. Third, the Komonos are noted for being conservative and resistant to change. They resisted Islam for centuries before finally accepting it as a group. Lastly, the acceptance of Christianity has required changes in cultural practices which are seen as unacceptable. This includes a reduced reverence and veneration for ancestors.

The Komono are clearly an unreached people group, almost totally Islamic, with few effective Christian witnesses who can communicate in the Komono language in culturally appropriate ways.

Process of Evangelism Among the Komono

I first heard about the Komonos over 20 years ago when I began to research the Gan tribe, a neighboring people group. I was told that the Gan, Dogosie and Komono were from the same language family. I became interested in the Komono and curious as to the state of Christianity among them. Occasional visits allowed me to see that Christianity was indeed largely unknown or misunderstood. In fact, I was not able to find one Christian among the Komono people, who all claimed to be Muslim.

In the late 1960s, with a group of Bible School students from the Lobi Tribe, I attempted to visit the Komonos, but this failed when our car went through a bridge and the road further on became impassable. Although our interest continued in evangelizing the Komonos, we made no further attempts to visit them until 1980. At that time, a young Swiss missionary was able to visit the Komonos by motor bike. He shared the message of Jesus Christ with them and received a polite hearing, but, in general, no response was seen.

In 1983, the Assemblies of God sent a young Massai couple to start a work among the Komonos. They live in Mangodara and have assumed a lifestyle similar to the Komono, as they attempt to live out their faith among the Komono as good community members and persons respectful of the land. This is an excellent testimony and has begun to lower the suspicion and barriers that separate the Komonos from hearing the gospel.

In 1984, a Lobi pastor, another missionary couple and I were again able to visit the Komono by motor bikes. There we met the Assemblies of God missionaries for the first time.

In 1986 I visited the Komonos in Mangodara to show the "Jesus film." This was well received and has given the Mossi Assemblies of God missionary couple opportunities to answer many questions about the gospel.

The Mossi missionaries have also been engaged in a healing ministry and have prayed for the sick with dramatic results. The results of the film, active witness of this couple, and display of God's power have begun to arouse the interest of the Komonos in Christianity.

Present Situation

The Komono are still unreached, and there are no known Komono Christians. Yet, Assemblies of God missionaries have begun to be accepted within the community, and have attracted the attention and respect of the Komono peoples. They are beginning to be heard as authentic witnesses of Christ among the people. There is yet a great work to be done in the establishment of a Komono church.

Chapter 11

REACHING THE NUBIANS OF EGYPT

by Steve Chism, Fran Hart, and Teresa Toms

I will never forget the expression on the face of Abdul Rafan, the Nubian schoolmaster, when I asked him, "Where did your family live in the old country?" Up until that moment, the distinguished old Nubian had been cordial but not emotive during our tour of a school built for relocated Nubians. He dressed in Western style clothes, his bespectacled face looking a bit haggard, but kind.

My question lit his eyes with deep longing. I could tell that he loved to dream about the old country, but he hated to think about recent events in his homeland. I was asking him to do both. He slowly lifted his long pointer to a map of Egypt and Sudan and pointed at a pale blue spot on the map which covered parts of both countries. "Our homes are submerged here." The word "submerged" was very precisely enunciated. He said it as if his home of carved and painted mud still stood under the reservoir of the Aswan dam.

Abdul Rafan spoke eagerly of the beauty of the narrow ribbon of fertile Nile valley called Nubia before it was inundated by the backwaters of the new Aswan dam in the early 1960s. He spoke longingly of evening dances under the dense date palms, and of the wonder of receiving gifts from his uncle, who worked as a servant in distant Cairo.

I asked him to tell me the story of his village. For some reason he felt that he had to begin the tale centuries ago. He gestured as if to warn me of an impending shock. "Once we were Christians, many years ago..."

Nubians: At One Time Christians

In 540 A.D., missionaries from Constantinople sailed up the Nile to the land of Nubia. Egyptian Christians who settled among the Nubians or conducted business with them had already spoken to them about Jesus Christ and prepared them for evangelization. Twenty years after the arrival of the missionaries, the king of Nubia decreed that their pagan temples be transformed into Christian churches. In this way, Nubians were converted to the Egyptian Coptic church.

About 100 years later, an Arab army invaded Egypt, forcefully introducing Islam to its Christian population. The Nubians refused to embrace the new religion or pay taxes imposed by the Arab leaders, and the Islamic tide was stopped at the first cataract of the Nile, the beginning of the ancient land of Nubia.

For the next 700 years, the Nubians resisted the onslaught of Islam, supporting the persecuted Copts in Upper Egypt. One king of Nubia even invaded Egypt to free the Coptic pope, who had been imprisoned for not having paid his tax to the Islamic conquerors.

Though they held out for almost seven centuries, the Nubians eventually accepted Islam. As they tell the story, one of their leaders in the sixteenth century gathered all the village sherifs (chiefs) together to decide what to do about the continuing skirmishes with the Muslim invaders. The sherifs agreed to pay tribute and thus buy protection. Following their leadership, the whole of Nubia converted to Islam in less than a month. The economic relief from war was accompanied by the instant protection from slave raids by Arab tribesmen, since Islam prohibited any Muslim enslaving another.

Nubians have retained some religious practices from the days when they were Christian, and some from their older traditional religion. For example, on the third day after a baby's birth, it is dipped into the Nile, in a style reminiscent of baptism. The Nubians make the sign of the cross as a protection against evil and decorate many of their doorways with a cross in mud relief. In the recent past, Nubian grooms carried a cross of twisted palm fibers in the wedding procession. But none of these symbols have any real meaning. Nubians acknowledge their Christian roots; in fact, some are strangely proud that their race held out against Islam for so many centuries. But they now say that Islam is the complete religion and Christianity was only a stepping stone to the full religion of Islam.

Geographical Relocation: "Nubia Drowned"

Portions of Nubian lands have been covered in successive manmade floods caused by damming the Nile at Aswan as early as 1897, 1912, and 1927. Each time, Nubians were compensated in some way, but in the early 1960s, they watched the last of ancient Nubia within the borders of present-day Egypt disappear under the backwaters of the latest dam. However, authentic Nubian villages still survive in northern Sudan, though most of the Nubians dwell in the major cities of Omdurman and Khartoum. Egyptian Nubians were all moved to resettlement villages in an area called "New Nubia" near the city of Kom Ombo. There are more than 650,000 Nubians living in both Egypt and Sudan.

Nubians find it hard to express their lingering horror at losing ancient homelands to floods of water. Although attempts were made to move entire villages to new locations, no land along the riverbank was available -- only plots of desert sand kilometers away from the river. Here, there was little to remind them of home. The houses built by the government, though adequate, failed to reflect any features of distinctive Nubian architecture, and government agriculture programs, which tried to help them scratch something from their new desert plots, could not bring back the lush date groves in the old country. They even lost some of their traditional ceremonies and dances during the move. Altogether, the relocation proved to be a massive crisis of identity, which is still unresolved.

Another kind of relocation is not new to Nubians: urbanization. For centuries, Nubian men have ventured from their homelands to the cities of Egypt for employment as servants, doormen, and waiters, sometimes staying away from home for years at a time. This practice has been so widespread that in some Nubian villages, females serve as heads of over half of the households.

Thousands of Nubians are found in the major cities of Alexandria and Cairo. Although most say they plan to return to their homes, the spartan resettlement villages lack the magnetic allure of the old homelands, and they remain in the cities. In addition, more and more Nubian women are staying in the cities with their husbands, resulting in a significant urban Nubian population in the two largest cities in Africa--Cairo and Alexandria. Although there are no distinct Nubian neighborhoods, special social clubs have kept Nubian tribal linkages intact in the urban environment.

Ethnic Distinctives: "We Are Not Arabs"

Nubians in Egypt take pride in being Egyptian citizens. Yet, even though all but a few of the older men are fluent in Arabic, visitors are often told, "We are not Arabs."

Nubians display the dark skin and tight curly hair of black African peoples, and most Egyptians refer to them as "black" people. But their color and features vary enough to indicate some intermarriage over the centuries with Arab and other Mediterranean races. Their dress is also distinctive. In "New Nubia," a Nubian man always stands out because of the narrow sleeves on his full length tunic.

In the rigidly stratified Egyptian society, such things as race, wealth, occupation, and education all work together to give each person a place of relative respect. Color-conscious Egyptian urbanites look on the black Nubians as a servant group and avoid intimate association with them. For centuries Nubians have held service occupations, first as slaves, and later as willing workers, and now as the most desirable and trustworthy doormen and waiters. However, their reputation as excellent servants has not changed their status. Even the Egyptian farming peasants of the delta look down on the Nubians as underclass.

Despite the mild contempt with which they are viewed by Egyptians, the Numbians quite proudly identify themselves as Nubians, speaking their own language which they call "Ratana," and marrying within their own people. Although the men are allowed to take a Muslim, non-Nubian mate, there are social strictures that prevent Nubian women from marrying non-Nubians. In fact, marriages of either Nubian men or women with non-Nubians are rare since prejudice against the Nubians is substantial, and they are not considered desirable mates by the rest of Egyptian society.

In upper Egypt, where as many as 10 percent of the population can be Christian, many Copts live near "New Nubia." But having a common heritage in the church does not open the communities to each other. Christians are perceived by Nubians as an insular society, withdrawn in selfishness or pride. And the feeling is shared by their Islamic neighbors. In one instance, an Egyptian, unable to understand two Nubians speaking in "Ratana," taunted them, saying "Why are you acting like Christians?" The comment reveals the subtlety of the barriers between the three communities of Arabs, Christians, and Nubians.

Within the Nubian community itself there are subdivisions. Most Nubians recognize three major groups, two of them speaking dialects of the "Ratana" language, and the other speaking only Arabic.

The Kenuz Nubians lived farthest to the north near Aswan before the dam ruined their homeland, but their distinctive patterns of architecture, such as arched mud-brick roofs, still appear whenever they build homes for themselves. Their building designs and certain special religious celebrations are so similar to the Dongolawi villages hundreds of miles to the south in Sudan that it is not surprising to find linguistic parallels as well. Their dialect is called "Kenzi" or "Metoki." They comprise about 39 percent of the Egyptian Nubians.

Fedija Nubians, who make up 52 percent of the Nubian population in Egypt, originally lived farther south than their Kenuz neighbors. The Fedija dialect is called "Mahas." Their architecture of pounded earth in wood frames is not distinctive from that of much of northern Africa. There are memories of hostility between the Fedija and Kenuz Nubians, but the shared tragedy of the dam deluge has softened any significant animosity. Although intermarriage is tolerated, they usually find more preferable matches within their own groups.

The Arab Nubians comprise about 9 percent of the Nubians in Egypt. Although they speak only Arabic, they are recognized by other Nubians and Egyptians as bona fide Nubians. The stability of this segment of the Nubian population, even after being displaced by the dam, casts into doubt the notion that distinctive Nubian culture will rapidly disappear into Egyptian society because of an increasing use of the Arabic language.

Evangelistic Directions: "In Our Language We Would be Pleased"

Nubians must be recognized as a distinct people group lacking any kind of meaningful force for evangelism. No church structure seeks or welcomes them. No missionaries focus efforts on them. There are no scriptures available in their mother tongue. Nubians fit the definition of an unreached people in every way even though they were at one time a Christian people.

As a people with a unique culture and distinct history, any successful evangelism strategy must include the following components.

(1) Use Nubian Language. The Nubian language has not died. It remains the central feature of Nubian identity despite education and business dealings in Arabic. Efforts to evangelize Nubians in their own language will prove to be more effective than if Arabic, the national language of Egypt, is used.

Old translations of portions of scripture exist. The Gospels were put into the Kenuzi dialect in 1912 and the British and Foreign Bible Society published a Gospel of Mark in the Fedija dialect in 1899. These scripture portions are neither in print nor distributed in any way. In fact, most Nubians have no idea that their language has ever been recorded. Because over 70 percent of Nubian men can read Arabic script, and many can read Roman script; they would have little trouble reading the Ratana language in either script.

Many Nubians would be very interested in anything published in "Ratana." One community leader stated, "If someone came and made books in our language, the people would be pleased-- it is our language." The Egyptian government does not encourage Nubian literature because of its effort to integrate Nubians into the national mainstream, and translations of Scripture into Nubian languages would likely be opposed. Distribution of Nubian scripture portions would be an even greater challenge, calling for creative approaches.

(2) Reach Urban Nubians. Evangelization of the Nubians could get a start among the thousands of Nubians working in major urban centers. Not only are they sprinkled throughout the cities, they tend to work in service jobs which puts them in natural, long-term relationships with expatriates. Nubian workers tend to be male heads of households with great potential impact on their families. Nubians in urban situations have greater freedom to make personal decisions and order their own lives, while at the same time keeping close contact with their home villages. The few known Nubian converts began to follow Christ while they were working or studying in the cities.

(3) Plant Churches Made Up of Nubian Converts. Evangelization of Nubians requires fresh churches to be planted which would use the Nubian language. Some Christians in Egypt estimate that there are hundreds of secret believers among the Nubian people. Yet, there are no Nubian churches, and the church as shelter and as proclamation point does not exist for the Nubians. Some have dreamed of Nubian worship celebrations where Nubian dance, song, and rhythm patterns would be used.

The churches need to be detached organizationally from the Coptic church. A supportive but quiet unity of Arabic and Nubian churches needs to remain. The evangelization of Nubians should not be based on the existing church for three reasons:

1. For a Nubian to attend one of the few local Coptic churches would be tantamount to cultural suicide. Public commitment by baptism would so severely damage the honor of family and village that severe sanctions could well drive a new believer away from village and kin.

2. The Egyptian government has recently put enormous pressure on non-Nubian converts in major cities, and hostile Muslim groups closely watch for conversions. Less visible home churches of some sort with minimal expatriate presence may be able to withstand such opposition.

3. Many Egyptian Christians have found it to be a problem when Muslim converts attend their churches because Christian-Muslim tensions are high and motives are suspect. Thus, the church has not actively sought Nubians as converts or members. There is, of course, the hope that the existing churches could take a key role in the evangelization of Nubians. Any efforts by expatriates should be done in careful consultation with select church leaders.

The Kenuz and Fedija sub-groups might well need separate church fellowships. Their languages are not mutually intelligible, and there is some evidence that the Kenuz and Fedija keep themselves separate on religious occasions. Mission efforts will need to make this an early point of research.

The main thrust of the church planting effort should be to prevent the Nubians from paying an artificially high price for repentance. A Nubian who decides to follow Christ usually leaves family, friends, honor, and all hope of meaningful life. An authentic Nubian church would testify that Christ calls Nubians to obey him as complete families and villages.

Reach Them Soon

Many scholars believe that the reference to "Cush" in Genesis 10:7 refers to peoples who have dwelt in the Nile valley south of the first cataract -- these are Nubians. Scholars believe there is a genetic continuity between these early peoples and present day Nubians. Nubians are one of the most ancient of unreached peoples -- now is the time to reach them.

To our knowledge, no one is now trying to reach the Nubians of Egypt, yet timing is critical. After the last relocation, Nubians were more responsive to the gospel. The resentment and disorientation resulting from the move still persists. This could be a time prepared by God for reaching them with his message of grace and hope.

Chapter 12

MUSLIM ZANZIBARIS OF SOUTH AFRICA

Lists of cultural and social groups by country or area are commonly found in works such as the *Unreached Peoples* series, the *World Christian Encyclopedia,* the *Encyclopedia of the Third World,* United States Government Area Handbooks, Human Relations Area Files indices, and a variety of volumes devoted to cultural and area overviews. Read uncritically, these lists can give us the impression that human societies or cultures are static and have always existed in the configurations in which they are presently found. This can lead us to the unwarranted assumption that human societies or groups do not change, in the sense of people groups either emerging as totally new or disappearing through time. Yet, human societies or groups have always been dynamic. Change can take place as humans move from area to area in response to environmental stress, in search of new opportunities or due to the pressure of other human populations.

The process of colonialism throughout the eighteenth and nineteenth centuries displaced hundreds of cultures and societies. Some were destroyed, such as the unfortunate inhabitants of Tasmania off the southeast coast of Australia. Others were displaced, such as the Caroline Islanders who were moved to Saipan and the Mariana Islands by the German colonial administration. These processes resulted in the formation of new people groups with newly defined needs for ministry. This case description concerns the Muslim Zanzibaris, who emerged as a new people group in South Africa within the last hundred years.

Description of Muslim Zanzibaris as a People Group

In the neighborhood of Chatsworth, an urban area close to Durban on the Natal coast of South Africa, can be found a community of Muslims referred to as Zanzibaris. These persons are the descendants of ex-slaves of Islamic Sultans who ruled coastal areas of East Africa and the island of Zanzibar itself. At present, this group consists of approximately 1,000 persons, growing at the same rate as the rest of the population of South Africa.

The process by which these people arrived at their present location and have become a distinct people group in the context of South African society has to be understood in light of the Islamization of East Africa. Islam had been carried to the coast of East Africa by Arab traders, slavers, and adventurers who established communities in coastal areas of East Africa. Islamic Arabs learned the language of the African people and intermarried with African women.

Descendants of these first Arab settlers became known as the Sawahila (*Sawahila* = coast), a community whose language became the lingua franca of the coastal areas and later of much of East Africa. This community lived and interacted with the African peoples. The result was an indigenous Islamic-African people which, although molded by Arab elements, preserved certain indigenous African cultural and religious features.

The Sawahila were traders and slavers. Their slave activity eventually penetrated to the area of northern Mozambique where the Makua were located, an influential people of the eastern coast of Africa. Many were captured and sold into slavery to Islamic Sultans of East Africa and Zanzibar. Eventually, most of these slaves accepted Islam.

It was from these slaves that the Zanzibaris originated. Britain, after abolishing slavery in her colonies in 1833, determined to stamp out the slave trade in the area. She had problems in carrying out her intent because of the importance of slaves for the commercial and social lives of the ruling Sultans. Eventually, however, this policy was successful, and in 1873 the Sultan of Zanzibar signed a treaty with Britain which committed him to stop the slave trade and to abolish slavery within his domain.

As a result of this agreement, freed slaves were brought to the British-controlled area of Natal in South Africa both to protect them from recapture by slave traders and to meet the need for cheap labor. The first group of 113 ex-slaves from Zanzibar and northern Mozambique arrived on August 4, 1873, and they continued to arrive through 1878, when immigration of Zanzibaris is ceased. Initially, the government of Natal planned to employ the new arrivals in public works projects but, due to the intervention of white settlers, decided to divide them equally between public works and private individuals, for whom they worked as indentured laborers. After a period of five years, a laborer received a "Freed Pass" and was allowed to settle permanently in Natal.

The ex-slaves soon formed their own separate community, concentrating in Kingsrest in the Durban area, where they became market gardeners for the growing urban communities of Durban. Government policy kept the Zanzibaris separate from the local black African population. This, plus the fact that the Zanzibaris saw themselves as different from the Christian or animist Blacks in the area, tended to enforce their separateness.

The Zanzibaris soon developed close links with Indian laborers, who lived in the same area. Their common allegiance to Islam drew them together in common worship in mosques and even burial in the same cemetery. Furthermore, the colonial government put both groups under the office of the "Protector of Indian Immigrants." Zanzibaris, thus, became closely aligned with Indian Muslims in Natal.

The link between Indian Muslims and Zanzibaris has remained strong to the present time, partly due to apartheid in South Africa. In determining where the Zanzibaris fit within its legally-recognized racial scheme, the South African authorities had to decide whether they were Asiatic, Blacks, or Coloureds. The Zanzibaris resisted the designation of Black or Coloured, for accepting either assignment would mean being subject to stricter regulations concerning movement and opportunities for employment. The Indian Muslim community supported the Zanzibaris' position and lobbied for their assignment with the Asian population. In 1961, the authorities classified the Zanzibaris within the Coloured groups, but in a special category known as "other Asiatics," under which they were to be treated on the same basis as the Indians. This has again intensified their links with the Indian Muslims.

In 1962, the South African government decreed that Kingsrest was to be reserved for White development and moved the Zanzibari en masse to the Chatsworth area in Durban. There they continue as a distinct community, working mainly in trade or as police, clerks, and laborers. Thus, they form a well-defined residential community of persons occupying a distinct economic niche.

Critical to the definition of Zanzibaris is their Islamic faith. They are ardent Muslims and adhere faithfully to the core practices of Islam, while mixing in many practices which reflect origins in African traditional religions. For example, Zanzibari medicine men are often called to help in cases of illness. They might suggest that the person is possessed by a malevolent spirit and require the patient to attend meetings where the spirit will be either exorcised or appeased.

The Zanzibari also practice *ratieh,* a ceremony done in remembrance of the prophet Mohammed in which participants work themselves into a state of ecstasy by repeating the name of Mohammed. Drums are also beaten and verses from the Koran are chanted repeatedly until a condition of ecstasy is achieved. Sharp metal objects are then stuck into the body while prayers are said to enable the devotees to overcome the pain. Zanzibaris say that the *ratieh* allows the devotee the obtain the "true feeling of Islam."

For the Zanzibari, respect for ancestors is of vital importance. They feel that the world of spirits is real and dynamic and that ancestors visit their progeny through dreams and visions to give help and guidance to the living. Their strong family structure includes those in the afterlife as active participants of the family, and propitiatory rites are then carried out with regard to ancestors. Thus, for Zanzibaris, ancestors play an important role in every-day life.

The Zanzibaris are clearly a people group in present-day South Africa. For over 100 years, they have been a well-defined residential community, first at Kingsrest, then at Chatsworth. Social interaction among the Zanzibaris is intense while contact with those outside the Zanzibari community is less frequent and not as meaningful. Zanzibaris stress that marriage should take place within the bounds of the community, and thus, intramarriage helps to distinguish them from other peoples living around them. Islam is of vital importance in defining them as a people group in that it has allowed them to keep a strong sense of self identity and to develop a political and economic strategy in the apartheid-ruled South African society. Official policies of the government have acted to distinguish them as a people group and keep them separate from the larger black African population.

Discussion of the Unreached Status of the Group

As Muslims, the Zanzibaris' knowledge of Christianity is based upon their contact with Christian groups in South Africa and the teachings of the Islamic religion. This is often superficial and prejudiced by the teaching of Islamic leaders and shaped through the Zanzibari cultural perspectives. To them, Christianity is the religion of outsiders, colonial and white leaders, who have often been seen as threats by the community. It is the religion of Blacks from whom the Zanzibaris attempt to maintain some distance due to the official policy regarding separation of races and cultural groups. Furthermore, Christianity, as practiced by either Whites or Black Africans, has been irrelevant to the cultural values and practices of the Zanzibaris. Islam has been a strong force for survival and has helped protect their sense of identity. It has allowed them to develop an alliance with Indian Muslims which has proved powerful as an adaptive strategy in South African society.

Christian outreach to the Zanzibaris began soon after their arrival in Natal. Roman Catholics began to work among Blacks in the Durban area in 1880, and the Saint Xavier Mission was established to work with Zanzibaris and Zulus in this region of Natal. The initial response from the Zanzibaris was favorable and soon a Roman Catholic community developed as a result of converts from the Zanzibari ex-slaves and Zulus. In 1897, Roman Catholics numbered 300 at the Saint Xavier Mission.

In contrast to their success among the Zanzibaris, the Roman Catholics had difficulty in their mission efforts among the Zulus in South Africa. Because of the persuasive influence that Zanzibari Christians had upon local Blacks in this area, the mission fathers became convinced that these converts should intermarry and thereby spread the gospel among them.

From this, there developed the idea of Catholic villages in Zulu areas. Twenty families from the Saint Xavier Mission, including some Zanzibari, settled among the Zulus in areas near Oakford, and they were integrated into churches with Zulu Christians. Together, they formed the nucleus of a new Christian community. Eventually, almost 2,000 Christians, predominantly Zanzibari but also Christian black Africans from the Natal area, were settled on Catholic mission lands by the latter part of the 1950s. The dispersal of Zanzibari Christians led to the spread of the church among the Zulus,but also the removal of Christian Zanzibaris from the Zanzibari community in Natal. Eventually, these Roman Catholic Zanzibaris lost their clear identity as Zanzibaris and were melded into the greater Zulu population. At the present, Zanzibari descendants cannot be distinguished as a separate people among the Zulus.

The remaining Zanzibaris in Natal are solidly Islamic. Their faith has been a strong factor in their retention of a separate identity in this area and it has also been important in their successful adaptation within the apartheid system of South Africa. The combined effect of apartheid and mission policies has been the strengthening of Islam among this group and the decrease in the force for evangelism among Zanzibari Muslims in Chatsworth.

Present Status

Presently, there are no Christian groups which are working directly with the Zanzibaris. However, there are a number of missions and churches in the area working among Indians. These include the Reformed Church in South Africa, Full Gospel Church, Church of the Nazarene, Lutheran Church, Roman Catholic Church, African Church and a number of small Pentecostal churches. They constitute potential forces for evangelism. Indeed, given the linkages between Indian Muslims and Zanzibari Muslims, there is some reason to believe that converted Indians can be effective in sharing the gospel with Zanzibari Muslims.

The Zanzibari Muslims of South Africa are an unreached people group in the midst of a heavily evangelized area. They are hardly unevangelized, but they are clearly unreached in the sense of having no indigenous community of believers which can effectively evangelize the rest of the group. As yet, there still exists a need for the development of a strategy to share the gospel with the Zanzibaris in such a way that it is seen as culturally relevant.

Based upon G.C. Oosthuizen's *The Muslim Zanzibaris of South Africa*, Durban: University of Durban-Westville, 1982, and personal correspondence.

Chapter 13

ASIANS OF NAIROBI, KENYA

by Archie Hensley

Asians in Nairobi, Kenya originally came from India, Pakistan, Bangladesh, Goa, and other South Asian regions. They were brought from India to Kenya by the British colonial government to build the East African railroad. After the railroad was completed, the migration from South Asia continued as others came to Nairobi in search of economic opportunity. Being a skillful people with excellent manual as well as clerical skills, they soon became the merchants and traders of Nairobi.

In the past, Asians in African cities have not been the primary focus of evangelization. Christian missions to Kenya have worked mainly with African peoples in rural locations. But with the continued growth of African cities, missions began to recognize the need for work among the growing urban population. Yet, even with this recognition, the focus of evangelization still remained upon the African population, to the neglect of Asians.

In the recent past there have been efforts to bring the gospel to Asians in African cities. One such effort is described here. This study focuses upon the "Asians" of Nairobi as an unreached people group and describes efforts to reach them for Christ.

Nairobi Asians as a People Group

There are at least 39,000 Asians in Nairobi, a city of 1.2 million. They form a people group made up of persons whose ancestors came from a number of South Asian ethnic and cultural backgrounds. The degree to which their countries of origin receive their primary loyalty varies. Approximately 70 percent identify themselves as "Kenyan Asians," based upon a stronger felt affiliation with Kenya than South Asian nations. Some subgroups, such as a few Islamic sects, have almost totally taken Kenya citizenship. Still, the fact that these persons are descendants of South Asian immigrants is an important determinant of their sense of a shared identity as a people group.

Asians are found throughout Nairobi, but there are certain areas in which they have concentrated, and it is in these areas that most of the Hindu and Muslim temples and mosques are found. Within residential areas there is further clustering in terms of housing. For example, Muslims tend to cluster within certain residential areas and enforce cultural practices which are dictated by the Islamic faith.

The Asian community is linguistically diverse. The major South Asian languages represented are Gujarati, Hindi, Tamil, and Urdu. Gujarati is the predominant South Asian language and is used by about 85 percent of Asian residents. Due to the use of English in the Kenyan educational system, English is becoming more widely used and, to some extent, binds this people group together.

Asians, in general, make up a significant percentage of the commercial community in African cities. This adaptive niche opened up as the British government recognized their usefulness as traders and merchants. In colonial society, it was the British who were usually in administrative positions, while Asians were in technical and shopkeeper professions and Africans were laborers. Asians were thus able to move easily into the middleman role and market Western goods to Africans while they ensured the flow of agricultural products from Africa to the West. This role continued and even expanded after independence to the point that many Asians are in import-export businesses and often own medium- to large-scale commercial enterprises. The result is a tightly integrated commercial community made up of Asians and based largely upon personal networks and inter-family ownership of businesses.

Although closely held together by religious, social, and community ties, Asians are not organized by any over-arching associations. There are, however, voluntary associations partly based on religious affiliation and partly on "caste." The role of caste differs from that found in South Asia in that occupational distinctions, though often influential, are not critical. Castes are primarily extended kin or family groups, and their importance has been reduced somewhat by the influence of Western cultural and social practices, the African context, and the fact that Asians are living outside the rural Indian environment. The influence of these voluntary associations, or castes, is not strong enough to cause internal divisions in the Asian community to the point of distinguishing separate people groups. Castes become most influential at the time of marriage when it is still common to find persons marrying within caste boundaries.

For the Asians, the sense of being a people group is partly based upon either Hinduism or Islam. Yet, because of contact with Western influences, such as educational and economic institutions, these religions have lost much of their pervasiveness in structuring social behavior and cultural values. Indeed, for some Asians, secularism or purely cultural forms of Hinduism or Islam are common. It can be accurately stated that the world view of many Asians in Nairobi is pragmatic. The role of supernatural forces is delimited, and primary concern is with financial and material security for oneself and one's family. Yet, for many others religion remains strong and all-embracing. Hindu, Muslim, and Sikh schools and activities abound. For these persons, core values continue to come from their religious beliefs.

The Asian population in Nairobi forms a pan-South Asian community united by the sense of common ethnic heritage, similar occupations, shared social status, and a political reality. In Nairobi, original differences between various ethnic communities and social groups are remembered, but there is a very real sense of being a minority population among a much larger African population. Asians in Nairobi are aware that their continued existence and livelihood depends upon the goodwill of local and national governments. Many in this people group have either personally suffered or have known someone who has suffered from the purges of Asian populations within Uganda or other African nations. Another important influence has been the role of English in establishing a semblance of linguistic homogeneity among the Asian population. Last, the impact of Western influences has diminished the importance of cultural particulars from a South Asian heritage and has, to some degree, highlighted newer, Western cultural forms and social behaviors.

Thus, Asians in Nairobi form a large and highly heterogeneous people group. They represent many South Asian ethnic, cultural and religious groups. Yet there is a shared sense of cultural and social origin along with a distinct set of behaviors and practices which presents a sharp contrast with their African neighbors.

The Status of Unreached Asians in Nairobi

It is presently estimated that a very small number of Asians, perhaps less than 1 percent, in Nairobi are evangelical Christians. There is a greater number of nonevangelical Christians. But by far the greatest portion of the population professes allegiance to Hinduism, Islam, or one of the many eastern mystical sects. Although evangelical efforts to reach these people began many years ago, it was not until the last ten years that significant advances began. It was thought that the difficulty in reaching Asians came from the fact that they had no interest in Christianity, but in reality, they had little if any knowledge of Christianity.

There are potential forces for evangelization of Asians in Nairobi. Hundreds of missions, organizations, churches, Bible schools, and theological seminaries are found in this city of over a million. Other evangelistic resources for evangelism include Christian radio and national television programs, which are broadcast in both English and Kiswahili, languages known to the Asian community. Many Christian bookstores exist, and a wide range of literature is available in South Asian languages which have been developed elsewhere and are available for use in Nairobi. Bible distribution and Christian literature have been directed toward the Asians of Nairobi for many years. Yet, in spite of these efforts, there has been proportionally less evangelistic effort directed toward them than toward the African national population. This has been especially true for evangelical churches and missions.

The primary reason for the presence of unreached Asians in Nairobi is not their rejection of Christianity, but rather, with notable exceptions, that their evangelization has not been given a high priority by either missions or churches. In fact, they are seen as "unreachable" by many Christians in Nairobi. One African pastor has even said, "Asians can not be saved."

Mission strategists in Kenya tend to focus on Africans, rural people, the poor and illiterate, and those considered open to the gospel. The South Asians of Nairobi fit none of the categories and thus have been effectively separated from hearing the gospel by a lack of strategy, methodology, and understanding of their needs as a people.

Moreover, the gospel has not been communicated in a way that respected Asian values or heeded Asian means or methods of communication. Either a Western gospel or an African gospel is communicated. To become a Christian means that an Asian is in danger of losing his or her cultural, social, and family identification. Western or African cultural factors which impede acceptance of the gospel by Asians are not well understood by mission strategists. There is a need to understand ideological, social, religious, and cultural factors affecting the communication of the Gospel with Asians. Christians concerned with Asians in Nairobi are more often moved by compassion than guided by understanding.

Development of a Ministry of Evangelism to Asians

This case description reports on how I, as a fledgling missionary, began to minister to Asians in Nairobi. I arrived in Nairobi in late 1981 to serve with the African Inland Mission (A.I.M.), in a support ministry as a purchasing agent for a number of missionary organizations. In the course of my work, I came into contact with many Asian businessmen. As our business relationships developed, so did our personal and social ties. Soon, my family and I were accepted as extended family members in many Asian homes, both Muslim and Hindu. As our associations increased, I began to realize that my Asian friends had not heard the gospel.

With a newly kindled burning to reach these people, my wife and I began to search for a place where we could worship with Asian Christians. Our search led us to a small garage in Nairobi South "B" area and to the house of a missionary with International Missions, Inc. There, we found a group of about 30 people, including some Asian believers, worshiping together. As I began sharing my burden with a colleague in my mission, we became excited and joined our forces to spread the good news among Asians.

My colleague became the first pastor of that small church. I was still employed full-time in the purchasing department of A.I.M., working with the church in the evenings and on weekends. Assisted by other A.I.M. personnel the work began to prosper, and we soon we outgrew the small garage and awning that was put up. The Lord provided a building in which we could continue our ministry. When the first pastor left on furlough, the church called me to be their pastor. I agreed, but, with my other job, it could only be on a part-time basis.

I soon realized that the Asian business community had accepted me as a friend. Most did not know that I was a pastor, and I purposely withheld that information while the Lord developed strong bonds of friendships with them. They only knew me as a purchaser who often wore jeans and sport shirts and rode a motorcycle.

Their acceptance gave me opportunities to ask questions of my Muslim and Hindu friends about their beliefs. They asked about mine, giving me a natural opportunity to share the gospel. I also found myself the center of attention at parties as they began asking questions about my faith. At times it seemed that I was back in my ordination council being grilled on doctrine and the faith. I was surprised by their thirst for knowledge for Christianity and their curiosity as to why I believed what I did. I found both respect and desire for understanding as I began to share my faith. I began to be tutored by a Muslim scholar and a Hindu priest, and these relationships developed into close personal friendships. Eventually, they too began asking questions about my faith in God-- their hunger for knowledge gave rise to an opportunity to share Christ with them.

To a Muslim or Hindu, Christian conversion means losing strong ties with family and culture and a sense of peoplehood. This presents a strong force against evangelism. Another hindrance is the African church's failure to see the spiritual needs of this group. They see them as unreachable or, at best, as resistant to the gospel. Other cultural problems separate the two populations. In colonial times Asians were given certain privileges over Africans. Today, resentment of this former favoritism leaves little desire on the part of the Africans to evangelize Asians. Communication between the two groups is basically limited to business or trade transactions, but this is beginning to change as Africans reach out to Asians.

Our church began to grow. After working full-time as a purchasing agent and part-time as a pastor for one and a half years, A.I.M. relieved me for full-time work with the church. There were then 210 persons actively involved in the church, representing nine different cultural groups.

Even more exciting, the Lord was opening doors for us to minister as a church to the Asians of Nairobi. One-third of our adult congregation was made up of Asian Christians, who began reaching other Asians and developing evangelistic programs to reach out to non-Asians. This program was developed by Asians to reach Asians. However, its primary emphasis has continued to be developing personal relationships with those in the Asian community in order to know them as friends.

Outreach was based on personal friendships and social interaction. Ladies' teas, church picnics in the park, sporting events, boys' and girls' clubs, youth camps, and businessmen's luncheons and lectures all were used to gain contact and credibility among Asians, who would not come to church for a regular service but would come for a "social function." This pattern fit well within their own religious traditions since temples and mosques have long been used for both religious and social functions.

Thus, the ministry was built upon "friendship evangelism," in which an openness to meet Christians and talk about important spiritual issues is fostered. We have found that Asians are not hostile to Christ but, in many ways, are open to a clear and sensitive sharing of the gospel.

Present Situation

We must find additional ways of contextualizing the gospel for the Asian in Nairobi. One possibility is to develop Christian literature in the South Asian languages. Yet, there is the even greater challenge of contextualizing the gospel into the British English of East Africa, with a Hindu or Muslim philosophical flair. This task, which we have started, will help us present Christ, as Sadhu Sundar Singh once said, "in an Indian cup." Literature must speak to the situation of the Asian in Nairobi in his or her own set of circumstances and needs.

We must also develop cell groups of Asian believers who can support one another and find culturally appropriate ways of sharing their faith in Christ. When they have indeed begun reaching other Asians, the process of people group evangelism will be a reality. Even now, the gospel is being heard by Asians in Nairobi, both from cross cultural missionaries and from members of the group itself. Pray for us as we train persons in Nairobi for this work and as we carry out personal ministries to Muslim and Hindu Asians who are yet without Christ, but not yet without hope.

Chapter 14

EVANGELIZING INDIAN MUSLIMS IN SOUTH AFRICA

Indians in South Africa? With worldwide concern and interest being shown in current political and social events in South Africa, little is mentioned of the country's Asian, primarily South Asian, population. Yet, there are almost 820,000 persons of South Asian ancestry living there. They are collectively called Indians, although many are descendants of immigrants from other South Asian countries. Most are non-Christian, and almost one-fifth are Muslim. Are there efforts to share the gospel with this largely unknown population? This case description reports on efforts to share the gospel of Jesus Christ with Indian Muslims in South Africa.

Description of Indian Muslims in South Africa as a People Group

Why do we talk about Indian Muslims as a people group? Why not just Muslims in South Africa? The Muslim population of South Africa is actually made up of at least two distinct people groups, separated by language, cultural traditions, history, and patterns of interaction. The two groups comprise over 300,000 people. Half of these live in the Capetown area and are predominantly of Malay origin. They were brought to the Capetown area from Java and other places in the East Indies as political prisoners and slaves approximately 300 years ago. The other half are predominantly persons of South Asian ancestry, referred to as Indians. They came either from East Africa or directly from India. At the present time, there are well over 170,000 Indian Muslims in South Africa, making up approximately 21 percent of the total Indian population in the country. Another 69 percent of the Indian population is Hindu, while around eight percent is Christian.

The two groups of Indian Muslims and Malay Muslims are clearly distinct from one another. First of all, they are separated residentially. Most Malay Muslims live in the Capetown region, although there are small populations in Johannesburg, Pretoria, Durban, and Port Elizabeth. Indian Muslims are predominantly found along the Natal coast and urban areas around Durban. In fact, as many as 80 percent of the Indians, both Hindu and Muslim, in South Africa live in this area. There is also a sizable Indian population in the Transvaal surrounding Johannesburg. Last, there is a sizable number of Muslims living in smaller towns throughout the country, where they serve rural and small town populations as local traders.

Besides differences in their histories in South Africa, areas of origin, and residential concentration, the two groups are also distinguished by language. Although Indian Muslims originated in northern India where Gujarati and Urdu are commonly used, few, outside of the elderly, use these languages today. Malay Muslims predominantly speak Afrikaans, while most Indian Muslims speak English.

The two groups also differ in terms of their modes of subsistence. The Indians are predominantly merchandisers and traders, although an increasing number have become integrated into industry and professional occupations, such as medicine and computers, and as clerical workers and craftsmen in many trades. Malays are more heavily involved in crafts, such as building, carpentry, and other similar trades. Overall, the

Indians are concentrated in more financially rewarding fields than the Malays.

In general, there tends to be little communication between the two groups. Each is well integrated and centered around its respective mosques. Although the ideology of Muslim unity is stated, in practice there is a clear social and cultural separation of the two groups.

How are the Indian Muslims distinct from the general Indian population in South Africa? The Muslims are clearly distinguished by their Islamic practices and beliefs. The sense of community is very strong, centering upon the *Umma*, or Islamic congregation, and the Imam, a religious leader. Islam is a social institution which provides sanctions for action, socialization of children, and symbols of collective relativity. Also there is a lack of substantial interaction between Muslims and other groups of Indians--intermarriage and substantive friendships are rare with non-Muslims. Last, according to Islamic beliefs, Hindus, Christians, and the non-religious are seen as inferior peoples. There is a strong sense of identity and pride in being Muslim.

The social organization of Indian Muslims is centered around Islam. This includes regular attendance at mosques and the practice of Islamic rituals and ceremonies in the homes. These practices generate community consenusregarding issues and reinforce uniform expectations of proper social behavior.

In spite of the central role of Islam, there is some evidence of tolerance for other religions. For example, one study found that 40 percent of those Indian Muslims responding felt that there is some truth in other religions. The survey also found that over two-thirds of the Muslim respondents believed that one should fully obey the religion they profess, whatever it may be. In the same study, as many as 73.5 percent of all Muslims were convinced that all religions should be studied.

Yet, it remains the case that Islam is seen as the only true religion. Christianity, in particular, is often portrayed in a very negative light.

The world view of the Indian Muslim is an amalgam of the Islam and western capitalism with core cultural elements coming from the former. It is seen as important to live in accordance with the demands of Islam, but at the same time, a heavy involvement in the business world is believed necessary for material reasons. The acquisition of wealth and property is of great importance because of the emphasis placed on the protection and the care of the family.

Indian Muslims make up a distinct people group in South African society. Their Islamic beliefs and practices separate them from the rest of the Indian population, while language, residence, and mode of subsistence distinguish them from other Muslims in South Africa. The governmental policies of apartheid, which calls for racial segregation, separates them from other populations in South Africa. Only an evangelistic strategy which recognizes these facts and builds upon them will be able to communicate the gospel effectively to South African Indian Muslims.

Unreached Status of Indian Muslims in South Africa

These people are partially defined by the very fact that they are Muslims. There have been few converts from the community because conversion, up until this time, has meant that one must leave the community and be excluded from other Indian Muslims. It has meant losing one's cultural identity, a costly undertaking for anyone. Accordingly, the rate of conversion is very low, approaching zero.

All Muslims have some knowledge of Christianity. Their knowledge, however, comes primarily from Islamic sources and is stereotypic and negative. In addition to the teaching carried out in Koranic schools, mosques, and homes, there are organizations which work to ensure the combined strength of the Islamic faith in South Africa. Two of these are the "Islamic Propagation Centre" and the "Islamic Missionary Society." The first organization produces anti-Christian booklets attacking the Bible, the crucifixion and divinity of Jesus, and similar issues. Most Muslims have seen this literature and are aware that Christians believe in the Trinity, which is anathema to Muslims, and the crucifixion of Jesus Christ, which is held to be a hoax. Such topics are the subject of training in polemics and debate for Muslims.

Indian Muslims have also learned something of Christianity through the observation of the behavior of Christians around them. For one who is schooled in the rigors of Islamic purity, Christians appear to be blatant violators of such standards. It is noted that Christians do not fast, rarely pray in public, and do not avoid impure food and drink, such as pork and alcohol. Christians appear to be "fallen peoples."

In general, there is great resistance and some hostility toward Christianity, which has long been associated with a foreign culture. There are indications, however, that younger persons among the Indian Muslims are open to new ideas, including Christianity, but it is difficult to evaluate these claims or to determine if the youth are attracted more to western cultural values or to Christianity.

There is a long history of Christian outreach to Indian Muslims. The Anglican Church began to evangelize Malay Muslims in South Africa at the beginning of the century. This advance was curbed, however, by Muslim hostility and resistance toward the gospel, and the effort was eventually abandoned. In 1950, the Dutch Reformed Church began to establish missionaries among Muslims. At the present, only one couple from the Dutch Reformed Church works with these people in South Africa. Also in the 1950s, a Brethren mission- ary began to work among the Malay Muslims in Capetown, but later moved to Durban where the emphasis of his work was on Indian Hindus. Two decades later, in the early 1970s, "Jesus to the Muslims," was established as a Baptist ministry to the Indian Muslims in and around Johannesburg, with some outreach in Durban. By 1983, the Baptist Mission had one woman working among Muslims in Capetown. This agency later placed a couple to train with the "Jesus to the Muslims" program in Johannesburg. They have now begun a ministry among Indian Muslims in Durban. In 1984, the Africa Evan- gelical Fellowship recruited a couple from Canada, who also began working among the Indian Muslims in Durban.

Africa Evangelical Fellowship has a history of working among Indian Hindus in and around Durban. As a result of an inten- sive survey which was carried out in 1982, they saw the need to expand this ministry. Last, the Roman Catholic Church has a strong history of ministry among Indian Hindus, but has done little with Muslims.

These evangelistic efforts are supported by scriptural and Christian literature written in English. There are also many radio and TV programs dealing with Christian life in South Africa. These are, however, not geared to Muslims and may, because of their strong doctrinal focus, do more harm than good.

The unreached status of Indian Muslims is largely a result of the tight community boundaries which have protected them from outside influences. It is also a result, to some extent, of the apartheid policies of South Africa, which have restricted communication across cultural barriers. Last, the continued unreached status of Indian Muslims in South Africa speaks of the lack of success by Christian missions and the church in South Africa in developing a strategy which, until recently, effectively speaks in their cultural and social contexts.

Following is a description of one attempt to develop an effective evangelistic effort focused on this group of Muslims. The effort has not solely targeted Indians or Malays, but is clearly a different model than the one found in the earlier case description dealing with Asians of Nairobi.

Evangelization of Indian Muslims

As of this date, the Sudan Interior Mission (SIM) has more than twice the number of outreach personnel committed to work with Muslims than all the other missions in the area combined. The work began when in 1975 a German missionary of the Deutsche Missionsgemeinschaft, after having completed his work in another field, was guided by God to Capetown, where he became aware of the need for work among the Muslim population. He knew that for over 60 years, Christians in Britain (FFM) had been praying that a missionary would begin work among the Malay Muslims in Capetown. He was convicted of the need to develop such a ministry with Muslims in South Africa. Another missionary from the same mission soon joined him.

Problems delayed the beginning of this work, and in 1978, God caused a change of emphasis for the mission, leading to a realization that more must be learned about Islam and the Muslim peoples in South Africa. The missionary began to study the situation and develop a strategy for working systematically and effectively among them. The result was the formation of a small mission called "Life Challenge."

The mission's work force trebled in the following seven years. In 1986, SIM, an agency with identical aims as Life Challenge and a larger administrative infrastructure, merged with it.

Life Challenge is designed to penetrate the tight cultural barriers of the Muslim population. It was obvious that an evangelistic strategy dependent upon reaching Muslims in the traditional evangelistic meetings would not work--the Muslim community is too strong and insular. Life Challenge was formed upon the principle of personal evangelism through house-to-house visitation or the building of friendships with Muslims in work situations or other environments.

Literature plays an increasingly big role in the sharing of the gospel, particularly as an aid for Christians who are not otherwise equipped to evangelize Muslims. Beginning in Capetown, and now country-and continent-wide, literature distribution and sales have been effective in sharing scriptural truths with the Muslim population.

One set of books was written to serve both the Muslims, who are interested in Christianity, and the Christians, who wish to get to know Islam and its polemical attacks on the Christian faith along with possible defences based upon biblical answers. Several booklets with pre-evangelistic and evangelistic content were particularly designed for Muslim readers, and several printed testimonies have been developed as initial tools for outreach. These are supplemented by a well received Bible correspondence course called "Al-Kitab." Now in planning are video productions for Muslims. In addition, advertising space has been bought in local indigenous newspapers to present spiritual thoughts to Muslims.

Life Challenge attempts to motivate, recruit, and train large numbers of local Christians so they will understand Islam and communicate with Muslims effectively. Central to the outreach are prayer groups of Christians, who meet together regularly to pray for Muslims. The members of the prayer group then reach out with programs of evangelism to their Muslim neighbors and fellow community members. The motto for this effort is "A Prayer Group for every Mosque."

A central focus of this outreach is systematic house-to-house visitation where the gospel will be shared on a one-to-one basis in a conversational style.

As an evangelistic strategy, Life Challenge focuses upon Muslims from both Indian and Malay backgrounds and centers upon a small missions concept where groups of believers are called to work systematically in a given area. Muslim residential areas are divided into specific fields, each consisting of approximately 50 Muslim households. Two Christian witnesses are then assigned to each of these fields and encouraged to pledge one evening a week to sharing the gospel on a personal basis at each house in their field.

In practice, this structure allows the formation of specific strategies of evangelism for each of the Muslim people groups since each "mission field" will tend to be homogeneous in the terms we have been using. Thus, one pair of Christian witnesses will usually work solely with either Indian or Malay Muslims.

After its initial start in Capetown, Life Challenge was extended to the Johannesburg area in 1984. The main target area was Lenasia, an Indian town near Johannesburg with approximately 100,000 inhabitants, of which about 60 percent are Indian Muslims.

Success has not come easily because of great resistance to this work from the Muslims. Yet, there have been converts to the Lord Jesus Christ. Some of these converts are being equipped to communicate to members of their own people group. They will help reduce the danger of cross-cultural misunderstanding.

The advantages of Life Challenge are clear. The financial burden is relatively small because most witnesses are people who volunteer their own time. The approach does not ask

Muslims to leave the security of their environment, but attempts to reach them where they are.

Plans for the future call for broadening the work to all the suburbs and cities in which Muslims reside. It is also essential to plan for reaching Muslims who live in smaller towns and rural areas. The greatest need at this time is to decrease the role of expatriate missionaries and to increase the centrality of South African Christians in this work.

Present Situation

Thus far, the number of converts has been low. Major breakthroughs are needed.

Life Challenge presently grapples with the major question of whether churches should be established specifically for Muslims. It may be expected that this could lead to a stronger witness by ex-Muslims within their own communities. Alternatively, converts could be encouraged to join existing churches, which are largely composed of ex-Hindus and Christians from other backgrounds. However, the step from the mosque to these churches is too big for most Muslims.

Yet, although major questions remain for the future growth of this ministry, a way to communicate the gospel with Muslims in South Africa has been developed. It is based upon people to people, or friendship, evangelism.

A concern for cooperation and exchange of experience and ideas as well as know-how and the desire to avoid competition and duplication has led to the formation of an umbrella body for all groups and individuals working among Muslims in South Africa. It is called "Christian Concern for Muslims" (CCM) and has been functional for several years. Much could be done to increase its impact, but even so, Christian outreach to Muslims in South Africa is no longer fragmented. Perhaps this can serve as a model for Christian missionary outreach among Muslims in other lands. This would open new perspectives and make us all "hasten his coming" (II Peter 3:12).

Based upon personal correspondence, interviews, and secondary research.

Chapter 15

BEGINNING A WORK AMONG THE UNREACHED BARAGUYU OF TANZANIA

by Doug Priest

Our mission, the Christian Missionary Fellowship (CMF), has been working among the Maasai people in Kenya since 1978. In the early 1980s, almost a dozen missionary families ministered to this colorful group of pastoral nomads, often living out with the people as part of their community. Several of us who were located along the Kenya-Tanzania border were aware of Maasai people in both countries--the Maasai readily crossed back and forth across the border. We began to think about the possibilities for evangelization of the Tanzanian Maasai. In Kenya, we were experiencing rapid growth among a people who had for nearly a century resisted the gospel and clung to their traditional ways. We were excited about this and wondered, "Could not the same thing happen in Tanzania?"

When we began to survey the Maasai of Tanzania, we found a need for evangelization among the Baraguyu, a group of pastoral people who at first glance resemble the Maasai. The realization that they are actually a separate people group was the first step in developing a ministry with them. This case description describes our strategy for sharing the gospel with the Baraguyu in a way that respects their culture and effectively communicates God's love for them. This work is just beginning; with God's help, it will bear fruit as a Baraguyu church.

The Baraguyu as a People Group

The Baraguyu are distributed across the breadth of Tanzania, from the Indian Ocean almost to Malawi. Even so, they number only about 30,000 people. They are widely scattered and live intermingled with other people groups. All Baraguyu speak Maa, the Maasai language, although a majority of them also speak Swahili, the national language of Tanzania and the trade language used to communicate with outsiders. Virtually no other African peoples can speak to the Baraguyu in Maa, a situation that heightens their sense of group identity. In all of our surveys among the Baraguyu, asking hundreds of people the same question, we were always told that we were the only foreigners they had heard speak to them in their own language.

Baraguyu livelihood comes primarily from their herds of cows, sheep, and goats. While some of them have small gardens, they consider themselves to be a pastoral people. On the whole, they refuse to till the earth, leaving that chore to other groups who do not mind receiving wages for such work. The fact that they do not practice agriculture again separates them from other peoples.

There are two dominant settlement patterns among the Baraguyu. On the one hand, there are scattered homesteads, bordering on areas inhabited by other peoples. Then, there are villages that have been specifically set aside for pastoral peoples. The majority live in these villages. Yet, dependence upon herds which need to forage over large areas to find grass and water means that the Baraguyu are not a settled people. They move with their herds. For this reason schools, clinics, and other such resources of more sedentary peoples are not available to the Baraguyu.

Baraguyu men marry women from other people groups, but almost no Baraguyu women marry men other than Baraguyus. In a patrilineal system, this ensures that children are not lost from the people group. The women marry soon after puberty, and the prevailing pattern is for a man to have more than one wife. Young men, from the time of their circumcision until they are about 30 years of age, are warriors. Some of them may marry earlier, but most wait until they have moved out of warriorhood status.

Traditionally, the Baraguyu do not believe in spirits--neither evil spirits, nature spirits, nor ancestral spirits. The limited knowledge that they have of spirits comes from contact with other groups who are animists. The Baraguyu worship a supreme God, *Enkai*, who is the creator of the world, the almighty and powerful one. He is both far and near, responds to people when they pray to him, provides for their needs, is to be feared and revered, and will punish bad behavior.

The Baraguyu are clearly a people group. Their language, nomadic lifestyle, patrilineal form of society, and strong sense of self identity distinguish them from other peoples. These people, who are called Maasai by almost everyone else, call themselves Baraguyu. They know that they are different from the Maasai and others around them. The Maasai are also quick to inform us that the Baraguyu are not to be considered Maasai. Thus, although those unacquainted with the two people groups would identify the Baraguyu as Maasai, the Baraguyu are clearly different.

Unreached Status of the Baraguyu

Our interest in the Baraguyu began with the question of the need for evangelism among the Maasai in Tanzania. One of our mission group in Kenya suggested that we travel into Tanzania to research this question. With the encouragement of our mission, two of us spent the summer of 1982 in Tanzania. Our goal was to learn to what extent the Maasai were being reached. We wanted to know if Maasai churches were largely confined to towns as was the case in Kenya, or if there were groups of believers meeting to worship the Lord in "bush" homesteads, underneath the shade of an acacia tree. It was these new homestead churches made up of traditional Maasai that were growing rapidly in Kenya.

We wanted to know which churches were represented among the Maasai and whether the worship services were in Maa or in Swahili.

All of these questions were asked over and over again as we traveled among the Maasai in Tanzania. We learned of two denominational groups with long-standing work among the Maasai. They were well spread out with catechists or evangelists in almost every "town." Both groups told us that while probably only three percent of the traditional Maasai were Christians, they were poised to push forward with their evangelistic efforts. We were heartened to find groups ready to evangelize the Tanzanian Maasai.

We also learned that there was a group of Maasai-speaking people in the central part of the country who had little Christian witness among them--the Baraguyu. We found that they have a limited knowledge of Jesus gained from surrounding peoples who are Christian. Even though some Baraguyu occasionally attend churches where the worship service is in Swahili, less than five percent of them are practicing Christians. Of those, the majority are women and young children.

Very few of the men claim to be Christian, probably because the gospel has not been presented to them in a culturally relevant manner.

There had been previous Christian witnesses to the Baraguyu, but few responded. The men informed us that no man would attend a Christian church, and that many women had no desire to attend. Among the reasons they offered was the fact that the church had ruled against such things as wearing beads, shaving heads, chewing tobacco, and drinking alcoholic beverages. Since all of these are cultural practices of the Baraguyu, they tended to equate Christianity with rules forbidding such behavior. Furthermore, the church services had been in Swahili, with the leader of the services being a young man who was not Baraguyu. Clearly, the gospel had been presented in a way that clashed with their cultural standards and expectations.

As we asked questions of the Baraguyu and the various denominations located in their area, we learned that here indeed was an unreached people group with little evangelistic work being done among them in their own language. Furthermore, none of the denominational groups had any plans to evangelize the Baraguyu in their own language. One group was interested in traveling out to Baraguyu areas for short periods of crusade-type evangelism in Swahili, although it had no plans to establish permanent work in the villages.

Fortunately, the New Testament and portions of the Old Testament, as well as song books, dictionaries and books of oral literature, are readily available in the Maasai language. Yet, it is only recently that these materials have been available in the Baraguyu areas. It is not an exaggeration to say that most of the literate Baraguyu have yet to read anything in their own language.

On the basis of this survey, our mission decided to initiate a work with the Baraguyu and asked our family to become the first resident missionaries. Specifically, we were invited to work with the Tanzania Church of God in church planting, evangelism, and community development among the Maa-speaking people in Tanzania. Since our arrival in Tanzania, we have made numerous follow-up surveys and done other research preparatory to beginning resident efforts at evangelism.

The Process of Evangelization of the Baraguyu

After identifying the Baraguyu as the unreached people group with whom we wished to minister, we moved to temporary housing in Tanzania, where we began learning how the Baraguyu lived in the different regions of the country. We learned that two regions had the smallest number of Christian witnesses, and that approximately 15,000 Baraguyu live in these regions. We made trips to the regions and became acquainted with the local officials.

The Morogoro Region, one of the two regions, is home to 10,000 Baraguyu. We noted that there were four villages within the region set aside strictly for pastoral peoples. Roughly half of the Baraguyu lived in the northern part of the region and the other half lived in the south. We traveled to each of the four villages and met the leaders. After learning of our intentions, they were all quick to ask us to consider beginning a mission at their location. We attribute this both to God's timing and to the fact that we spoke to them in their own language.

Over an eight month period, we visited one of the villages in the southern section of the Morogoro Region almost a dozen times. On each occasion, we were welcomed and encouraged to locate in that village. The village had about 1200 people when there was adequate grass, but its population dwindled drastically during the dry season. The long distance to the nearest well, almost three miles, also accounted for fewer people in the area during the drier time of the year when surface water disappeared. Yet, another 3,500 Baraguyu lived within a two hours drive on rough roads.

On one of our visits to the village, the leading men of the area, who had heard of our desire to locate among the Baraguyu, invited us to come and live in their village. Their official invitation included an offer of land for a house. We thanked God for his leading and decided that we would accept this invitation.

In the past, the village had a small church, attended by a few women and children, but now abandoned. Of course, we wished to learn more of this church, as well as the Baraguyu response to having another church in their area. They explained that the former church had rules which were too foreign and stringent to be pleasing to them. We prayed that the antipathy toward that church would not be directed at our efforts.

The people enjoyed discussing religion with us and listened willingly to cassette tapes with short talks and songs in the Maa language. Many of the songs were traditional Maasai tunes with Christian words rather than translations of western songs with the accompanying western tune. The talks, which were recorded by missionaries who had lived with the Maasai in Kenya for many years, presented the gospel in a framework acceptable to the Maasai. They featured simple stories with a scriptural moral, and we used them as a test to see how the Maasai responded to hearing part of the gospel in their own language. These were first used in the homestead of the Baraguyu government leader, although anyone was allowed to listen to the tapes if they wished.

Our house is now being constructed. While waiting for its completion, we will visit every homestead in the village to become acquainted with the people. We intend to become accepted as members of the community, but first the people must see that we will speak to them in their own language and will not exploit their cattle or use them as subjects for a "book of photographs." Whenever possible, we will also provide assistance when asked. As time goes by, we hope to begin community development projects that the people desire and for which they ask. Such projects must arise from within the entire community and not as something we have initiated on our own.

Present Situation

Our mission presently has plans for four or five families working with the Baraguyu. We will concentrate initially on two regions but may expand later to other regions with significant Baraguyu populations. All of the mission families will first learn to speak Maa, although some may also choose to learn Swahili. To be part of the Baraguyu community, all will locate in the "bush" rather than the cities. They will concentrate primarily on evangelism, church planting, and leadership development. Small scale community development projects will be considered and some will likely be undertaken.

Evangelistic efforts among the Maasai in Kenya show that the best responses came when attempts were made to win the men who were the leaders of the community. These efforts also show the importance of worship celebrations that make use of Maasai practices. Such things as Western-style buildings, three-point homiletical sermons, and musical instruments (which are not used by Maasai-speaking people), hinder initial response to the gospel. Meeting in the shade of a tree, using Maasai proverbs in "mini-sermons," spending much time discussing Christ around the cooking fire prior to going to sleep, and showing an interest in traditional veterinarian practices all help in the communication of the gospel. We will apply these lessons in our work with the Baraguyu.

Four years have gone by since our first survey trip into Tanzania. During that time we have, as a mission, taken the necessary steps to enter Tanzania. Numerous trips have been made to determine the area of highest concentration of the Baraguyu. We have been invited to begin to work in a specific location and have, together with our mission, determined the number of missionary personnel needed. We are ready to begin our work with the Baraguyu. With God's help and by his grace our strategy for reaching the Baraguyu will be successful!

Chapter 16

EVANGELIZING THE BASSARI OF SENEGAL

by James Stanley

Among the large, powerful people groups of West Africa such as the Fulbe, Wolof, and Hausa, are many smaller groups, long overshadowed and dominated by their more prominent neighbors. One such group is the Bassari, of whom approximately 6,000 live in Senegal and another 8,000 in Guinea. The political border separating them has placed an "artificial" barrier between these two populations, dividing them into clearly distinct people groups.

This case description focuses upon the process of evangelism among the Bassari of Senegal. It points out lessons we have learned in our work.

Description of the People Group

The population of the Bassari is growing much slower than that of the rest of the peoples in Senegal. There are two reasons for this. First, there is a high mortality rate. But also of importance is the intermarriage that takes place between Bassari women and men from Fulbe and other surrounding people groups. The children of these marriages are taken into these neighboring peoples. Thus, even though Bassari men do not marry women from other groups, there is a gradual out-flow of persons from the Bassari to other people groups.

Today, over half the Bassari have migrated to towns and cities with Kedougou and Tambacounda the primary destinations. In such urban areas, men labor at bamboo fence-making and women work as domestic workers in the homes of wealthier city dwellers. Approximately one to two hundred per year travel to towns in search of work, but return to their villages in June to cultivate their crops. Only three percent or so of those that migrate to towns stay permanently.

The rural Bassari in Senegal are now cultivators of millet, ground nuts, fonyo, and beans. Previously, they were hunter-gathers. Their means of livelihood changed when the national government established a park in the area and moved them to their present location. Although some hunting and gathering continues, it now provides only a minor portion of the Bassari diet. As agriculturalists, the Bassari cultivate small plots of land, primarily at a subsistence level. Government programs have begun to encourage them to enter the cash market with ground nuts. In addition, the programs provide improved agricultural implements and draft animals.

The Bassari are matrilineal, tracing kinship relationships through women. Six "lineages" or clans are found in Senegal. Two of these were formerly found only in Guinea, but, because of migration, all six are now represented in Senegal. In any single village one of these groups tends to predominate. Each Bassari village has a recognized chief and elders chosen on the basis of seniority within the dominant kinship group. They make decisions for the village, but the process is actually one of consensus. Problems are discussed at length until all the elders agree upon a solution.

In Senegal, the Bassari are considered to be of low status by the surrounding Fulbe. In fact, some 50 years ago they were almost decimated by the Fulbe in warfare. Only the intervention of the Konyagi, a neighboring group, saved them. Today, the Bassari carry on trade with the nomadic Fulbe, providing chickens, goats, and meat in exchange for cloth. Generally, the Bassari do not do well in these exchanges as they have no well developed tradition of trade.

The traditional religious system of the Bassari is animism. They know of a god, but this god is remote and little involved in their daily lives. Essential religious practice is centered on the recognition and ownership of family idols to whom offerings are given and from whom blessings asked prior to important activities such as hunting or other tasks having a degree of uncertainty as to their success. Blessings are also asked when an animal is killed or butchered. There are no recognized religious leaders.

Among the Bassari, sorcerers play important roles sometimes reserved for religious leaders in other societies. Anyone within the tribe can become a sorcerer and direct evil spirits against others. It is believed that a sorcerer has a wide range of powers, including the power of death over others. As with many other groups, the role of sorcery is one of social control. In a small society like the Bassari one takes care not to offend a neighbor. Such an act could bring retribution or revenge through sorcery.

Another important element of the Bassari religious system is male dancing. Men over the age of 18 or so are eligible to participate. They disguise themselves with masks and change their voices to hide their identities from the women and children, who are said to see the dancers as spirits. Dancing is a way of acting out important spiritual truths such as initiation rites and other procedures known only to men. It also is used to discipline children who are "naughty", by chasing them with whips and threatening to beat them.

The Bassari are distinct from surrounding peoples. They have their own well developed sense of cultural identity and a distinct language. Their low status in the Senegalese society further distinguishes them.

The Unreached Status of the Bassari

We are Assemblies of God missionaries, and began our work among the Bassari in 1962. Prior to this, some evangelistic efforts had been made with neighboring peoples, but there had been no direct outreach to the Bassari, who consequently had little knowledge of Christianity. There was also no Scripture available in their language.

Previous contact with white people had actually raised barriers to the sharing of the gospel among the Bassari. When we arrived we learned from the older men that white men had told them a story of a flood. The Bassari knew the story was important because it was taught by "the men from the water," yet they had heard stories of how these same men had taken people as slaves in the Gambia. They also knew how other people had been taken as forced laborers to build roads and sisal plantations. The gospel was strongly identified with this history and had a negative, fearful reputation even though it was known to be important.

This raised a barrier to the gospel. It was identified as foreign, and furthermore, linked with danger. This, along with the physical isolation of the Bassari created barriers to evangelization.

The Process of Evangelism Among the Bassari

We arrived in Senegal in 1962 and settled temporarily in Tambacounda where we came into contact with Bassari youth who had migrated to the city. There was a good deal of openness to the gospel and some of them became Christians and returned to their home land. However, when they returned once again to Tabacounda, they reported that they had faced intense persecution for their new found faith.

We investigated the possibility of living among the Bassari in their home area. Although the area is completely isolated from the rest of the country from June through December due to washed out roads, we knew this was not a problem for God. In 1965, we moved to the Bassari village of Edane with the goal of establishing a Bassari church within three years. In living there, we wanted to cause as little social and cultural disruption among the people as possible so that a Bassari pastor could take over our work without pause when we left.

Our mission began by meeting with the chief and elders. We asked them two questions: "Do you know God?" and "What do you know about him?" The chief and elders told us that they realized that there was a God, but they did not know him. They understood that they had to meet him sometime, but they were afraid and uncertain. We used this opportunity to address some of their questions with answers from the Bible.

We were asked to stay among the Bassari. We agreed that during our stay we would submit to the authority of the chief while in Edanc village, and he agreed that we were to be in charge of church activity.

The initial reception of the Bassari was open, although we progressed slowly in our work. Everything that was done was explained in light of scripture to insure that our Christian practice and verbal witness were consistent and biblically based.

At length, several Bassari came forth and asked to be baptized. We consulted the chief and other elders, who agreed that if the new converts lived according to the Scripture, they would be exempt from customs involving sacrifice to idols and other related religious practices. However, the converts would be subject to all other customs of the Bassari.

To reinforce the fact that this was a true Bassari church, we consulted the new Bassari Christians about all church matters. Eventually, with their help a mud brick church and parsonage were built for Edane village.

Meanwhile, opposition arose. Sorcerers cursed us and our work and even tried to kill us. Sadly, Christian workers in neighboring areas who were motivated by denominational differences and jealousies opposed the growing church among the Bassari. Because some of the Bassari had nominal affiliation with these neighboring churches, our presence was resented. This has continued to be a problem.

Yet, progress was made. Even though many of the Bassari felt that Christianity was hard to follow and seemed to go against much of their culture, most felt it was true and admitted that those who accepted Christ demonstrated a strengthening of spirit and mind. Lives were being changed.

In 1970, we moved to Obadji, a new area, to plant a church. But problems soon began in the church we had left behind at Edane. Most of the church members were young people and we had left a young man in charge. He took over the work from us along with our house, food, and other forms of support. Our intent was that he would work on church business for one year without outside support.

We had been gone only a short time when sorcerers began to oppress the young leader, and others in the village began to oppose the work of the church. The leader moved away and soon all the other church leaders left the area to search for work elsewhere. Because they were young people, they had none of the status that comes with age, and were, therefore, not accepted by the community as leaders of the church.

We learned a lesson from this. When we planted a new church in Obadji, we worked among older persons in the community and concentrated on building a church around them. This gave the church a much firmer foundation. Soon another church was also established at Ekess, five kilometers from the church which failed at Edane. We continued our work until 1973, when we left the area.

In 1981, we returned to teach and support the growing church. Our work has concentrated on training leaders and helping develop new skills and techniques in agriculture. The core of the discipling work has centered on a group of leaders, who are sent to Bible school for training. When they return home, the new leaders conduct evangelistic programs. Their training schedule is arranged so that some of the leaders are always available to serve the church.

Present Situation

A growing church has been established among the Bassari. Although they find that old ways and customs can come into conflict with their new Christian life, they are growing in the faith. Their church is maturing to the point of becoming a sending church with a completely indigenous and self-supporting evangelistic outreach to the Bassari in Guinea. We, as foreign missionaries, now take a supporting role by concentrating on agricultural work, translation, and the distribution of scriptures. The Bassari have come to know Jesus Christ.

Chapter 17

KOMAS OF GHANA

by Howard Brant

A group of people known as the Koma live in northern Ghana. Who are these people? None of the tribal groups around them admit to having ethnic ties with them. Interestingly, another people in Nigeria are called the Koma. Is there an ethnic connection?

We do not know. Yet, we do know that there are about 1,500 Koma hunter-gatherers who have been pushed deeper into the bush by more powerful neighbors, the Sissala, Builsa, and the Mamprusi. Times are hard for the Koma. Many have moved away because of difficult living conditions, and only the older people and those who have no education remain in the tribal homelands. The Koma are under increasing pressures of modernization and Islam -- their days of independence are over. This case description describes our work as missionaries among the Koma of Ghana. It is a work that is timely, in that the Koma are at a crossroads and Jesus provides a direction for their future.

God at Work Among the Koma

In 1977, my wife and I were forced to leave our missionary post with the Gurage people in the Ethiopian highlands. Returning to the United States, we felt that God had not closed a door to us without opening another. We prayed earnestly that he would take us again to some part of the world where there were unreached people and that we might be the first ones to take the gospel to those who have never heard. By 1978, we had been reassigned to the northern part of Ghana, West Africa.

That same year, two Wycliffe missionaries, doing a linguistic survey in Northern Ghana, stumbled upon a small ethnic group called the Koma. The group was spread out in five small villages and had a population that did not exceed 1,500 people. Pressed back beyond swamps and rivers, these people were cut off from civilization -- coming out infrequently from the African bush to sell tuber yams or smoked meat.

The Wycliffe missionaries told us of this contact, and we determined to find these people and preach the gospel to them. Finding a guide to take us into their remote area was not easy, and it was six months before we made our first contact with a young man named Isifu who, though not a Koma himself, knew a chief near the area who would send someone with us to the Koma.

Three of us missionaries, along with two of our Ghanaian brothers, packed up a van and set off. We were supplied with sleeping and cooking gear, maps, a motorcycle, and a winch to pull us through the numerous sandy river beds. When we reached Isifu's village, after a difficult trip, we were surrounded by hundreds of curious children, most of whom had never seen foreigners. No car had ever before ventured into their world.

After giving respectful greetings to the chief, we asked about the Koma. The chief acknowledged that he knew of them but asked why we wanted to go to their villages. We assured him we had something very important to share with them. His response was, "What about us?" Three hundred brown bodies pressed close around us as we explained the message of the gospel to Isifu's chief. Only then did he give us a guide to the first Koma village.

We parked the van, and three of us set off on a motorcycle through 14 kilometers of dense bush. Thorns and sharp branches of scrub brush tore at our ankles and legs as we pressed along. We lost the trail many times, and often we had to dismount and walk the motorcycle up rocky slopes or through narrow paths. After many hours we reached the first Koma village of Nangurma.

The effect of our arrival was dramatic. Little children, who had been taught that ghosts were white, ran screaming to their mothers, who in turn walked away, for they were lowly women and not "worthy" to meet such strangers. We sought out the chief's hut and immediately noted several men lying on logs inside the hut. We soon learned that they were victims of onchocerciasis, river blindness.

Soon a group of men gathered around us. They were obviously sick, weak people. We gave customary greetings through interpreters and explained that we had come a long way to find them because we wanted to hear about their problems, and we had a message we wanted to share with them. They agreed to talk to us. What did we want to know?

We asked them about their livelihood. They told us that they were basically hunters. They hunted the bushcow with poison arrows. They also farmed yams and planted guinea corn. Their biggest problem was a lack of clean water. In the dry season, the water backed up in the local river and became infested with guinea worms and other parasites. Their older men suffered from river blindness, but worst of all, measles came every year and killed many of their children.

I looked around that day and saw human suffering at its worst. Though I had spent 20 years in Africa, I had never been so moved. Of the men over 40 years of age, half were already blind with onchocerciasis. We asked why they did not move away from the river where black flies, the carriers for the disease, live. Their stoical view of life accepted such misfortune as part of their personal destiny. I asked one blind man what he did for a living. He explained that each morning a child led him out to the millet fields so that he could kneel down in the dirt to weed the millet by touch. Others showed clear signs of bilharzia (schistosomiasis). A lad of 15 sat on a stump nearby, a tumor almost pushing his left eye out of its socket.

After listening to them, I tried to share the gospel with them, but they were so overwhelmed by their plight that they were not able to hear what I was saying. As we left, I turned to my friend Joseph and asked with a sigh, "How will these people ever hear the gospel." His response was prophetic, "God will make a way."

We returned to Isifu's village that night and again preached to his people. The following day we again left our car and the six of us -- three foreigners, our two Ghanaian brothers and the guide -- set off for the second Koma village of Yikpobongo. The road was somewhat better and we covered the eight kilometers with little trouble.

As we neared the village, we came up out of the river bed and saw a man working in a field of yams. He gazed at us intently as we approached. After we had introduced ourselves, he told us his name was Ali. We explained to him that we had come to his village to tell his people about the Son of God. As soon as we said this, he grew even more intense, telling us that the people of his village would be very interested in what we had to say.

We walked the last few hundred meters into a village of about 750 people. Again, little children went screaming to their mothers. Women ducked out of view. But we had expected this from our first contact. What surprised us were the white crosses drawn on the side of every hut in the village. When we asked the meaning of this, Ali told us, "Our people believe that God (Mung) has lost his son. One day Mung will come to our village and look for His son. If he looks in a house and does not find his son, he will strike the people dead unless they have the sign of the cross on their house."

After we had greeted the chief with the customary greetings, and he had gathered his elders, we learned that there was another chief who lived on the other side of the village. I went to greet that chief, while one of my fellow missionaries, David Pitman, sat with the first group to tell them of the Son of God.

Halfway through David's presentation, the chief stopped him and said, "We have a book in our village." David was surprised and asked to see the book. It was a small booklet produced by the Jehovah's Witnesses. On seeing the book, David told the chief, "We too have a book. In fact," he went on, "if the chief will give us his book, we will give him ours." Now the chief, a very intelligent man, could see that he would get a much newer and bigger book in the trade. He made an astute decision and surrendered his book for our Bible.

Having made this initial contact, we left the Koma, promising that we would return as soon as we could. But, in fact, because the seasonal rains made the rivers uncrossable, it was five long months before we could return.

On our return trip, it was late afternoon before we reached Yikpobong. We sat with the chief and his tribal elders in their conference hut. Slowly, we began again to tell them about the Son of God. We had just started when the chief again interrupted. Were we not the people who had brought them the book? "Go, and get the book!" A small child went scrambling to the chief's hut for the book.

"While you were away," the chief explained, "a trader came into our village. He stayed in my house and found the book. He read it to us. "Do you know," he asked me, "that the very stories which you told us about the Son of God are written down in this book?" We quickly acknowledged that it was the source of our story. "Furthermore," the chief went on to say, "my elders have been discussing this news. Seventeen of them have decided that they would like to follow the Jesus that is spoken of in the book."

I could not believe my ears. We had done nothing but tell them the simple story of the gospel and brought them a Bible. God was indeed "finding a way." With the temperature at 110 degrees and the sweat dripping off the end of my nose, I had the wonderful joy of hearing 17 elders of a tribe confessing their sins to God, renouncing the worship of Satan and evil spirits, and asking Jesus to be their Lord and Savior. Ali, the first Yikpobongo villager we had met, was among them.

Growth of the Koma Church

Time passed. Within two years the 17 converts had turned into 140 and had built their own little church. An evangelist from a nearby tribe was now leading their little group. Feeling that it was time for in-depth Bible training, we invited six of the older men at Yikpobongo to come the 70 miles to our home. They stayed with us for a week before going back.

During the training, we asked one of our nurses, Pat Robertson, to give them instruction on health care. After asking about their most pressing problems, she decided to teach them about measles, a killer in their communities. As it is a foreign disease, their systems have no natural immunity to it and many of their children die each year in measles epidemics.

Pat asked them what they do when one of the children contracts it. They explained that because the sickness comes from sores in the stomach, they force the child to drink small amounts of scalding water to wash out the sores. They also withhold cool water as they believe it causes diarrhea. Fearing the blindness that sometimes results from measles, they keep the child in the hot sun and wash out pus out of its eyes with distilled whiskey made from their own grain.

Carefully, Pat explained that there are no sores in the stomach of a child with measles. The child needs cool water to drink so that it does not become dehydrated. It also needs to be in a cool, dark room to protect its eyes. As she talked to them, Ali listened intently. Suddenly, he jumped up, and pointing to the sky, called out, "Now I believe in God." None of us could understand what he meant until he told us this story:

> "Five years ago, measles came to Yikpobongo. My first son died. Then my second and third son died. When my fourth son got sick, I ran to the local soothsayer and offered him a sheep if he could keep my son from dying. In case he could not help, I went to the second soothsayer and offered him a ram. To make very sure, I went to a third soothsayer and offered him a large rooster to protect my son. But, with all of this, my fourth son died.
>
> "That night they buried my fourth son. Everyone in the village cried. My two wives had both lost

sons; they tried to console each other. I had lost
four sons now and I was heartbroken. I knew
that the soothsayers could no longer help us."

Ali told us that in his distress he walked out of his compound
and pondered the starry heavens. He and his people all knew
that there was a creator God, Mung, who lives in the sky. But
they knew that all communication with him had been cut off,
leaving no contact except through the soothsayers. Now the
soothsayers had proven that even they could not get an answer
from Mung.

As he looked into the sky, he called out to Mung.

"Oh, Mung. Our children are dying from measles
and we have lost our way to you. Please send
someone to tell us how to find our way
back to you -- and how to keep our children
from dying."

Ali said he tossed on his mat all that night. He dreamed that
he was out working in his yam field when suddenly, three
white strangers came walking up to him. Someone in his
dream told him, "Ali, these will be the men who will tell you
about me, and they will also tell you how to keep your children from dying from measles." Now his dream had been fulfilled and his faith was complete.

As Ali told this story, my mind flashed back to the time five
years ago when we had been forced out of Ethiopia and were
praying, "Lord, send us to someone who has never heard the
gospel." Here, thousands of miles away, among a people unknown to us and the outside world, Ali had been praying, "Oh
Mung, please send someone..." God had answered both prayers.

Current Situation

The Koma churches are moving along well. There is still an outside evangelist among them, but efforts are being made to train Koma elders to pastor and lead their own people in the churches. The outside evangelist circulates around four different Koma groups. He is now training younger men to take his place and become leaders of the churches in the area. Some of these new church leaders travel over 30 kilometers on bicycle each week for theological extension courses taught by one of our missionaries. Our plans to develop local leadership are beginning to bear fruit.

A potential problem for the Koma has developed because of the discovery of deposits of terra-cotta in this area in 1981. European archaeologists, who came into the area to do minerals research, gave a generator to the people and opened up roads. They told the Koma that they would build a hospital and bring other developments to the area. What will be the effects of modernization for the Koma? Often, such sudden changes are devastating for hunter-gatherer peoples such as these.

Our greatest challenge has been the advance of Islam into the area. In 1981, when we went to work with the Koma, four of the five villages had no Muslims. Since then Islamic teachers have moved in, building mosques in each of the villages. Many of the young men who were initially open to our approach have turned to Islam along with some of the Christian converts.

Today, there are Christians in four of the five Koma villages. Ali is one of the leaders in his church but has not been made an elder because he, like many of the Koma believers, has chosen to remain polygamous. Mission work among the Koma has as its goal holistic development along with presentation of the gospel. Each year, our nurses give measles vaccinations. A road into the area has made transportation easier. Wycliffe has a couple ready to enter the tribe for scripture translation. God continues to work among the Koma. He graciously prepared them for the gospel even before our arrival, and he will continue to guide the new Koma church.

Chapter 18

KONKOMBA PEOPLE OF NORTHERN GHANA

by Ross F. Gaskin

The Konkomba of West Africa are a people group situated mainly in Ghana. Earlier in this century most of the Konkomba were semi-nomadic agriculturists, abandoning their mud homes and surrounding fields every few years to search for more fertile lands and water. Being poor, unsettled, often hired as low paid, occasional laborers, they were viewed by surrounding peoples as occupying the lowest rung of the social ladder. In 1946, one of the first missionaries of the Worldwide Evangelization Crusade (WEC) described the Konkomba as among the least developed and most despised peoples in their region. However, he admired them for their physical strength, generosity, and honesty.

This image is changing today. The Konkomba have mastered new, productive farming techniques and have become more settled. They are seen as ambitious and hard working with a growing reputation as a prestigious and well-to-do people. Thus, although traditionally having occupied the position of the underdog, they are assuming roles of higher status in the society of northeastern Ghana.

Definition and Description of the Konkomba

The Konkomba people, also known as the Bikpakpaln, are situated in the northeastern section of Ghana, adjoining the Togo border and near the original ancestral home of the Konkombas. Almost 30,000 Konkomba reside in Ghana, most of them in the area in which WEC is ministering. On the Togo side of the border it is estimated that there are an additional 30,000 Konkomba.

The Konkomba speak Likpakpaln in one or another of its many dialects, all of which are mutually intelligible. Like most Africans, they are also multilingual, often speaking Twi, Bassari, Hausa, or English.

Recent social changes, including the growing number of people competing for a fixed amount of land and the advantages of schooling which is only available to sedentary peoples, have put pressure upon the Konkomba to become more settled. Although some Konkomba have moved into towns where they sell produce from their gardens, the majority continue to live in rural areas and produce primarily for subsistence, but even among these there has been an increasing involvement in market exchange and cash cropping.

The Konkombas have a patrilineal system in which the males form the linkages of the descent group. From the time a child is born, his or her closest associations are with brothers, sisters, and the children of his or her father's brothers. The Konkomba are also patrilocal, preferring to reside with the husband's father, if possible. Thus women, upon marriage, leave the company of their patrilineal-linked relatives and enter the world of their husband's relatives. A small hamlet or neighborhood group consists of several family dwellings of men closely related patrilineally, along with the men's wives and children.

The senior man of the compound is the dominant figure. He is the village headman, or chief and the village bears his name. All village members respect his authority, while at the same time requiring that decisions be made by consensus of all senior males of the village.

The Konkomba are predominantly followers of African traditional beliefs and practices, which form a strong component of their cultural- and self-identity. Spirits are believed to be localized in the sense of relating to and are important only for the Konkomba. Although Islam attracts the allegiance of a growing number of persons in northeastern Ghana, with estimates of Muslims in all tribes in this area ranging from 15 percent up, few Konkombas have converted to Islam. Christianity seems to have more appeal through the witness of missionaries and Christians in neighboring groups. Nine percent of the Konkombas are practicing Christians, either Roman Catholics or Protestants, and 15 percent are Christian adherents.

The Konkomba world view transcends the secular-sacred distinction known in the Western world. Their view of the universe tends to fuse everything into one whole. For example, morality and agriculture are linked, with crop failure meaning that there has been moral failure. One's life is preoccupied with gods, spirits, and ghosts, which are present not only in the other world, with its "living dead" (the tribal ancestors), but also in this world. Because the past is of much importance to the Konkomba, they have little interest in the future, which is seen to be of shorter duration.

Historically, the Konkomba have occupied a position of low status in the political and social system of Ghana. They have been looked upon as an uneducated, laboring class. Until colonial times they were subservient to the conquering Damongo, but with the defeat of the Damongo by the French, the Konkomba were freed from their political servitude.

After World War II, however, they became subservient to the neighboring Nummumba as shareholders and tenant farmers on Nummumba land. In 1981, many Konkomba began to feel that this was an unjust arrangement and rebelled against the Nummumba. Much animosity remains from this period of rebellion and warfare.

The role of the Konkomba in the society of northeastern Ghana is now changing. By their willingness to adopt new, improved farming techniques, they have increased their economic standing, becoming suppliers of farm produce, particularly yams, in northeastern Ghana. Politically, they have shaken free of their subservient roles to the Damongo and, by becoming land owners, are no longer dominated by their former Nummumba landlords.

The Konkomba of northeastern Ghana are clearly a people group with a common cultural heritage. They are geographically localized near the town of Saboba, a central gathering place historically linked to the center of Konkomba life. The Konkomba speak one language, with all its dialects mutually intelligible. They practice traditional religious beliefs which have given them a sense of being a people with a long history. Finally, the Konkomba are demarcated from surrounding people groups by the special characteristics of their architecture, their reputation as yam growers, and their rise from low cultural status to a position of social prestige.

The Unreached Status of the Konkomba

When WEC first started work in northeastern Ghana in 1940, there were no known Christians. Since that time there has been a slow growth in the number of Konkomba Christians in this area, although even now most are practitioners of traditional African religion. Because it is difficult for them to abandon these religious practices, only 9 to 15 percent profess

Christianity, either as Roman Catholics or Protestants. However, their attitude towards Christianity is open.

The Evangelical Church of Ghana, affiliated with WEC, has approximately 200 Konkomba members, 500 adherents, and seven Konkomba pastors. The Assemblies of God, which also works in this area, has a small number of churches in northeastern Ghana. Other Christian missions include the Roman Catholics, who have worked among the Konkomba around the Yeji-Salaga area since 1970, and the Presbyterians, who have a small work in the Saboba area, also since 1970.

The Ghana Institute of Linguistics, WEC, and the Roman Catholic Church are all involved in literacy programs. Translation of the New Testament was completed by the Ghana Institute of Linguistics in 1977. The first edition was sold out by 1982. A reprint is needed and expected soon. In general, literacy programs have made substantial impact among the Konkomba, opening their culture to the gospel and to social changes. In addition, medical and agricultural programs have been implemented by the churches and missions in the area as a way of evangelical witness.

In 1960, the Konkomba were clearly unreached, but today, small Konkomba churches are beginning to develop. As missionaries learn how to communicate cross-culturally and truly identify with the Konkomba lifestyle, world view, and mind set, they will be more accepted and the gospel will have gained greater credibility. This is beginning to happen.

The Process Of Evangelization Among the Konkomba

My family and I worked and lived in the Konkomba area from 1960 until 1971. In 1982, we came back to the same area for a short-term assignment. In our first years there, we concentrated on learning the language and the culture of the Konkomba. The more we lived among them, the more we saw their tremendous need and openness to the gospel. We also saw that there was no viable church among them.

In looking for a way to reach this people group, we initially attempted to share the gospel by taking a small group of Christian Ghanaians to remote Konkomba villages and staying overnight with the people. Warm welcomes were always given to us on these visits.

In these early years of 1960-65, there were a small number of Konkomba converts. It was our plan to start them in Bible training immediately so that, as the first Konkomba Christians, they could become pastors. Our hopes were fulfilled when they began to exercise effective outreach ministries to their own people.

The Konkomba language at that time was unwritten and known by few Europeans, but we saw that translation of the language and literacy programs were vital tools needed for the communication of the gospel. We therefore worked diligently at learning the language and developing our skills at communicating gospel truths to the Konkomba. In about 1967, the Ghana Institute of Linguistics began work on a translation of the scriptures into the Konkomba language.

We found that we had to help the Konkomba people with other problems if they were to see a true Christian witness and open their hearts to the message of Christ. Among their felt needs were treatment for widespread leprosy, reduction of high infant mortality, and increased agricultural production. WEC addressed these problems through a program of leprosy control, the establishment of general and midwifery clinics, and a program to increase the people's agricultural potential.

Resistance to the work of church and mission has come from powerful chiefs who exercise strong authority over the Konkomba. They oppose both the acceptance of the gospel and the presence of outside influences among their people. While their attitude has slowed acceptance of the message of Jesus Christ, it points to the need of relying upon Konkomba pastors for the process of evangelization once such pastors have been called and trained. The work will accelerate as more pastors are trained. Although missionaries are still needed to work in this region, their role has become that of supporter and enabler of Konkomba Christians, instead of front line worker and evangelist.

Present Situation

Results in our work with the Konkomba was at first slow in coming. Yet, seeing the message of Jesus Christ lived out in the lives of Konkomba Christians and pastors profoundly affected and encouraged us. The first Konkomba Christians worshiped in churches with a mixture of other tribal peoples, but gradually, churches began to develop which were more fully Konkomba, using their own language and working within their cultural values and patterns of behavior. The reality of a Konkomba church is beginning to come true.

Work continues among the Konkomba on the part of WEC, the Roman Catholic Church, Assemblies of God, and Presbyterians. The development of a truly viable church is still a priority for this work. Yet God has truly blessed the work and with God's grace, it will continue to bear fruit.

Chapter 19

AARI PEOPLE OF
CENTRAL GAMO GOFA, ETHIOPIA

by Brian Fargher

The complex physical environment of Ethiopia, with its deep ravines, soaring mountains, parched plains and bleak coastlines, is matched by a complex array of people groups. Ethnic and social lines crisscross to produce a social system which is not only staggering in its complexity but also constantly changing in relationship to political and environmental stresses. Some of the larger people groups, such as the Amhara peoples and the Ormo, Tigre, and Sidama, are well-known. Yet, there are many smaller people groups who are virtually unknown to anyone outside the local area. One such group is the Aari people.

There has been a long history of evangelistic efforts among the Aari. Although these began in earnest in the early 1930s, it was not until the mid-1960s that mission expansion and growth began to take place. The success of this work is evidenced by the 90 flourishing congregations that exist today. Following is a description of the process of evangelism and outreach among the Aari people of Ethiopia.

Description of the Aari as a People Group

The Aari people live on the southern tip of the Ethiopian plateau. They number around 86,000 people and are surrounded by a number of other small people groups. In general, they and their immediate neighbors have long been on the fringes of Ethiopian society. They are far removed geographically from the center of the national government and are thus often forgotten or ignored when major political and social events take place. Not only are they a fringe people in terms of their location, they are also a fringe people in terms of greater Ethiopian society.

The Aari belong to a larger grouping of peoples which have long been referred to by the dominant peoples of Ethiopia as *Shankilla* (also spelled Shanqila). This is a derogatory term, referring to black African peoples in a negative sense, and is used by the dominant Amharic-speaking peoples of Ethiopia. Aari is the term the people use to refer to themselves.

The Aari live on the Ethiopian plateau in south central Gamo Gofa province, surrounded on three sides by precipitious slopes. On the north they are bounded by Gofa peoples, who are also plateau dwellers. On the east, south, and west are lowland peoples, the Mali, Bunna, Murisee, Podi, and Deme. Although they have occasional contact with these people, the Aari do not like to travel or live in their area. In fact, they are noted for strong attachment to their traditional homeland. Outside of short visits for the purpose of trade, they rarely travel in large numbers to the nearby towns or to major cities such as Addis Ababa. Essentially, they are still a distinct, independent people living in a relatively remote area of Ethiopia.

For 95 percent of the people, Aari is the language of the home and the marketplace. Other languages which are used to some extent are Amharic and Gofa, the latter mostly for trading.

Aari people who have lived either in the household of an Amhara person or in one of the cities will speak Amharic.

Traditionally, the Aari people have been cultivators. Many of them supplement the products of their fields through small-scale trading in local markets. Also, a few are involved in cottage industries.

In traditional times the Aari social system was a kinship-based system. Clans, structured along patrilineal lines, were the basis of social organization, with the oldest male members of the clan being the leaders of society. This changed significantly when the central Ethiopian government began to impose tighter control at the beginning of the twentieth century. Today, kinship is still a strong local organizing force, but the central government provides the basic structure for law and order, political decision making, and economic interactions.

Because the Aari have had long contact with Christianity, it is somewhat difficult to describe their traditional religion with any degree of confidence. It is argued by anthropologists that the Aari people have two main deities, one of which is male and the other female. It is unclear as to whether this is still true today. It seems more likely that the people possess the concept of a creator god, *Sabi*, who although remote, has maintained contact with the world. This contact is through intermediary deities, or *Beri*, which often appear to be equal with *Sabi*, but inhabit the unseen world which exists between *Sabi* and mankind. *Beri* and lesser spirits are believed to possess humans to pass on messages and convey minor revelations.

The world view of the Aari centers around the notion of punishment. They believe that mankind has offended *Sabi*, which has driven a wedge between human beings and him. As a result of this offense there is suffering. Thus, the Aari have no concept of suffering caused by a personalized evil power, rather they themselves bear the blame for the suffering they find in the world.

The relations of the Aari with surrounding lowland peoples is somewhat complex and have often been tense. On occasion, they have had to defend their land, crops, cattle, and women from predatory raids of lowland people. Although, the Aari do trade with people of the lowlands, it is a delicate relationship.

The Aari language is not closely related to neighboring languages, and their religion is distinct from neighboring people groups. Their physical features set them apart from the greater Ethiopian society and their strong sense of identity further distinguishes them from the surrounding peoples. They are clearly a people group distinct in Ethiopian society.

The Unreached Status of the Aari

It is difficult to determine how much interaction the Aari have had with Christian peoples. We do not know whether Christianity reached as far as central Gamo Gofa during its spread throughout Ethiopia in the twelfth and thirteenth centuries. It is known that after Emperor Menelik conquered Gamo Gofa in the late 1890s, Amharic-speaking government officials slowly moved into the area. They were Christian, but their Christianity was confined to stockades in which they lived and from which they ruled. This created the impression among the Aari that Christianity was the religion of ethnic colonizers.

Thus, when Ethiopian evangelists and expatriate missionaries arrived in the area in the mid-1900s, the Aari were already aware of the existence of Christianity. These early Christian workers had some basis for communicating to the Aari the tenets of Christianity, and they found some degree of openness to the message. By 1954, non-Ethiopian Orthodox churches had been established in Gofa, as well as in Gamu and Wolayta. These were churches financed and administered by Ethiopians who shared the work willingly with expatriate missionaries in the area. Most of the Ethiopian evangelists who went into this area did not speak the Aari language but, being Ethiopians, were seen as related to the Aari.

During the first years they were in the area, the expatriate missionaries erected buildings, first housing for themselves and then a clinic for their medical work, and later, a school. They wanted to travel among the people to establish relationships and begin to share the gospel. However, strict government policy limited the amount of itineration they were allowed to do. In addition, they were not allowed to learn the Aari language and had to carry on all their work in Amharic. This was in line with the Ethiopian government's policy of furthering the process of Amharization in the area.

Thus, the early years of missionary work were spent getting to know people and being available so that rapport would be developed. This was difficult since the missionaries were required to be associated with government officials, who were Amharas. The Aari saw this as close identification, and the missionaries had to struggle to establish their separate identity in order to be accepted by the Aari people.

No translation work had been done among the Aari people. The only Bible available was the Amharic Bible. This meant that anyone who wanted to read the Bible first had to become literate in Amharic. It was a hurdle that was accepted as one of the givens of the situation by missionaries working in the area. Looking back now, it may well be that it worked in favor of the spread of the gospel since Amharic became the lingua franca of the area.

Although the more progressive officials of the central government wanted missionaries to be present in rural areas, the local

Amhara population, including government officials, soldiers, and priests, opposed expatriate missionaries for a number of reasons. They were afraid that the Aari people would be supported by the missionaries in establishing and maintaining their own ethnic identity, which ran counter to the designs of these Amhara officials. They suspected that once the Aari became Christian, they would begin to question previous dogma imposed upon them.

The early work of the missionaries was also hindered by the Aari tradition that "salvation" and relief from problems came from obedience to shamans who then kept the spirit world contented. The Aari feared that any violation of these traditional methods of appeasing spiritual forces would bring death and disaster. They were therefore reluctant to change and accept Christianity.

On the other hand, there were a number of cultural factors that aided the spread of the gospel among the Aari. Within their traditional religion there was a deep desire to find reconciliation, usually sensed as a gulf between them and *Sabi*, the creator god. In addition, the increasing influence of Christian Amharic-speaking peoples and the fact that some of the Aari people had become members of the Orthodox church signalled the beginning of a time of religious change. Last, the people longed for social harmony and an escape from the problems of feuding, fighting, and alcohol consumption. The gospel offered a way to achieve this harmony.

The Aari were clearly an unreached people group. Christianity was known to them through the Ethiopian Orthodox church. Yet, it was seen as foreign and irrelevant. Traditional animistic beliefs continued to have powerful effects on their lives. There was a need for clear presentation of the gospel in ways that were culturally and socially relevant to the Aari people.

The Process of Evangelization of the Aari

As far back as the 1930s, missionaries working to the north of
the Aari region knew that there was an area south of them in
which there had been little proclamation of the gospel. They
wanted to go there but were unable to do so. Except for the
Ethiopian Orthodox, church there were no other churches
present, and little direct evangelism was being carried out.

In the early 1950s, mission agencies began to work to establish
a presence at Bako, the government center of the region. They
had the support of the Ethiopian government in this endeavor.
The first missionaries at Bako felt no need to research the
situation. They assumed that because no non-Ethiopian Orthodox churches had been established, there was a need to
enter the area and preach. This evangelistic strategy called for
the conversion of individuals and encouragement of the new
converts to worship together and to reach out to their own
people. It was modeled on mission work in Wolayta, where
the church had grown rapidly. (see *Fire on the mountain* by
Ray Davis, and *Born at midnight* by Peter Cotterell). Similar
results were expected among the Aari people.

Government policy restricted the early missionaries to one
location, but they were allowed to build houses near the
government center and operate an academic school. Because
they were convinced that it was only the local people who
could reach the larger masses, they worked toward the conversion of individuals and discipled these individuals to then work
with their neighbors. Evangelistic meetings were not used
since they were seen as culturally inappropriate. Since the
great majority of the Aari were illiterate, it was not practical
to distribute literature. The missionaries used conversation as
the media for spreading the gospel.

From 1954 to 1964, the work grew slowly. These were years
of preparation both by expatriate and national evangelists.

However, from 1964 to 1974, the individuals who had been disciples in the previous decade moved out and began to establish churches, and there were soon scores of new churches.

In 1962, there was a significant change in the way the work was carried on. At that time the scattered believers that existed throughout the area were organized into their own evangelistic association. Each group of about ten converts was formed into a congregation, and the congregations were assigned to a parish. The parish representatives gathered for monthly meetings. This led to the formation of the Aari churches, which later became part of the Kala Hiywat church, the national Ethiopian denomination with roots in the evangelistic work of Sudan Interior Mission (SIM).

When there were too few Christians in an area for a church, additional Ethiopian evangelists were brought in from Gofa and Wolayta. These evangelists did not know the Aari language, but they were experienced church planters, familiar with the culture and customs of the peoples. They easily fit into the local scene.

At every opportunity, the home of a believer became the residence of an evangelist whose task was to establish a church. The expatriate missionaries acted as catalysts in this process, providing no funds and doing very little of the preaching. Every Christian was encouraged to give what he or she could for the support of Ethiopian evangelists, and whatever was given was immediately passed on to the evangelists. If no money was available, the evangelists did not get paid and had to rely upon the generosity of their hosts. They trusted completely in the Lord.

The work developed along four significant lines: (1) Local Bible schools were established so that students need never be sent out of their own area for training. The schools were as self-sufficient as possible, taught by local teachers, and supported by local money. (2) Visiting evangelists, both expatriate and national, were reduced in number so that the evangelistic outreach could be taken over entirely by local people. The church provided, trained, and supported its own evangelists. (3) Expatriate involvement in handling finances, teaching, and administration was gradually reduced. (4) The structure of the national Kala Hiywat church was strengthened.

Property was purchased for a headquarters near the town of Jinka, the new administrative center of the government, and a Bible school was erected there. By 1977, the theological training program had entirely moved off the mission compound. The Kala Hiywat church is now found throughout Ethiopia and has approximately 3,000 congregations.

Christianity is now an authentic expression of the culture of the Aari people. The form of Christianity that exists is neither Amhara nor European, but rather Aari. Christians among the Aari argue that biblical Christianity is what their traditional religion had groped for in vain. It has fulfilled all their hopes and aspirations.

There have been times of difficulty for the Aari Christians. From 1977 through 1983, there was a wave of persecution when churches and Bible schools were closed and Christians were forbidden to meet. Some of the church leaders defected in order to obtain lucrative government jobs. Conditions have now changed and there has been no overt opposition for the past four years. Through it all, the church thrived and continued to grow. In 1986, there are now close to 90 Aari congregations.

Current Situation

In 1983, after the years of persecution, the congregations were able to hold public meetings again. A new leadership was elected to guide their work. Aari churches now have a central Bible school and two district schools. They continue to send and support evangelists to work among people groups south of them and among the Murisee people, traditional enemies in the Omo River valley to the west of them.

The church is well established among the Aari people and has become a sending church. God has richly blessed the work among these people.

PART THREE

REGISTRY OF THE UNREACHED

This year's registry of unreached peoples and people groups consists of a single listing of entries sorted by country. If the reader compares this year's listing with those in previous volumes of the *Unreached Peoples* series, it will be seen that there are many changes. The registry is dynamic in that it attempts to display our best and most current information.

Thus, some of the changes are due to updated information which readers and co-workers have so generously submitted to us. There is a second reason for the changes. This year we have decided to only list those peoples and people groups for whom it has been reported that there is less than 20% of the population who have any affiliation with a Christian church.

Again, we have not done this to offer a new definition of unreached. Instead, it is done to ensure that we list those groups for which there is the strongest justification for further evangelistic efforts. So, the listing is not presented as a total listing of unreached peoples and people groups, but rather, it is a representative listing of unreached peoples and people groups of highest priority for the task of world evangelism.

Explanation of columns and codes

The registry contains 6 columns. The meaning of these is as follows:

1.   **Name** --   This column lists, in alphabetical order sorted by country, those peoples and people groups

identified as unreached. Two types of listings are found.

Ethnolinguistic peoples are listed in medium type.

Sociologically defined people groups are listed in bold type.

2. **Scripture** -- This column indicates the known state of translation of Christian Scriptures in the vernacular language.

3. **Language** -- This column lists the language used as the vernacular.

4. **Group size** -- This column indicates the population size of the people or people group in the country indicated.

5. **Primary religion** -- This columns notes the main or dominant religion of this people or people group as measured by proportion of the population professing affiliation to it.

6. **ID** -- This column lists the identification number of the people or people group in the MARC data base and is to be used when communicating to MARC about this data.

GROUP NAME	SCRIPTURE	LANGUAGE	GROUP SIZE	PRIMARY RELIGION	ID
Afghanistan					
Afshar	Bible	Azerbaijani	5,000	Islam	2545
Aimaq	portions	Dari (Farsi)	5,000,000	Islam	55
Amulah	none	Amulah	nr	Islam	3289
Arabs	Bible	Arabic, Balkh	2,000	Islam	4824
Ashkundi	none	Ashkundi	7,000	Islam	3297
Baluch	portions	Baluchi	200,000	Islam	4103
Bangaru	none	Bangaru (Jati)	167	Islam	4827
Bashgali	none	Bashgali	10,000	Islam	2546
Bashkarik	none	Bashgali (Bashkarik)	nr	Islam	3298
Brahui	portions	Brahui	10,000	Islam	4024
Darwiz	none	Darwazi	10,770	Islam	5205
Gawar-Bati	none	Gawar-Bati	8,000	Islam	2548
Ghori	none	Ghorani	nr	Islam	4075
Grangal	ncne	Nangalami (Grangal)	nr	Islam	4830
Gujuri	none	Gujuri	10,000	Islam	2549
Hazara	none	Hazaragi	500,000	Islam	4093
• Hazara in Kabul	+none	Hazaragi	300,000	Islam	5021
Ishkash	none	Sanglech-Ishkashim	2,000	Islam	3299
Jati	none	Jati	835	Islam	2550
Kantwai	none	Kantwai	nr	Islam	3294
Karakalpak	none	Karakalpak	2,400	Islam	2653
Kashgari	none	Qashqari(Uighur Dial.)	nr	Islam	2637
Kazakh	portions	Kazakh	2,400	Islam	2771
Kordar	none	Kordar	nr	Islam	3295
Lahnda	Bible,NT	Lahnda	10,000	Hinduism	4828
Logari	portions	Pushto	2,000	Islam	4831
Malakhel	none	Malakhel	2,100	Islam	3141
Mogholi	none	Mogholi	2,000	Islam	2552
Munji-Yidgha	none	Munji-Yidgha	14,000	Islam	2553
Naroj	none	Naroj	nr	Islam	3160
Narwizi	none	Narwizi	nr	Islam	3159
Nijrau	portions	Pashto	600	Islam	4018
Nishe	none	Nishe	nr	Islam	3193
Pahlavani	none	Pahlavani	nr	Islam	5013
Parun	none	Prasuni	nr	Islam	3220
Pashayi	none	Pashayi	96,000	Islam	2554

GROUP NAME	SCRIPTURE	LANGUAGE	GROUP SIZE	PRIMARY RELIGION	ID
Prasuni	none	Prasuni	2,000	Animism	2555
Punjabi Sikhs	Bible,NT	Punjabi	10,000	Sikhism	4829
Pushtun, Abdali	none	Pushtun	2,000,000	Islam	2521
Pushtun, Afridi	none	Pushtun	nr	Islam	2606
Pushtun, Durrani	none	Pushtun	2,400,000	Islam	2589
Pushtun, Ghilzai	none	Pushtun	3,000,000	Islam	2551
Pushtun, Mangal	none	Pushtun	nr	Islam	2630
Pushtun, Mohmandi	none	Pushtun	nr	Islam	2557
Pushtun, Shinwari	none	Pushtun	nr	Islam	2625
Pushtun, Waziri	none	Pushtun	nr	Islam	2612
Pushtun, Wenetsi	none	Pushtun	nr	Islam	2631
Pushtun, Yusefzai	none	Pushtun	nr	Islam	2595
Qatar	none	Qatar	nr	Islam	5424
Ramgal	none	Ramgal	nr	Islam	3032
Sau	none	Sau	1,000	Islam	2556
Share	none	Share	nr	Islam	5350
Shatul	portions	Pashto	600	Islam	4023
Shekhani	stories,portions	Shekhani	67,000	Islam	3296
Shughni	none	Shughni	3,000	Islam	2558
Sindhi	Bible,portions	Sindhi	600,000	Hinduism	4107
Tajik	portions	Pamiri	3,600,000	Islam	4040
Tangshi	none	Tangshewi	nr	Islam	5246
Tatar	portions	Tatar	350	Islam	2828
Tekke	portions	Chaghatai (Dial Uzbek)	300,000	Islam	2547
Tirahi	portions	Pashto	5,000	Islam	4030
Turkmen	portions	Turkmeni	380,000	Islam	26
Uighur	Bible	Uighur	3,000	Islam	2559
Uzbeks	portions	Uzbeki, Turkic	1,188,000	Islam	1229
Wadah	none	Wadah	nr	Islam	5377
Waigali	none	Waigali	40,000	Islam	4015
Wakhi	none	Wakhi	7,200	Islam	5166
Wardaj	none	Warduji	nr	Islam	5349
Wotapuri	none	Wotapuri-Katarqalai(Nurst)	nr	Islam	4046
Yarkand	none	Yarkandi(dial.Uighur)	nr	Islam	2652
Zargar	none	Zargar	nr	Islam	4063

GROUP NAME	ID	GROUP SIZE	PRIMARY RELIGION	LANGUAGE	SCRIPTURE
Albania					
• Muslims	4000	2,000,000	Islam	Albanian Tosk	New Testament
Algeria					
Berber	9186	1,200,000	Islam	Tamazight	portions
Kabyle	145	2,000,000	Islam	Kabyle	+Bible
Riff	9183	1,000,000	Islam	Riff	portions
Shawiya	2207	150,000	Islam	Shawiya	none
Shilha	9184	3,000,000	Islam	Shilha	portions
Tuareg	9185	10,000	Islam	Tamasheq	portions
• Western Sahara Refugees	9012	70,000	Islam	Arabic	+Bible
Angola					
Bushmen (Kung)	9193	1,000	Animism	Kung-Ekoka	portions
Hukwe	511	9,000	Animism	Xun	none
O'Kung	9195	1,000	Animism	O'Kung	none
Argentina					
• Chilean Refugees	9031	1,850	Roman Catholic	Spanish	+Bible
• Lao Refugees	9037	1,500	Ancestor Worship	Lao	+not reported
• Universitarios - Rosario	5003	10,000	Roman Catholic	Spanish	+Bible
Australia					
• Aborigines in Brisbane	5000	8,000	Secularism	English	+Bible
• Chinese	747	30,000	Traditional Chinese	Hakka	Bible
• Chinese Students	2119	6,000	Secularism	Chinese Dialects	**Bible**
Gugu-Yalanji	430	5,000	Animism	Gugu-Yalanji	portions
Iwaidja	390	150	Animism	Iwaidja	not reported
• Japanese in Sydney	5937	2,000	**Buddhism**	Japanese	Bible
Turks	312	60,000	Islam	Turkish	portions,NT,OT,Bible
• Vietnamese Refugees	2126	8,000	Folk Religion	Vietnamese	**Bible**
Yanyula	230	150	Other	Yanyula (Yanjula)	portions

GROUP NAME	LANGUAGE	SCRIPTURE	GROUP SIZE	PRIMARY RELIGION	ID
Austria					
Chinese	Cantonese	Bible	1,000	Traditional Chinese	753
• Turkish Guest Workers	Turkish	Bible,NT,portions	60,000	Islam	2193
Bahrain					
Arabs	Arabic	Bible	320,000	Islam	4845
Iranians	Persian	Bible	53,000	Islam	4843
Pakistanis	Urdu	Bible,OT,NT	22,000	Islam	4844
Bangladesh					
Assamese	Assamese	Bible,NT,portions	7,700	Islam	1406
Baluchi, Eastern	Bengali	New Testament	200	Islam	1407
Banai	Bengali	Bible	2,000	Buddhist-Animist	63
Barua	Barua	not reported	nr	Buddhist-Animist	1405
• Bengali Sufis	**Bengali**	not reported	70,000	Islam	4820
• Burmese Muslim Refugees	**Bengali**	+portions	200,000	Islam	9001
Chakma	Chakma	New Testament	533,731	Buddhist-Animist	302
Darlong	Darlong	none	5,000	Animism	1408
Hajong	Bengali	Bible	17,000	Hindu-Animist	61
Ho	Ho	portions	nr	Unknown	1409
Hodi	Bengali	not reported	nr	Hindu-Animist	4198
• Keot-Muslim of Rangpur	**Keot**	**not reported**	nr	**Islam**	4196
Koch	Bengali	Bible	35,000	Hindu-Animist	62
Mandai	Mandai	not reported	nr	Hindu-Animist	4199
Marma	Arakanese	portions	nr	Hindu-Animist	1403
Mirung	Mirung	none	12,000	Animism	650
Mru	Murung	not reported	50,000	Animism	3
Oriya	Oriya	Bible,NT	nr	Unknown	1412
Pangon	Meithei	Bible	nr	Islam	4197
Pankhu	Pankhu	none	600	Islam	2563
Punjabi, Eastern	Punjabi	Bible	nr	Unknown	1413
Rajbangsi	Rajbangsi	none	nr	Hindu-Animist	1401
Rakhaine	Arakanese	Bible	10,000	Hindu-Animist	1404
Santali	Santali	Bible,portions	100,000	Unknown	2562
Shendu	Shendu	none	1,000	Animism	1415
Sylhetti	Sylhetti	portions	3,000,000	Unknown	1416

NAME	SCRIPTURE	LANGUAGE	GROUP SIZE	PRIMARY RELIGION	ID
Tangchangya	none	Tangchangya	8,000	Islam	2564
Tippera	none	Tippera	38,000	Islam	2565
Tripuri	NT,portions	Tripuri	50,000	Animism	1417
Belgium					
• North Africans	Bible	Arabic	90,000	Islam	4019
• Turkish Workers	Bible	Kurdish	60,000	Islam	4020
Belize					
• Salvadoran Refugees	+Bible	Spanish	2,000	Roman Catholic	9059
Benin					
Adja	Bible	Ge	323,000	Animism	423
Aizo	none	Ayizo-Gbe	165,000	Animism	9198
Anii	none	Anii	2,375	Islam-Animist	9199
Bariba	NT,portions	Bariba	342,000	Animism	246
Biali	none	Berba	48,000	Animism	5165
Boko	+NT,portions	Busa	50,000	Islam	444
Dendi	none	Dendi	46,000	Islam	445
Dompago	portions,NT	Dompago	41,800	Animism	515
Dyerma	NT,portions	Dyerma	9,000	Islam	5315
Fon	portions	Fon-Gbe	957,000	Animism	5232
Fulbe	BI,OT,NT	Fulfulde, Benin-Togo	224,000	Islam-Animist	446
Gun-Gbe	Bible	Gun-Gbe	247,000	Animism	5167
Gurma	NT,portions	Gourma	38,000	Animism	447
Kabiye	portions	Kabiye	47,000	Animism	5168
Kotokoli	portions	Tem	34,200	Islam	448
Lamba	portions	Lamba	29,000	Animism	5169
Mbelime	none	Mbelime	20,000	Unknown	5162
Mina	NT,portions	Gen-Gbe	250,000	Unknown	5158
Mokole	portions	Mokole	15,200	Animism	449
Nateni	none	Nateni	35,000	Animism	5171
Pila	NT,portions	Pila-Pila	53,800	Animism	237
Save	Bible	Yoruba	15,000	Animism	451
Sola	none	Sola	3,000	Animism	453
Somba	portions	Ditamari	262,000	Animism	452

GROUP NAME	SCRIPTURE	LANGUAGE	GROUP SIZE	PRIMARY RELIGION	ID
Tofi	none	Tofin-Gbe	33,000	Animism	422
Waama	portions	Waama	50,000	Animism	5172
Watchi	none	Waci-Gbe	83,600	Animism	454
Yoruba	Bible	Yoruba	500,000	Animism	5233
Bhutan					
Drukpa	New Testament	Sharchagpakha	960,000	Buddhism	2022
Kebumtamp	none	Kebumtamp	517,000	Unknown	1418
Lepcha	portions	Lepcha	9,100	Unknown	8634
Nepali	Bible	Nepali	400,000	Hinduism	2566
Schachop	none	Sharchagpakha	400,000	Islam	2567
Tibetans	Bible	Tibetan	2,000	Buddhism	7017
Tseku	none	Tseku	nr	Unknown	1419
Bolivia					
• Aymara in La Paz	NT,portions	Aymara	220,000	Syncretic Christian	44
• Mestizos in La Paz	+Bible,NT,OT,portions	Spanish	400,000	Syncretic Christian	5001
• Mororata	none	Aymara	1,000	Animism	6568
• Professionals in La Paz	+Bible,OT,NT,portions	Spanish	200,000	Roman Catholic	439
• Quechua in La Paz	+NT,OT,portions	Quechua	53,000	Syncretic Christian	347
Tacana	portions	Tacana	4,000	Animism	2142
Tsimane	portions	Tsimane	6,000	Animism	2143
Botswana					
Au ei	none	Au ei dialects	5,000	Animism	5173
Buka-khwe	none	Local dialects	9,000	Animism	5174
Bushmen	none	Buka-Khwe (Ko,Hu,Xu)	10,500	Animism	509
• Dukwe Refugee Camp Residents	not reported	Tribal Languages	800	Animism	9022
Kwe-etshori	none	Kwe-etshori	3,000	Animism	5176
Nharon	none	Nharon	3,000	Animism	5177
Shua	portions	Shua	400	Animism	5178
Tswana	Bible	Tswana	830,000	Animism	9190
Yei	none	Yei	10,000	Animism	1162

Brazil

GROUP NAME	SCRIPTURE	LANGUAGE	GROUP SIZE	PRIMARY RELIGION	ID
Asurini	portions	Asurini	nr	Animism	153
Atruahi	none	Atruahi	500	Animism	2149
Bororo	portions	Bororo	500	Animism	441
Cinta Larga	none	Cinta Larga	500	Animism	2154
•Copacabana Apt. Dwellers	Bible	Portuguese	400,000	Roman Catholic	4116
•Drug Addicts in Sao Paulo	+Bible	Portuguese	200,000	Roman Catholic	5022
•Favelados-Rio de Janeiro	+Bible	Portuguese	600,000	Syncretic Christian	5043
Kayapo	portions	Kayapo	600	Animism	1158
Kuatinema	portions	Asurini	100	Animism	1159
•Spiritists	Bible	Portuguese	9,000,000	Folk Religion	28
•Students in Cuiaba	Bible	Portuguese	20,000	Secularism	712
Waimiri	none	Waimiri	1,000	Animism	3134
Zuruaha	portions	Zuruaha	520	Animism	2198

Burkina Faso

GROUP NAME	SCRIPTURE	LANGUAGE	GROUP SIZE	PRIMARY RELIGION	ID
Bella	+portions	Tamachek	350,000	Islam	5240
Birifor	NT	Birifor	90,000	Animism	5664
Bolon	ncne	Bolon	4,000	Islam-Animist	5661
Dagaaba	none	Dagari	150,000	Islam-Animist	5663
Doghosie	none	Doghosie	12,000	Animism	5665
Dyan	none	Dyan	18,400	Islam-Animist	5666
Frafra	portions	Gurenne	10,000	Animism	5469
Fulbe (Macina)	portions	Fufulde, Macina	250,000	Islam	140
Fulbe, Sokoto	none	Fufulde, Sokoto	258,000	Islam	5468
Gouin	NT,portions,Bible	Gouin	90,000	Animism	5669
Gourmances	portions	Gourma	300,000	Animism	5670
Karaboro	portions	Karaboro	45,000	Islam-Animist	4139
Kasena	none	Kasem	55,000	Islam	5671
Komono	none	Komono	8,000	Islam	5672
Kurumba	New Testament	Kurumba	27,000	Islam-Animist	5673
Kusasi	New Testament	Kusaal	20,000	Animism	5148
Lobi	New Testament	Lobi	1,285,000	Animism	5467
Manenka	none	Maninka	54,400	Islam	5466
Marka	none	Marka	136,000	Islam	5675
Natioro	none	Natioro	1,500	Islam-Animist	5676

GROUP NAME	SCRIPTURE	LANGUAGE	GROUP SIZE	PRIMARY RELIGION	ID
Nouna	portions	Nouni	130,000	Animism	4129
Puguli	none	Puguli	5,000	Islam-Animist	5678
Senoufo, Nanerge	portions	Senoufo, Nanerge	33,800	Unknown	5463
Senoufo, Tagba	none	Senoufo, Tagba	30,000	Animism	5462
Siamou	portions	Siamou	20,000	Animism	5519
Sisala	New Testament	Sisala	25,000	Islam-Animist	5681
Songhai	none	Songhai	136,000	Islam-Animist	5682
Tiefo	none	Tiefo	10,000	Islam-Animist	5683
Toussian	none	Toussian	30,000	Islam	4123
Tuareg	none	Tuareg	13,600	Islam	94
Vige	none	Vige	4,000	Islam-Animist	5684
Wara	none	Wara	3,000	Islam-Animist	5685

Burma

GROUP NAME	SCRIPTURE	LANGUAGE	GROUP SIZE	PRIMARY RELIGION	ID
Akha	New Testament	Akha	51,000	Animism	2285
Arakanese	portions	Arakanese	310,000	Buddhism	214
Chaungtha	none	Chaungtha	40,000	Buddhist-Animist	2568
Chinese	Bible	Cantonese	600,000	Traditional Chinese	751
Dai	portions	Dai	60,000	Buddhist-Animist	2576
Danu	Bible	Burmese	70,000	Buddhism	4148
Hallam	portions	Hallam	11,000	Buddhist-Animist	2578
Hkun	portions	Shan	20,000	Buddhism	4144
Intha	none	Intha	80,000	Buddhist-Animist	2580
Kachin in Shan State	**Bible**	**Burmese**	**80,000**	**Buddhism**	**4154**
Karen, Padaung	none	Padaung Karen	4,000	Buddhist-Animist	2577
Lama	none	Lama	3,000	Buddhist-Animist	2581
Lu	New Testament	Lu	223,000	Buddhist-Animist	725
Moken	none	Moken	5,000	Animism	157
Mon	Bible	Mon	426,000	Buddhist-Animist	2583
Mun	none	Mun	10,000	Buddhist-Animist	2584
Norra	none	Norra	10,000	Buddhist-Animist	2585
Palaung	none	Palaung	150,000	Buddhism	156
Pao	not reported	Pao	100,000	Buddhism	4149
Purum	none	Purum	300	Buddhist-Animist	2587
Riang-Lang	portions	Riang-Lang	20,000	Buddhist-Animist	2590
Senthang	none	Senthang	10,000	Buddhist-Animist	2591
Shan	not reported	Shan	800,000	Buddhism	4143

GROUP NAME	SCRIPTURE	LANGUAGE	PRIMARY RELIGION	GROUP SIZE	ID
Taman	none	Taman	Buddhist-Animist	10,000	2592
Taungyo	none	Taungyo	Buddhist-Animist	200,000	2593
Taungyoe	Bible	Burmese	Buddhism	18,700	4147
Tawr	none	Tawr	Buddhist-Animist	700	2594
Thai-Ney	not reported	Shan	Buddhist-Animist	5,000	4158
Wa	not reported	Wa	Animism	50,000	4155
Yangbye	none	Yangbye	Buddhist-Animist	330,000	2596
Yin-Kyar	not reported	Shan Dialects	Animism	2,000	4146
Yin-Nett	not reported	Shan Dialects	Animism	2,000	4145
Yinchia	none	Yinchia	Buddhist-Animist	4,000	2597
Yos	none	Yos	Buddhist-Animist	5,000	2598

Burundi

GROUP NAME	SCRIPTURE	LANGUAGE	PRIMARY RELIGION	GROUP SIZE	ID
Batwa Pygmy (Binga)	Bible	Rundi	Animism	45,000	211
	none	Local dialects	Animism	30,000	508

Cameroon

GROUP NAME	SCRIPTURE	LANGUAGE	PRIMARY RELIGION	GROUP SIZE	ID
Babinga	none	Babinga	Animism	2,000	9134
Baka	none	Baka	Animism	25,000	5212
Bamum	NT,portions	Bamum	Unknown	215,000	5215
Buduma	none	Buduma	Unknown	60,000	5228
• Chad Refugees from N'Djamena	not reported	Tribal Languages	Islam	100,000	9005
Daba	portions	Daba	Animism	35,700	7051
Dugun	portions	Pape	Animism	3,000	5279
Duru	portions	Duru	Animism	47,000	7040
Fali, North	none	Fali, North	Islam	16,000	7054
Fali, South	New Testament	Fali, South	Unknown	20,000	9072
Fulbe, Adamawa	Bible	Fufulde, Adamawa	Animism	470,000	507
Glavda	portions	Glavda	Unknown	2,800	9077
Gouwar	none	Gouwar	Animism	5,000	7057
Gude	portions	Gude	Animism	17,700	502
Guduf	portions	Guduf	Unknown	21,300	5237
Hausa	Bible	Hausa	Unknown	23,500	9079
Jimi	none	Jimi	Animism	3,500	9080
Kadam	none	Kadam	Animism	3,000	7060
Kanuri	portions	Kanuri	Unknown	56,500	9081

GROUP NAME	SCRIPTURE	LANGUAGE	GROUP SIZE	PRIMARY RELIGION	ID
Karang	portions	Karang	10,000	Unknown	9083
Koh	portions	Koh	5,000	Unknown	9085
Kolbila	portions	Kolbila	1,600	Islam-Animist	1155
Kompara	none	Kompara	3,000	Unknown	9086
Konja	portions	Konja	4,000	Unknown	9087
Kotoko-Kuseri	none	Arabic	2,100	Islam	9089
Kotoko-Logone	none	Kotoko-Logone	38,500	Islam	5248
Laamang	portions	Laamang	9,000	Unknown	5251
Mandara	New Testament	Mandara	23,500	Islam	5249
Matakam	portions	Matakam	136,000	Animism	498
Mbembe	none	Mbembe	36,000	Animism	5258
Mbuko	New Testament	Mbuko	6,700	Unknown	9095
Mofu, North	portions	Mofu, North	27,500	Animism	8503
Mofu, South	none	Mofu, South	20,000	Animism	5263
Molokwo	portions	Molokwo	8,300	Unknown	8504
Ngemba	none	Ngemba	70,000	Animism	5270
Njanyi	portions	Njanyi	7,500	Animism	8511
Parekwa	none	Podoko	17,500	Animism	496
Saa	none	Saa	3,500	Animism	5277
Sakpu	none	Sakpu	7,000	Unknown	8514
Tikar	portions	Tikar	15,800	Animism	5285
Tupuri	New Testament	Tupuri	70,000	Animism	5286
Voko	not reported	Woko	2,400	Islam-Animist	1154
Wuzlam	none	Wuzlam	10,500	Unknown	5288

Canada

GROUP NAME	SCRIPTURE	LANGUAGE	GROUP SIZE	PRIMARY RELIGION	ID
•Chilean Refugees, Toronto	+Bible	Spanish	10,000	Roman Catholic	9023
•Chinese Indonesians-Vancouver	portions,NT,Bible	Indonesian	1,500	Protestant	15
•Chinese Students, Thunder Bay	+Bible	Mandarin	500	Secularism	9113
•Chinese, Calgary	+Bible	English	30,000	Traditional Chinese	9171
•Chinese, Halifax	+Bible	Mandarin	3,000	Buddhism	9120
•Chinese, Metro Toronto	+Bible	English	40,000	Buddhism	9100
•Chinese, Thunder Bay	+Bible	Various dialects	1,000	Buddhism	9109
•Chinese, Vancouver	Bible	Cantonese	80,000	Traditional Chinese	758

GROUP NAME	SCRIPTURE	LANGUAGE	GROUP SIZE	PRIMARY RELIGION	ID
• Ex-Mental Patients, Hamilton	+Bible	English	800	Secularism	9116
• Fur Trappers	+Bible	French	8,000	Secularism	9115
• Greeks, Toronto	+Bible	Greek	85,000	Orthodox	9150
• Haitians, Montreal	+Bible	Creole	32,000	Folk Religion	9111
• Homosexuals, Toronto	+Bible	English	60,000	Secularism	9203
• Indians, CN Rail Lines	+Bible	English	20,000	Roman Catholic	9267
• Indians, Cold Lake Reserve	+Bible	English	1,250	Roman Catholic	9266
• Indians, Eden Valley	+Bible	English	300	Protestant	9258
• Indians, Edmonton	+Bible	English	30,000	Folk Religion	9251
• Indians, Interlake Region	+Bible	English	10,000	Christianity	9169
• Indians, Kinistino Reserve	+Bible	English	250	Animism	9256
• Indians, London	+Bible	English	8,000	Protestant	9264
• Indians, Lower Mainland	+Bible	English	2,500	Roman Catholic	9260
• Indians, Northern Sask.	+Bible	Various dialects	100,000	Protestant	9254
• Indians, Northwestern Ontario	+Bible	English	250,000	Protestant	9261
• Indians, Regina	+Bible	English	33,000	Roman Catholic	9265
• Indians, Saskatoon	+Bible	English	10,000	Protestant	9268
• Indians, Thunder Bay	+Bible	English	10,000	Roman Catholic	9257
• Indians, Vancouver	+Bible	English	40,000	Roman Catholic	9262
• Indians, White Bear Reserve	+Bible	English	500	Protestant	9259
• Indians, Winnipeg	+Bible	Various dialects	70,000	Roman Catholic	9170
• Indo-Canadians, Vancouver	+Bible	Urdu	70,000	Sikhism	9127
• Iranians, Montreal	+Bible	Farsi	1,500	Islam	9208
• Japanese, Toronto	+Bible	Japanese	20,000	Buddhism	9151
• Jews (Non-Sephardic), Montreal	Bible	English	120,000	Judaism	384
• Jews (Sephardic), Montreal	not reported	French	26,000	Judaism	724
• Jews, Toronto	+Bible	English	120,000	Judaism	9118
• Jews, Vancouver	+Bible	English	12,000	Judaism	9108
• Jews, Winnipeg	+Bible	Yiddish	20,000	Judaism	9121
• Kampuchean Refugees, Ontario	+Bible	Khmer	1,200	Buddhist-Animist	9046
• Khmer Refugees, Montreal	+Bible	Khmer	3,000	Buddhism	9122

GROUP NAME	SCRIPTURE	LANGUAGE	GROUP SIZE	PRIMARY RELIGION	ID
• Khmer Refugees, Toronto	+Bible	Khmer	300	Buddhism	9123
• Khmer, Ottawa	+Bible	French	400	Buddhism	9124
• Koreans	+Bible	Korean	40,000	Buddhism	9167
• Lao Refugees, Toronto	not reported	Cantonese	3,000	Buddhism	9167
• Lao-Chinese Refugees, Edmonton	+Bible	Lao	2,000	Buddhism	9207
• Laotian Rfugees-Montreal	not reported	Hmong	6,000	Buddhist-Animist	257
• Lebanese, Beamington	+Bible	French	1,500	Islam	9269
• Macedonians	OT,NT	Macedonian	100,000	Orthodox	306
• Metis, Elizabeth Settlement	+not reported	Cree	1,000	Animism	9130
• Micmac Indians, Eskasoni Rsv.	+portions	English	2,000	Roman Catholic	9285
• Moroccan Jews	+Bible	French	10,000	Judaism	9103
• Muslim Lebanese Refugees	+Bible	French	29,000	Islam	9025
• Oil Executives, Calgary	+Bible	English	5,000	Secularism	9206
• Okanagan Indians	none	Okanagan	3,000	Syncretic Christian	270
• Portuguese, Cambridge	+Bible	Portuguese	15,000	Roman Catholic	9154
• Portuguese, London/Strathroy	+Bible	Portuguese	14,000	Roman Catholic	9155
• Portuguese, Metro Toronto	+Bible	Portuguese	150,000	Roman Catholic	9158
• Portuguese, Vancouver	+Bible	Portuguese	15,000	Roman Catholic	9157
• Portuguese, West Lorne Village	+Bible	Portuguese	250	Roman Catholic	9156
• Rastafarians, Edmonton	+Bible	English	100	Other	9205
• Shopping Bag Women, Toronto	+Bible	English	500	Secularism	9165
• Sikhs, Toronto	+Bible	Punjabi	20,000	Sikhism	9119
• Street People, Thunder Bay	+Bible	Various dialects	10,000	Secularism	9253
• Street People, Victoria	+Bible	English	1,900	Secularism	9126
• Theater Arts Performers	+Bible	English	6,000	Secularism	9114
• Tibetan Refugees	+portions	Tibetan	400	Buddhism	9160
• Ugandan Asian Refugees	+not reported	Gujarati	7,000	Islam	9011
• Ugandan Asian Refugees, Tor.	not reported	Various dialects	15,000	Islam	9164
• Ukrainians, Toronto	+Bible	Ukrainian	100,000	Orthodox	9152

GROUP NAME	SCRIPTURE	LANGUAGE	GROUP SIZE	PRIMARY RELIGION	ID
• University Students, Edmonton	+Bible	English	20,000	Secularism	9101
• Vietnamese Refugees, Regina	+Bible	Vietnamese	500	Buddhism	9105
• Vietnamese, Edmonton	+Bible	Chinese	8,000	Buddhism	9125
• West Indian Migrant Workers	+Bible	English	400	Hinduism	9102
• West Indians, Toronto	+Bible	English	200,000	Protestant	9166
• Youth, Toronto Peanut District	+Bible	English	3,500	Secularism	9163

Central African Republic

GROUP NAME	SCRIPTURE	LANGUAGE	GROUP SIZE	PRIMARY RELIGION	ID
• Arab Immigrants in Bangui	+Bible	Arabic	5,000	Islam	5045
• Fulbe, Bagirmi	none	Fulfulde, Bagirmi	28,000	Islam	8519
• Mbaka, Zairuan Immigrants	+Bible	Lingala	250,000	Secularism	665
• Mbati	none	Mbati	15,000	Animism	5190
• Monjombo	none	Monjombo	11,000	Animism	5191
• Pygmy (Binga)	none	Gundi	2,000	Animism	512
• Runga	none	Runga	13,000	Animism	5199

Chad

GROUP NAME	SCRIPTURE	LANGUAGE	GROUP SIZE	PRIMARY RELIGION	ID
Abou Charib	none	Abou Charib	25,000	Islam-Animist	2208
Arabs	New Testament	Arabic, Shua	728,000	Islam	8527
Asongari	none	Sungor	57,200	Islam-Animist	2259
Bagirmi	none	Bagirmi	57,200	Islam-Animist	2209
Bilala	none	Bilala	67,600	Islam-Animist	2210
Boudouma	none	Boudouma	31,200	Islam-Animist	8528
Bua	portions	Bua	20,000	Animism	513
Dadjo	none	Daju, Dar Sila	82,000	Islam-Animist	2213
Dangaleat	none	Dangaleat	31,600	Islam-Animist	2215
Daza	not reported	Dazaga	180,000	Islam-Animist	4044
Fulbe	none	Fulfulde, Bagirmi	52,000	Islam	8531
Haddad	not reported	many languages	156,000	Islam	8684
Jongor	none	Jongor	16,000	Islam-Animist	2223
Kanembu	none	Kanembu	93,600	Islam-Animist	2224
Kenga	none	Kenga	364,000	Islam-Animist	2227
Kibet	none	Kibet	22,000	Islam-Animist	2229

GROUP NAME	SCRIPTURE	LANGUAGE	PRIMARY RELIGION	GROUP SIZE	ID
Kotoko	none	Kotoko-Logone	Islam	44,000	8535
Kuka	none	Kuka	Islam-Animist	62,400	2233
Maba	none	Arabic	Islam	235,000	2236
Mararit	none	Mararit	Islam-Animist	62,400	2239
Masalit	none	Masalit	Islam	78,000	2241
Massalat	none	Massalat	Islam-Animist	36,400	2242
Mimi	none	Mimi	Islam-Animist	26,000	2247
Moubi	none	Mubi	Islam-Animist	41,600	2249
Rounga	none	Runga	Islam-Animist	20,800	2256
Sokoro	none	Sokoro	Islam-Animist	8,000	2251
Tama	none	Tama	Islam-Animist	26,000	2260
Teda	none	Teda	Islam	183,000	4012
Zaghawa	none	Zaghawa	Islam	56,000	2265

Chile

GROUP NAME	SCRIPTURE	LANGUAGE	PRIMARY RELIGION	GROUP SIZE	ID
Mapuche	NT,portions	Mapuche	Syncretic Christian	400,000	48

China

GROUP NAME	SCRIPTURE	LANGUAGE	PRIMARY RELIGION	GROUP SIZE	ID
Ach'ang	none	Ach'ang	Traditional Chinese	10,000	2807
Atsi	portions	Atsi	Traditional Chinese	50,000	2808
Bai	none	Bai	Buddhist-Animist	1,130,000	7008
Buriat	portions	Buriat	Traditional Chinese	30,000	2809
Burig	portions	Burig	Traditional Chinese	148,000	2810
Ch'iang	none	Ch'iang	Traditional Chinese	77,000	2811
Chuang	none	Chuang	Animism	12,000,000	7014
Chungchia	portions	Chungchia	Traditional Chinese	1,500,000	2814
Dagur	none	Dagur	Traditional Chinese	23,000	2816
Ewenkis	not reported	Altaic	Animism	10,000	7020
Hani	none	Hani	Traditional Chinese	138,000	2818
Hui	not reported	Hui-hui-yu	Islam	5,200,000	4006
Jinuos	none	Tibeto-Burman	Animism	10,000	7021
Jyarung	none	Jyarung	Traditional Chinese	70,000	2819
Kalmytz	New Testament	Kalmytz	Traditional Chinese	70,000	2820
Kam	none	Kam	Traditional Chinese	830,000	2821
Kang	none	Kang	Animism	nr	794
Kazakhs	New Testament	Kazakh	Islam-Animist	700,000	7013
Kelao	none	Kelao	Traditional Chinese	23,000	2822

GROUP NAME	SCRIPTURE	LANGUAGE	PRIMARY RELIGION	GROUP SIZE	ID
Khalka	New Testament	Khalka	Traditional Chinese	68,000	2823
Kham	none	Kham	Traditional Chinese	11,000	2824
Kirgiz	not reported	Kirgiz	Islam	90,000	4039
• Koreans in Manchuria	none	Korean	Secularism	3,000,000	7007
Lahul	none	Lahul	Traditional Chinese	2,000	826
Laka	portions	Laka	Traditional Chinese	6,000	2827
Lati	none	Lati	Traditional Chinese	500	2829
Li	none	Li	Traditional Chinese	1,000,000	2830
Lolo	not reported	Yi	Animism	4,800,000	7006
Lu	New Testament	Lu	Buddhist-Animist	105,600	2831
Manchu	New Testament	Manchu	Traditional Chinese	2,430,000	2832
Miao	New Testament	Miao	Animism	2,800,000	7000
Mien	NT,portions	Mien (Yao)	Animism	825,000	780
Mongour	none	Mongour	Traditional Chinese	50,000	2833
Nahsi	portions	Nahsi	Traditional Chinese	160,000	2834
Nanai	portions	Nanai	Traditional Chinese	1,000	2835
Nosu	New Testament	Nosu	Traditional Chinese	556,000	2837
Nung	none	Nung	Traditional Chinese	100,000	2838
Nung, (Thai)	portions	Thai Nung	Animism	100,000	796
Oirat	none	Oirat	Traditional Chinese	60,000	2839
Oronchon	none	Oronchon	Traditional Chinese	2,000	2840
Paongan	none	Paongan	Traditional Chinese	8,000	2841
Pu-I	none	Pu-I	Traditional Chinese	1,311,000	2842
Punu	none	Punu	Traditional Chinese	220,000	2843
Rawang	New Testament	Rawang	Traditional Chinese	60,000	2844
Salar	none	Salar	Traditional Chinese	31,000	2845
Santa	none	Santa	Traditional Chinese	200,000	2846
Sibo	none	Sibo	Traditional Chinese	21,000	2847
Sui	none	Sui	Traditional Chinese	160,000	2848
Tai, Black	portions	Black Tai	Animism	250,000	789
Tai, White	portions	White Tai	Animism	100,000	790
Tibetans	not reported	Tibetan	Buddhism	4,000,000	127
Tung-Chia	not reported	Tung	Animism	1,100,000	7031
Uighur	Bible	Uighur	Islam	5,900,000	4013
• University Students	+Bible	Mandarin	Secularism	600,000	6567
• Vietnamese Refugees	-Bible	Cantonese	Traditional Chinese	2,000	9000
Wa	New Testament	Wa	Traditional Chinese	300,000	2849
Yellow Uiguir	none	Yellow Uiguir	Traditional Chinese	4,000	2850
Yuku	none	Yuku	Traditional Chinese	4,000	2851

GROUP NAME	SCRIPTURE	LANGUAGE	GROUP SIZE	PRIMARY RELIGION	ID
Colombia					
Barasano, Northern	portions	Barasano, Northern	450	Animism	474
Barasano, Southern	portions	Janena	400	Animism	289
Carapana	portions	Carapana	200	Syncretic Christian	2184
Coreguaje	none	Coreguaje	500	Animism	397
Cuiba	portions	Cuiba	2,000	Animism	2192
Guajiro	portions	Guajiro	82,000	Animism	177
Guanano	portions	Guanano	800	Syncretic Christian	442
Ica	none	Ica	3,000	Animism	280
Inga	portions	Inga	6,000	Syncretic Christian	3143
•Llaneros--Cattle Ranchers	+Bible	Spanish	25,000	Syncretic Christian	4807
Macu	none	Macu	1,000	Animism	242
Malayo	portions	Kogi	1,000	Animism	696
Paez	portions	Paez	40,000	Syncretic Christian	1196
Tatuyo	portions	Cubeo	300	Animism	621
•University Students	Bible	Spanish	3,000	Roman Catholic	9188
•Urban Elites, Bogota	Bible	Spanish	nr	Roman Catholic	8649
Yucuna	portions	Yucuna	500	Syncretic Christian	1185

GROUP NAME	SCRIPTURE	LANGUAGE	GROUP SIZE	PRIMARY RELIGION	ID
Comoros					
Comorians	not reported	Comorian (Shingazidja)	400,000	Islam	139
Costa Rica					
Chinese	Bible	Mandarin	4,000	Secularism	4141
• Nicaraguan Refugees	+Bible	Spanish	55,000	Roman Catholic	9053
Denmark					
• Muslims	NT,JT	Turkic	30,000	Islam	1340
Djibouti					
Afar	portions	Afar	110,000	Islam-Animist	8550
Eritrean Refugees	+Bible	Somali	25,000	Islam	9018
Somali	Bible	Somali	181,420	Islam	8551
Dominican Republic					
Caribs	+Bible	Patois	3,000	Animism	4825
Ecuador					
Cayapa	portions	Cayapa	3,000	Animism	3158
• Military Officers	+Bible	Spanish	1,000	Roman Catholic	4817
• Military Personnel	Bible	Spanish	80,000	Protestant	4119
Quichua, highland, Salasaca	New Testament	Quichua,Highland,Salasaca	15,000	Syncretic Christian	4070
• Urban Mestizos	Bible	Spanish	800,000	Roman Catholic	4032
Egypt					
• African Students in Cairo	Bible	Various dialects	700	Islam	2100
Arab Bedouins (Marubbet)	not reported	Arabic	nr	Islam	167
Arab Bedouins (Walid Ali)	none	Arabic	nr	Islam	168
• Egyptians, Middle Class	Bible	Arabic	16,000,000	Islam	1107

GROUP NAME	SCRIPTURE	LANGUAGE	GROUP SIZE	PRIMARY RELIGION	ID
Nubians	portions	Kenuzi-Dongola	500,000	Islam	8691
Siwians	none	Siwi	nr	Islam	169

Ethiopia

GROUP NAME	SCRIPTURE	LANGUAGE	GROUP SIZE	PRIMARY RELIGION	ID
Aari	portions	Aari	86,000	Christianity	8693
Afar	portions	Afar	300,000	Islam-Animist	21
Alaba	none	Alaban	50,000	Islam	358
Amaro	none	Amar	15,000	Animism	3190
•Ansar Sudanese Refugees	+New Testament	Arabic	11,000	Islam	9010
Anuak	NT,portions	Anuak	56,000	Animism	516
Arbore	none	Arbore	2,000	Animism	3191
Argobba	none	Argobba	3,000	Animism	3192
Bambeshi-Mao	none	Bambeshi-Mao	5,000	Unknown	8552
Beni-Amer	portions	Beja	39,000	Islam	3195
Bilen	portions	Bilen	32,000	Islam	3197
Boran	New Testament	Boran	95,000	Islam-Animist	3198
Bworo	none	Bworo	5,600	Animism	3230
Dasenech	portions	Dasenech	27,500	Animism	3202
Dime	none	Dime	2,000	Animism	3203
Falasha	Bible	Qimant	5,000	Judaism	159
Galla, Harar	none	Gallinya	1,310,000	Islam	367
Gawwada	not reported	Gawwada	50,000	Animism	3205
Ghimeera	none	Gimira	50,000	Animism	364
Gobeze	none	Gobeze	22,000	Animism	3209
Gumuz	none	Gumuz	23,000	Animism	3210
Gurage	New Testament	Gurage Dialects	750,000	Islam-Animist	274
Komo	none	Komo	20,000	Animism	678
Konso	portions	Konso	115,000	Animism	517
Majang	none	Mesengo	33,000	Islam-Animist	428
Me'en	none	Me'en	38,000	Animism	3223
Mocha	none	Mocha	70,000	Animism	429
Murle	portions	Murle	6,000	Unknown	3222
Mursi	none	Mursi	6,000	Animism	3225
Nara	none	Nara	25,000	Islam-Animist	3227
Nuer	New Testament	Nuer	70,000	Animism	519
Oromo, Borana-Arusi-Gusi	Bible	Oromo, Borana-Arusi-Guji	4,809,000	Islam-Animist	277
Saho	none	Saho	120,000	Unknown	520
Somali	Bible	Somali	1,000,000	Islam	90

GROUP NAME	LANGUAGE	SCRIPTURE	GROUP SIZE	PRIMARY RELIGION	ID
Suri	Suri	portions	10,000	Animism	521
Turkana	Turkana	portions	10,000	Islam	8554
Zayse	Zayse	none	21,000	Animism	3237
Zilmamu	Zilmamu	none	3,000	Animism	3238

Fiji

GROUP NAME	LANGUAGE	SCRIPTURE	GROUP SIZE	PRIMARY RELIGION	ID
Indians	Hindustani	Bible	265,000	Hinduism	131

France

GROUP NAME	LANGUAGE	SCRIPTURE	GROUP SIZE	PRIMARY RELIGION	ID
• Algerian Arabs	Arabic	BI	816,873	Islam	1086
• Chinese Refugees	Mandarin	Bible	100,000	Traditional Chinese	1226
• Chinese Restaurant Wrkrs.	Won Chow	Bible	50,000	Traditional Chinese	1227
• Moroccan Arabs	Arabic	not reported	444,472	Islam	8628
• Portuguese	Portuguese	Bible	750,000	Secularism	1186
• Tunsian Arabs	Arabic	not reported	193,203	Islam	8629
• Univ.Students in Montpellier	French	OT,NT,portions	40,000	Secularism	92
• University Students	French	Bible	800,000	Secularism	702

French Polynesia

GROUP NAME	LANGUAGE	SCRIPTURE	GROUP SIZE	PRIMARY RELIGION	ID
Chinese	Hakka	Bible	12,000	Secularism	82
• French Expatriates	French	+Bible	20,000	Roman Catholic	32

Gabon

GROUP NAME	LANGUAGE	SCRIPTURE	GROUP SIZE	PRIMARY RELIGION	ID
Bapunu	Punu	portions,OT,NT	150,000	Animism	64
• Equatorial Guin. Refugees	Tribal Languages	not reported	60,000	Roman Catholic	9033
Eshira	Sira	none	15,000	Roman Catholic	299
• Guinean Refugees	Tribal Languages	not reported	1,200,000	Islam	9047
Tsogo	Tsogo	+NT,portions	15,000	Animism	5316

GROUP NAME	SCRIPTURE	LANGUAGE	GROUP SIZE	PRIMARY RELIGION	ID
Gambia					
Bayot	none	Bayot	1,800	Islam-Animist	2266
Dyola	portions	Dyola	216,000	Islam-Animist	2267
Fulbe	BI	Fulacunda	70,000	Islam-Animist	2268
Mandingo	portions	Manding	600,000	Islam	8559
Mandinka	portions	Manding	250,000	Islam	1144
Soninke	none	Soninke	10,000	Islam	2271
Toucouleur	portions	Toucouleur	50,000	Islam	8560
Wolof, Gambian	portions	Wolof, Gambian	70,000	Islam-Animist	2272
German Federal Rep.					
Chinese	Bible	Mandarin	5,000	Secularism	1228
Gypsies	+none	Romany	50,000	Syncretic Christian	283
• Students	Bible	German	850,000	Secularism	1106
• Turkish Immigrant Workers	Bible	Turkish	1,200,000	Islam	134
Ghana					
Banda	New Testament	Ligbi	44,000	Animism	654
Bimoba	New Testament	Bimoba	72,000	Animism	5323
Birifor	portions	Birifor	36,000	Animism	1075
Builsa	portions	Buli	129,000	Animism	522
Busansi	New Testament	Bissa	87,500	Animism	1082
Chala	none	Chala	1,000	Islam-Animist	5324
Dagomba	New Testament	Dagbani	458,000	Animism	525
Deg	portions	Deg	14,000	Animism	8566
Fante Juju People	+Bible	Akan	1,900,000	Protestant	9189
Fra-Fra	New Testament	Gurenne	300,000	Animism	656
Fulbe	portions	Fufulde, Macina	45,000	Islam	1081
Gonja	portions	Gonja	129,000	Islam	1102
Hausa	portions	Hausa, Ghana	128,000	Islam	1083
Kasena	portions	Kasem	86,000	Animism	657
Koma	portions	Komung	1,000	Animism	1078
Konkomba	New Testament	Konkomba	229,000	Animism	528
Kulango	New Testament	Kulango	10,000	Unknown	527
Kusasi	New Testament	Kusaal	257,000	Animism	1183
Mamprusi	portions	Mampruli	128,000	Animism	529

-236-

GROUP NAME	LANGUAGE	SCRIPTURE	GROUP SIZE	PRIMARY RELIGION	ID
Mo	Mo (Degha)	none	14,000	Animism	1100
Nankansi	Gurenne	New Testament	110,000	Animism	8666
Nawuri	Nawuri	none	10,000	Animism	1068
Nchumburu	Chumburu	New Testament	28,600	Animism	1069
Ntrubo	Delo	portions	5,000	Animism	1065
Sisaala	Sisaala, Tumulung	New Testament	129,000	Animism	658
Tampulma	Tampulensi	New Testament	8,000	Animism	1077
Wala	Wali	New Testament	100,000	Islam	1076
Zowla	Ewe	Bible	1,860,000	Animism	1101

Greece

GROUP NAME	LANGUAGE	SCRIPTURE	GROUP SIZE	PRIMARY RELIGION	ID
• Greek Turks	Turkish Greek	portions,NT,OT	80,000	Islam	278

Guatemala

GROUP NAME	LANGUAGE	SCRIPTURE	GROUP SIZE	PRIMARY RELIGION	ID
Black Caribs	Garifuna	New Testament	2,000	Syncretic Christian	251
Cakchiquel, Central	Cakchiquel, Central	portions	120,000	Animism	8003
Cakchiquel, Northern	Cakchiquel, Northern	portions	40,000	Animism	3196
Chorti	Chorti	portions	25,000	Animism	8004
Ixil, Chajul	Cuyolbal	portions	5,000	Syncretic Christian	646
Kekchi	Kekchi	New Testament	361,000	Syncretic Christian	4034
Mam, Todos Santos	Mam (Todos Santos)	portions	13,000	Animism	310

Guinea

GROUP NAME	LANGUAGE	SCRIPTURE	GROUP SIZE	PRIMARY RELIGION	ID
Badyara	Badyara	none	5,000	Islam-Animist	8567
Baga	Baga	none	27,000	Islam-Animist	8568
Basari	Basari	none	6,500	Animism	5341
Diallonke	Dyola	portions	123,500	Islam	8569
Fulbe, Jalon	Fuuta Jalon	BI,OT,NT	1,836,000	Islam	406
Kissi	Kissi, Northern	NT,portions	266,000	Animism	478
Konyagi	Konyagi	none	11,200	Islam-Animist	5342
Konyanka	Maninka	NT,portions	108,000	Islam-Animist	8570
Kpelle	Kpelle	New Testament	250,000	Islam-Animist	5343
Kuranko	Kuranko	New Testament	108,000	Islam-Animist	8571
Landoma	Landoma	none	12,100	Islam-Animist	5344
Limba	Limba	New Testament	3,000	Islam-Animist	8572
Loko	Loko	New Testament	3,000	Islam-Animist	5345

GROUP NAME	SCRIPTURE	LANGUAGE	GROUP SIZE	PRIMARY RELIGION	ID
Loma	New Testament	Loma	172,800	Animism	479
Nalu	none	Nalu	6,700	Islam-Animist	5346
Papel	none	Papel	2,000	Animism	8573
Susu	NT,portions	Susu	702,000	Islam	6562
Toucouleur	portions	Toucouleur	17,600	Islam	8574

Guinea-Bissau

GROUP NAME	SCRIPTURE	LANGUAGE	GROUP SIZE	PRIMARY RELIGION	ID
Balanta	portions	Balanta	257,000	Animism	594
Banyun	none	Banyun	5,000	Animism	593
Bayot	none	Bayot	1,800	Islam-Animist	5348
Biafada	none	Biafada	25,000	Animism	592
Dyola	portions	Dyola	14,000	Islam	590
Fulbe	none	Fulacunda	185,000	Islam	421
Kasanga	none	Kasanga	400	Islam-Animist	5351
Mandingo	NT,portions	Maninka	96,000	Islam-Animist	5355
Manjaco	portions	Mandyako	100,000	Animism	589
Nalu	none	Nalu	6,500	Islam	8577
Sarakole	none	Soninke	4,000	Islam	8578
Susu	New Testament	Susu	2,400	Islam-Animist	5358

Haiti

GROUP NAME	SCRIPTURE	LANGUAGE	GROUP SIZE	PRIMARY RELIGION	ID
• Rural Vodun Believers	not reported	Creole	5,400,000	Animism	4819
Urban Elite Haitians	+Bible	Creole	300,000	Roman Catholic	68

Honduras

GROUP NAME	SCRIPTURE	LANGUAGE	GROUP SIZE	PRIMARY RELIGION	ID
• Arabic Speaking Hondurans	**Bible**	**Arabic**	**5,000**	**Roman Catholic**	4104
Jicaque (Tol)	portions	Jicaque	250	Secularism	4130
Salvadoran Refugees	+Bible	Spanish	30,000	Roman Catholic	9058

Hong Kong

GROUP NAME	SCRIPTURE	LANGUAGE	GROUP SIZE	PRIMARY RELIGION	ID
Chinese Businessmen	Bible	Cantonese	10,000	Traditional Chinese	2111
Chinese Villagers	Bible	Cantonese	500,000	Traditional Chinese	742
Drug Addicts	Bible	Cantonese	90,000	Secularism	2114
Factory Workers	Bible	Cantonese	40,000	Unknown	1010
High School Students	Bible	Cantonese	453,000	Traditional Chinese	2113

GROUP NAME	SCRIPTURE	LANGUAGE	PRIMARY RELIGION	GROUP SIZE	ID
New Territories People	Bible,NT,OT	Cantonese	Secularism	1,400,000	2112
Police	+Bible,NT,OT	Cantonese	Buddhist-Animist	30,000	337
Refugee Doctors	+Bible	Cantonese	Traditional Chinese	2,000	9039
Water Surface People	not reported	Cantonese dialects	Islam-Animist	11,000	4822

India

GROUP NAME	SCRIPTURE	LANGUAGE	PRIMARY RELIGION	GROUP SIZE	ID
Abujmaria (Madhya Pradesh)	none	Abujmaria	Hindu-Animist	17,839	2600
Adi	portions	Adi	Animism	288,000	1027
Adivasis of Dang	none	Dangi	Animism	131,650	2013
Adiyan in Kerala	NT,OT,portions	Kanarese	Hinduism	3,000	2601
Agariya in Bihar	none	Agariya	Hinduism	12,600	2602
Ahir in Maharashtra	none	Ahiri	Islam	183,675	2603
Ajmeri in Rajasthan	none	Ajmeri	Hindu-Animist	1,000	2605
Alars	Bible	Allar	Folk Religion	475	2017
Andha in Andhra Pradesh	none	Andha	Animism	144,625	2608
Anga in Bihar	none	Anga	Hinduism	587,000	2609
Angami Area Hindus	Bible	Angami	Hinduism	42,600	375
Apatani in Assam	none	Apatani	Hinduism	13,700	1026
Aranadans	Bible	Aranadan	Animism	830	2014
Arya in Andhra Pradesh	none	Are (Arya)	Hinduism	4,465	2611
Asuri in Bihar	none	Asuri	Animism	6,078	2613
Awadhi	portions	Awadhi	Unknown	42,836,000	126
Badaga in Nilgiri	portions	Badaga	Animism	145,417	2614
Bagata	none	Bagata	Hindu-Animist	57,607	2615
Baghati in H.P.	none	Baghati	Animism	6,850	2617
Bagheli in M.P.	New Testament	Bagheli	Hindu-Animist	320,486	2616
Bahawalpuri in M.P.	none	Bahawalpuri	Animism	1,100	2618
Baiga in Bihar	none	Baiga	Animism	15,400	2619
Balti in Jammu	portions	Balti	Animism	55,628	2620
Baluchi, Eastern	portions	Baluchi, Eastern	Islam	6,082	374
Bareli in Madhya Pradesh	none	Bareli	Hinduism	318,827	2622
Batal, Mochies	Bible,NT,portions	Punjabi	Islam	2,000	222
Bathudi in Bihar	none	Bathudi	Hinduism	104,542	2623
Bazigar in Gujarat	none	Bazigar	Animism	215	2626
Bediya in Bihar	none	Bediya	Animism	85,719	2627
• Bengali Refugees, Assam	not reported	Bengali	Islam	4,000,000	9054
Bharia in Madhya Pradesh	none	Bharia	Animism	7,458	2628

GROUP NAME	SCRIPTURE	LANGUAGE	PRIMARY RELIGION	GROUP SIZE	ID
Bhattri	none	Bhattri	Hindu-Animist	144,000	7047
Bhil	Bible	Bhili	Animism	1,750,000	291
Bhilala	none	not reported	not reported	342,000	7048
Bhotia	portions	Bhotia	Hinduism	50,000	86
Bhoyari in Maharashtra	none	Bhoyari	Hindu-Animist	5,627	2632
•Bhuiya in Bihar	none	Bhuiya	Animism	7,640	2633
Bhuiya, Orissa	not reported	Bhuiya	Hindu-Animist	1,500,000	226
Bhumij in Assam	none	Bhumij	Hindu-Animist	66,866	2634
Bhunjia in Madhya Pradesh	none	Bhunjia	Hindu-Animist	5,468	2635
Binjhwari in Bihar	none	Binjhwari	Hindu-Animist	51,000	2639
Birhor in Bihar	none	Birhor	Hindu-Animist	1,017	2640
Bodo Kachari	New Testament	Bodo	Hindu-Animist	726,500	2007
•Bodo in Assam	NT,portions	Bodo	Animism	654,600	2641
Bondo in Orissa	none	Bondo	Hinduism	2,470	2642
•Brahmins in Tirunelveli, T.N.	not reported	Tamil	Hinduism	8,000	225
Braj in Uttar Pradesh	New Testament	Braj	Animism	13,988,000	2643
Bunan in Kashmir	portions	Bunan	Animism	2,712	2644
Burig in Kashmir	portions	Burig	Animism	259,000	2645
Chakma	NT,portions	Chakma	Buddhist-Animist	95,235	2646
Chakmas, of Mizoram	New Testament	Chakma	Buddhist-Animist	23,800	2011
Chamar of Bundelkhand	+portions	Bundelkhandi	Buddhism	nr	2003
Chamari in Madhya Pradesh	none	Chamari	Hindu-Animist	7,379	2647
Chameali in H.P.	portions	Chameali	Hindu-Animist	73,420	2648
Chang-Pa of Kashmir	Bible	Tibetan Dialect	Buddhist-Animist	9,700	7011
Chenchu in Andhra Pradesh	none	Chenchu	Hindu-Animist	18,400	2649
Chero in Bihar	none	Chero	Animism	29,635	2650
Chik-Barik in Bihar	none	Chik-Barik	Animism	99,500	2651
Chin, Thado	portions,NT	Chin,Thado	Hindu-Buddhist	58,700	2791
Chodhari in Gujarat	none	Chodhari	Hindu-Animist	192,625	2654
Chulikata	none	Chulikata	Unknown	7,377	1387
Churahi in H.P.	none	Churahi	Hindu-Animist	48,000	2655
Dafla	portions	Dafla	Unknown	21,650	1388
Dal	none	Dal	Unknown	10,300	1389
Dandami Maria	none	Dandami Maria	Unknown	60,000	1390
Dangi	none	Dangi	Unknown	111,618	1391
•Dawoodi Muslims	Bible	Gujarati	Islam	268,000	2004
•Deccani Muslims	Bible	Dakhni (Urdu)	Islam	nr	4047
•Deccani Muslims-Hyderabad	not reported	Deccan	Islam	557,500	5027

GROUP NAME	SCRIPTURE	LANGUAGE	GROUP SIZE	PRIMARY RELIGION	ID
Degaru	none	Degaru	nr	Unknown	1392
Deori in Assam	none	Deori	20,702	Animism	2656
Dhanka in Gujarat	none	Dhanka	14,177	Animism	2657
Dhanwar in Madhya Pradesh	none	Dhanwar	36,418	Animism	2658
Dhodia	none	Dhodia	104,860	Unknown	1393
Dhurwa	none	Parji	23,300	Hindu-Animist	4059
Dog-Pa of Ladakh	none	Shrina	2,280	Animism	7005
Dorli in Andhra Pradesh	none	Dorli	33,700	Hindu-Animist	2661
Dubla	Bible	Gujarati	207,000	Hindu-Animist	122
Ezhava in Kerala	Bible	Malayalam	3,700,000	Hinduism	4068
Gadaban in Andhra Pradesh	none	Gadaba	22,750	Hindu-Animist	2662
Gaddi in Himachal Pradesh	none	Gaddi	97,320	Hindu-Animist	2663
Galong in Assam	none	Galong	51,100	Hindu-Animist	2664
Gamti in Gujarat	New Testament	Gamti	188,785	Hindu-Animist	2665
Gangte, Assam	New Testament	Gangte	5,320	Hindu-Animist	2666
Gawari in Andhra Pradesh	none	Gawari	50,520	Hindu-Animist	2668
Girasia in Gujarat	none	Girasia	37,640	Hindu-Animist	2669
Gonds	portions	Gondi	2,145,000	Animism	641
Gorkha	New Testament	Napali	215,200	Hinduism	2009
Gowlan	none	Gowlan	nr	Hindu-Animist	2076
Gowli	none	Gowli	nr	Hindu-Animist	2075
Gujars of Kashmir	New Testament	Gujari	171,000	Islam-Animist	7012
Halam in Tripura	BI,NT	Tripuri,Halam(Chin)	23,300	Animism	4062
Halbi in Madhya Pradesh	none	Halbi	484,100	Hindu-Animist	2671
Harauti in Rajasthan	New Testament	Harauti	463,450	Hindu-Animist	2673
• Harijanas of Andra Pradesh	none	Telugu	nr	Animism	4078
• Harijans in Kannilam, T.N.	Bible	Tamil	1,140	Hinduism	224
• Hindus in Andhra Pradesh	+Bible,NT,OT	Telugu	43,000,000	Hinduism	362
Ho in Bihar	portions	Ho	1,039,200	Hindu-Animist	2674
Holiya in Madhya Pradesh	none	Holiya	5,329	Hindu-Animist	2675
Irulas	Bible	Irula	11,900	Hinduism	2012
Jagannathi in A.P.	none	Jagannathi	2,250	Hindu-Animist	2677
• Jains	Bible	Hindi	2,400,000	Jain	2005
Jarawa	-none	Jarawa	2,000	Animism	4836
Jatapu in Andhra Pradesh	-none	Jatapu	50,500	Hindu-Animist	2678
Jaunsari in Uttar Pradesh	portions	Jaunsari	78,400	Hindu-Animist	2679
Jharia in Orissa	none	Jharia	3,540	Hinduism	2680

GROUP NAME	GROUP SIZE	PRIMARY RELIGION	ID	LANGUAGE	SCRIPTURE
Juang in Orissa	16,900	Hindu-Animist	2681	Juang	none
Kachchi in Andhra Pradesh	652,800	Hinduism	2682	Kachchi	portions
Kadar in Andhra Pradesh	855	Hindu-Animist	2683	Kadar	none
Kahluri in Andamans	91,750	Hindu-Animist	2684	Kahluri	none
Kaikadi in Maharashtra	16,400	Hindu-Animist	2685	Kaikadi	OT,NT
Kaipeng-Koloi	265,400	Animism	88	Kaipeng	none
Kamar in Madhya Pradesh	12,300	Hindu-Animist	2686	Kamar	not reported
Kamma in Andhra Pradesh	1,150,000	Hinduism	115	Telugu	Bible
Kanarese	26,700,000	Hinduism	119	Kannada	portions
Kanauri in Uttar Pradesh	49,100	Hindu-Buddhist	2687	Kanauri	none
Kanikkaran in Kerala	10,500	Islam	2688	Kani	none
Kanjari in Andhra Pradesh	76,765	Hindu-Animist	2689	Kanjari	none
Karbis	350,000	Hindu-Animist	2120	Mikir	none
Karmali in Bihar	96,500	Hindu-Animist	2690	Karmali	none
• Kashmiri Muslims	3,641,000	Islam	1231	Kashmiri	Bible,portions
Katakari in Gujarat	8,530	Hindu-Animist	2691	Katakari	none
Kawar in Madhya Pradesh	36,050	Hindu-Animist	2692	Kawar	none
Keer in Madhya Pradesh	3,100	Hindu-Animist	2693	Keer	none
Khadia, Orissa	122,500	Hindu-Animist	227	Oriya	Bible,NT,OT
Khamti in Assam	400	Protestant	2694	Khamti	none
Khandesi	20,000	Hindu-Buddhist	2695	Khandesi	none
Khirwar in Madhya Pradesh	36,600	Hindu-Animist	2698	Khirwar	none
• Khojas, Agha Khani	208,000	Islam	2006	Gujarati	Bible
Khowar	14,300	Hindu-Animist	2699	Khowar	none
Kisan in Bihar	102,350	Hindu-Animist	2700	Kisan	none
Kishanganjia in Bihar	78,900	Hindu-Animist	2701	Kishanganjia	none
Kishtwari in Jammu	16,900	Hindu-Animist	2702	Kishtwari	none
Koda in Bihar	19,600	Hindu-Animist	2703	Koda	none
Kolam	92,700	Hindu-Animist	1040	Kolami	portions
Kom in Manipur	10,000	Hindu-Animist	2705	Kom	portions
Kond	1,168,000	Animism	294	Kui	portions
Konda-Dora (Andra Pradesh)	21,700	Hindu-Animist	2706	Konda-Dora	portions
Koraga in Kerala & Karnataka	1,600	Hindu-Animist	2709	Koraga	none
Korku in Madhya Pradesh	357,000	Animism	198	Korku	portions
Korwa in Bihar	19,750	Hindu-Animist	2710	Korwa	none
Kota in Tamil Nadu	1,500	Hindu-Animist	2711	Kota	none
Kotta	1,485	Animism	1098	Kota	none

GROUP NAME	LANGUAGE	SCRIPTURE	GROUP SIZE	PRIMARY RELIGION	ID
Koya in Andhra Pradesh	Koya	+portions	293,660	Hindu-Animist	2712
Kudiya	Kudiya	none	110	Hindu-Animist	2713
Kukna	Kukna	New Testament	173,250	Hindu-Animist	701
Kuluis in Himachal Pradesh	Kului	portions	238,000	Hinduism	2015
Kumauni in Assam	Kumauni	NT,Bible	1,711,600	Hindu-Animist	2714
Kupia in Andhra Pradesh	Kupia	portions	4,270	Animism	2715
Kurichiya in Kerala	Kurichiya	NT,OT,portions	13,000	Roman Catholic	2716
Kuruba in Tamil Nadu	Kannada	portions	11,000	Hindu-Animist	2717
Kusava	Kusavan	New Testament	nr	Roman Catholic	1357
Kutia Kords	Kui (Distinct from Kuvi)	NT	97,300	Animism	383
Kuvi in Orissa	Kuvi	portions	334,500	Hindu-Animist	2719
Labbai	Tamil	Bible	nr	Islam	4045
•Labourers of Jhoparpatti	Marathi	Bible	2,000	Hinduism	2001
Ladakhi in Jammu	Ladakhi	portions	78,650	Hindu-Buddhist	2720
Lahoulis in Punjab	Lahouli	not reported	21,400	Buddhism	2016
Lalung in Assam	Lalung	none	14,760	Hindu-Buddhist	2721
•Lambadi in Andhra Pradesh	Lambadi	portions,NT	1,057,000	Hinduism	2018
•Lambadi of Karnataka	Lambadi	portions	880,000	Hinduism	58
•Lambadi of Maharashtra	Lambadi	portions	880,000	Hinduism	56
Limbu	Limbu	none	32,850	Unknown	1394
•Lingayath of Karnataka	Kannada	Bible	6,850,000	Hinduism	160
Lodhi in Bihar	Lodhi	none	61,100	Hindu-Animist	2723
Magar	Magar	portions	1,960	Unknown	1395
Mahali in Assam	Mahali	none	19,800	Hindu-Animist	2725
Mahar	Marathi	Bible,NT,portions	2,000,000	Buddhism	360
Majhi in Bihar	Majhi	none	nr	Unknown	1397
Majhi in Panjab	Majhi	none	nr	Unknown	1396
Majhwar in Madhya Pradesh	Majhwar	none	29,900	Hindu-Animist	2726
Malamuthas	Malamutha	Bible	1,200	Hindu-Animist	2019
Malankuravan in Kerala	Malankuravan	none	5,340	Hindu-Animist	2727
Malapanaikans	Malapandaram	Bible	1,200	Hindu-Animist	2021
Malapandaram in Kerala	Malapandaram	none	535	Animism	2728
Malaryan in Kerala	Malaryan	none	5,340	Hindu-Animist	2729
Malavedan in Kerala	Malavedan	none	2,135	Hindu-Animist	2730
Malayalars	Malayalam	Bible	120	Hinduism	2020
Mali in Andhra Pradesh	Mali	none	1,670	Animism	2731
Malki in Bihar	Malki (Dial.Malto)	portions	152,700	Hindu-Animist	2733
•Malpaharia in Assam	Malpaharia	none	10,700	Hindu-Animist	2732

GROUP NAME	SCRIPTURE	LANGUAGE	GROUP SIZE	PRIMARY RELIGION	ID
•Malpaharia in Bihar	none	Malto	59,500	Animism	5385
Malvi in Madhya Pradesh	New Testament	Malvi	892,600	Hindu-Animist	2734
Manda	none	Manda	nr	Unknown	1398
Mandeali	portions	Mandeali	241,700	Unknown	1399
Mangelas in Maharashtra	none	Mangelas	nr	Unknown	1400
Manipuri	NT,portions	Manipuri	178,000	Buddhism	5546
Manna-Dora in A.P.	none	Manna-Dora	9,050	Hindu-Animist	2735
Mannan in Kerala	none	Mannan	8,600	Hindu-Animist	2736
Mappillas	Bible,stories,tracts	Malayalam	5,240,000	Islam	4026
Maria in Andhra Pradesh	none	Maria	108,800	Hindu-Animist	2738
Marwari in Gujarat	NT,portions	Marwari	9,435,400	Hindu-Animist	2739
Matharis	Bible	Telugu	232,909	Hinduism	4069
Mawchis	none	Mawchi	61,311	Hindu-Animist	4061
Meitei	Bible	Manipuri	1,140,000	Hinduism	293
Meos of Rajasthan	not reported	Rajasthani	500,000	Islam	4017
Miching	Bible	Miching	359,737	Hindu-Animist	2002
Mikir	Bible	Mikir	235,000	Unknown	8654
Mina in Madhya Pradesh	none	Mina	2,000,000	Hindu-Animist	2741
Mirdha in Orissa	none	Mirdha	10,000	Hindu-Animist	2742
Mishmi	none	Mishmi	27,800	Animism	1028
Monpa	none	Monpa	27,400	Buddhist-Animist	1037
Mualthuam	none	Mualthuam	11,400	Animism	647
Mukha-Dora	none	Mukha-Dora	10,600	Unknown	2023
Multani in Punjab	none	Siraiki (Multani)	21,750	Hindu-Animist	2744
Mundas in Bihar	Bible	Munda	29,750	Animism	2010
Muria in Andhra Pradesh	none	Muria	17,900	Hindu-Animist	2746
•Muslims in Draksharama, A.P.	not reported	Urdu	3,420	Islam	223
Muthuvan (Andra Pradesh)	none	Muthuvan	7,500	Hindu-Animist	2747
•Muthuvan in Kerala	NT,OT,portions	Tamil	3,570	Hinduism	5380
Muwasi in Madhya Pradesh	none	Muwasi (Dial.of Kurku)	29,300	Hindu-Animist	2748
Naga, Zeme	New Testament	Zeme	28,375	Animism	7002
Nagar in Madhya Pradesh	none	Nagar	9,800	Hindu-Animist	2761
Naidu of Tamil Nadu	OT,NT	Telugu	1,863,000	Hinduism	106
Nepalese	Bible	Nepali	1,344,000	Hinduism	4060
Nihali in Madhya Pradesh	none	Nihali	2,000	Hindu-Animist	2762
Nimadi in Madhya Pradesh	none	Nimadi	1,101,000	Hindu-Buddhist	2763
Nishi	portions	Dafla	22,000	Animism	1038

GROUP NAME	SCRIPTURE	LANGUAGE	GROUP SIZE	PRIMARY RELIGION	ID
Ojhi in Madhya Pradesh	none	Ojhi	1,835	Hindu-Animist	2764
Ollari in Orissa	none	Ollari	2,600	Hindu-Animist	2765
Ong	none	Ong	200	Hindu-Animist	2766
Oriya	Bible,NT	Oriya	26,000,000	Unknown	4839
Oriya, Adivasi	portions	Oriya, Adivasi	15,000	Animism	4840
Pahari Garhwali (U. Pradesh)	portions	Pahari Garhwali	1,770,000	Hinduism	2667
Panika	none	Panika	81,700	Hindu-Animist	2770
Paniyan of Kerala	NT,OT,portions	Paniyan	8,767	Hindu-Animist	2772
Pao in Madhya Pradesh	none	Pao	40,500	Hindu-Buddhist	2773
Pardhan in Andhra Pradesh	none	Pardhan (Takankar)	780	Hindu-Animist	2774
Pardhi in Andhra Pradesh	none	Pardhi	14,000	Hindu-Animist	2775
Pardhi in Maharashtra	none	Pardhi	1,100	Hindu-Animist	361
Parengi in Orissa	none	Parengi	7,000	Hindu-Animist	2776
Parsees	ncne	Gujarati	142,800	Secularism	2121
Parsis in Bombay	Bible	Parsi	89,200	Zoroastrianism	5039
Patel	+Bible	Gujarati	2,000,000	Hinduism	392
Patelia in Gujarat	BI,NT,portions	Patelia	62,000	Hindu-Animist	2778
Pengo in Orissa	none	Pengo	2,200	Hindu-Animist	2779
Poouch in Kashmir	none	Poochi	582,000	Islam	4079
Prisoners in Kerala	+Bible	Malayalam	10,000	Protestant	400
Purig-Pa of Kashmir	none	Purig-Skad	nr	Islam	7010
Rabha in Assam	portions	Rava	48,000	Hinduism	295
Raj, Thulunge	none	Raj, Thulunge	5,700	Hindu-Animist	2722
Rajasthani Muslims-Jaipur	BI	Jaipuri	39,000	Islam	5033
Raji	none	Raji	406	Animism	87
Sadani in Madhya Pradesh	portions	Sadani	1,120,000	Hindu-Animist	2783
Saiva Vellala	Bible	Tamil	1,785,000	Hinduism	2000
Santali	Bible,NT	Santali	5,119,000	Unknown	2767
Satnamis (Madhya Pradesh)	none	Chattisgarhi	35,000	Animism	4076
Sauria Pahari	+not reported	Malto	84,600	Animism	4801
Sherdukpen	none	Sherdukpen	1,250	Unknown	2781
Sherpa	portions	Sherpa	17,500	Buddhism	2740
Shina	portions	Shina	13,750	Islam	2785
Shom Peng	none	Shom Peng	100	Animism	8648
Sikkimese	none	Sikkimese	63,000	Hindu-Buddhist	2786
Sindhis	New Testament	Sindhi	3,800,000	Hinduism	13
Slum Dwellers in Madras	Bible	Tamil	1,270,000	Hinduism	695

GROUP NAME	SCRIPTURE	LANGUAGE	GROUP SIZE	PRIMARY RELIGION	ID
Sondwari in M.P.	none	Sondwari	43,650	Hindu-Animist	2787
Sora in Orissa	New Testament	Sora	294,500	Hinduism	2788
Sourashtra	portions	Sourashtra	278,000	Hinduism	341
Tagin	portions	Tagin	31,000	Animism	1045
Tamaria in Bihar	none	Tamaria	5,385	Hindu-Buddhist	2790
• Tamil Laborers in Bombay	+Bible	Tamil	3,345	Hinduism	5017
• Tamil Muslims in Madras	-Bible	Tamil	55,750	Islam	5028
• Tamil in Ambirli Hills	0	Tamil	3,000	Hinduism	93
• Tamil in Yellagiri Hills	Bible	Tamil	4,000	Hinduism	4025
• Tea Garden Workers-Darjeeling	Bible,NT	Nepali	25,000	Hinduism	1356
Thakuri	none	Thakuri	103,400	Hindu-Animist	2792
• Tibetan Refugees	+New Testament	Tibetan	100,000	Buddhism	2033
Tripuri in Assam	portions,NT	Tripuri	416,000	Animism	648
Tulu	New Testament	Tulu	1,603,500	Unknown	2795
Ullatan in Kerala	none	Ullatan	1,550	Hindu-Animist	2796
Urali in Kerala	none	Urali	1,860	Hindu-Animist	2797
Vaagri Booli	portions	Vaagri Booli	nr	Unknown	2793
Vadval (Phudagi)	none	Vadval	nr	Hindu-Animist	2708
Varhadi-Nagpuri	none	Varhadi-Nagpuri	nr	Unknown	2672
Varli	none	Varli	nr	Hindu-Animist	2676
Vishavan in Kerala	none	Vishavan	200	Hindu-Animist	2799
Vohras of Yavatmal	New Testament	Gujarati	119,000	Islam	2008
Waddar in Andhra Pradesh	none	Waddar	50,000	Hindu-Animist	2800
Wagdi in Rajasthan	none	Wagdi	1,303,900	Hindu-Animist	2801
• Western Alienated Youth	+Bible	French	1,500,000	New Eastern	5234
Yanadi in Andhra Pradesh	none	Yanadi	215,000	Hindu-Animist	2802
Yerukala in A.P.	none	Yerukala	93,650	Hindu-Animist	2804
Zanskari	none	Zanskari	9,000	Buddhism	4834
Zoliang	not reported	Naga, Zoliang	59,500	Animism	1085

Indonesia

GROUP NAME	SCRIPTURE	LANGUAGE	GROUP SIZE	PRIMARY RELIGION	ID
Abung	not reported	Abung	200,000	Islam	2984
Acehnese	portions	Acehnese	2,200,000	Islam	97
Aji	not reported	Aji	40,000	Islam	355
Alas	none	Gayo	30,000	Islam-Animist	1133
Andio	none	Andio	1,600	Islam	820

NAME	LANGUAGE	SCRIPTURE	PRIMARY RELIGION	GROUP SIZE	ID
Ansus	Ansus	none	Animism	3,000	2864
Ara	Konjo (Ara dialect)	none	Islam	75,000	2865
Asmat	Asmat	portions	Animism	38,000	205
Baburiwa	Baburiwa	none	Animism	200	2872
Bacan	Bacan	none	Islam	3,000	824
Badui	Badui (Sundanese)	none	Animism	5,000	4812
Bajau, Indonesian	Bajau, Indonesian	none	Islam	50,000	2874
Balaesan	Balaesan	none	Islam	4,000	827
•Balantak	Balantak	none	Islam-Animist	30,000	2875
Balinese	Balinese	portions	Hindu-Animist	3,683,000	1094
Balinese in So.Sumatra	Balinese	OT,NT	Hinduism	110,000	1350
Bana	Bana	none	Animism	nr	828
Banggai	Banggai	none	Islam	86,000	2876
Bangka Malay	Malay	OT,NT,portions	Islam	40,000	49
Bangka Mapur	Chinese	not reported	Animism	600	47
Bantik	Bantik	none	Animism	nr	830
Bapu	Bapu	ncne	Animism	nr	831
Baras	Baras	not reported	Animism	4,000	832
Bare'e	Bare'e	New Testament	Animism	325,000	2878
•Batak in So. Sumatra	Batak	Bible,OT,NT	Islam	50,000	1353
Batak, Angkola	Batak, Angkola	NT,OT,Bible	Islam	750,000	4002
Batak, Mandailing	Batak, Mandailing	none	Islam	nr	838
Batawi	Batawi	Bible,OT,NT,portions	Islam	500,000	18
Bathih	Jambi	BI	Islam	100,000	357
Bauzi	Bauzi	portions	Animism	1,000	840
•Becak Drivers, Bandung	Sundanese	+Bible	Islam-Animist	10,000	331
Beketan	Beketan	none	Animism	nr	841
Belagar	Belagar	none	Animism	nr	842
Belide	Belide	not reported	Islam	20,000	351
Belitung Malay	Belitung Malay	Bible	Islam	170,000	823
Benggaulu	Benggaulu	none	Islam	5,000	843
Bengkulu	Bengkulu	none	Islam	55,000	6563
Bengoi	Bengoi	none	Animism	nr	844
Berau	Berau	none	Islam	8,000	67
Biha	Biha	none	Animism	nr	847
Bimanese	Bima	none	Islam	177,000	1096
Bingkokak	Bingkokak	none	Islam	150,500	2886
Bipim	Bipim	none	Syncretic Christian	500	1119
Bira	Bira	none	Islam-Animist	75,000	2887

GROUP NAME	SCRIPTURE	LANGUAGE	GROUP SIZE	PRIMARY RELIGION	ID
Bojo	portions	Bima	5,000	Animism	290
Bolano	none	Bolano	1,600	Animism	850
Bolongan	none	Bolongan(a Tidung Dialect)	15,000	Animism	851
Bonerate	none	Bonerate	nr	Islam	853
Bugis	portions,Bible	Wajo,Pangkep,Bone,Soppeng	3,000,000	Islam-Animist	7
Bugis in So. Sumatra	Bible	Bugis	70,000	Islam	1354
Bulanga-Uki	none	Bulanga-Uki	nr	Animism	858
Buli	none	Buli	2,000	Islam-Animist	2893
Bunak	none	Bunak	50,000	Animism	2894
Bungku	none	Bungku	35,000	Islam	2895
Buol	none	Buol	65,000	Islam	2892
Butung	none	Butung	200,000	Islam-Animist	2898
Campalagian	none	Campalagian	nr	Islam	860
Chinese	Bible,NT,OT	Mandarin	4,000,000	Traditional Chinese	733
•Chinese in So. Sumatra	Bible,OT,NT	Chinese	400,000	Traditional Chinese	1351
Cirebon	Bible,NT,OT	Javanese, Cirebon	2,500,000	Islam-Animist	1135
•Civil Servants in Bengkulu	Bible,OT,NT,portions	Indonesian	1,000	Islam	22
Dagada	none	Dagada	30,000	Animism	2901
Dampelasa	none	Dampelasa	9,500	Animism	864
Dani, Balliem	portions	Dani, Grand Valley	50,000	Animism	1219
Dayo	not reported	Dayo	50,000	Islam	1338
Dondo	none	Dondo	9,000	Animism	869
Embaloh	none	Embaloh	nr	Animism	874
Enim	not reported	Enim	70,000	Islam	353
Erai	none	Erai	nr	Animism	877
Erokwanas	none	Erokwanas	300	Animism	2910
Galoli	none	Galoli	nr	Animism	880
Gamkonora	none	Gamkonora	2,000	Islam	881
Gane	none	Gane	2,900	Animism	2913
Gebe	none	Gebe	2,000	Islam	882
Gesa	none	Gesa	200	Animism	2914
Gorontalo	none	Gorontalo	250,000	Islam	2915
Hahutan	none	Hahutan	nr	Animism	885
Hatue	none	Hatue	nr	Animism	887
Helong	none	Helong	5,000	Animism	2917
Hoamol	none	Hoamol	nr	Animism	888

GROUP NAME	SCRIPTURE	LANGUAGE	GROUP SIZE	PRIMARY RELIGION	ID
Horuru	none	Horuru	nr	Animism	889
Hoti	none	Hoti	nr	Animism	890
Idate	none	Idate	nr	Animism	893
Iliwaki	none	Iliwaki	nr	Animism	895
Isal	none	Isal	nr	Animism	896
Jahalatane	none	Jahalatane	nr	Animism	1324
Jambi	Bible	Sumatra Malay	800,000	Islam	4088
•Javanese (Rural)	Bible	Javanese	60,000,000	Islam-Animist	73
•Javanese	Bible,OT	Javanese	nr	Islam	372
Migrants/E.Kalimantan					
•Javanese in Sumatra	Bible,NT,OT	Javanese	5,200,000	Islam	170
•Javanese of Central Java	Bible	Javanese	31,000,000	Islam-Animist	125
•Javanese of Pejompongan	Bible	Bahasa Jawa	5,000	Islam	319
Kadai	none	Kadai	500	Animism	900
Kaibubu	none	Kaibubu	nr	Animism	901
Kaidipan	none	Kaidipan	nr	Animism	902
Kajang	none	Konjo	50,000	Animism	2930
Kalabit	none	Kalabit	nr	Animism	905
Kalaotoa	none	Kalaotoa	nr	Islam	907
Kalumpang	none	Kalumpang	8,000	Christianity	908
Kamariang	none	Kamariang	nr	Animism	910
Kasimbar	none	Kasimbar (Tajio)	7,000	Animism	3053
Kaur	none	Mulak	50,000	Islam-Animist	4084
Kawe	none	Kawe	300	Animism	2947
Kayu Agung	not reported	Kayu Agung	35,000	Islam	967
Kedang	none	Kedang	nr	Animism	916
Kei	none	Kei	30,000	Animism	2950
Kelimuri	none	Kelimuri	nr	Animism	918
Kemak	none	Kemak	50,000	Animism	2951
Kendari	portions	Kendari	500,000	Islam-Animist	2952
Kerinci	none	Kerinchi	300,000	Islam	2954
Koba	none	Koba	nr	Animism	926
Kodi	portions	Kodi	40,000	Animism	2956
Kofei	none	Kofei	nr	Animism	928
Komering	portions	Komering	700,000	Islam	4086
Komfana	none	Komfana	nr	Animism	933
Konjo	none	Konjo	200,000	Islam	935
Krui	none	Krui	nr	Islam	938

GROUP NAME	SCRIPTURE	LANGUAGE	GROUP SIZE	PRIMARY RELIGION	ID
Kubu of Jambi	portions	Kubu	6,000	Animism	7026
Kubu of Lubuk Linggau	portions	Local dialects	4,000	Animism	1093
Kwandang	none	Kwandang	nr	Animism	943
Lahanan	none	Lahanan	nr	Animism	946
Laiyolo	none	Laiyolo	nr	Animism	947
Lampung	portions	Lampung Pesisir	5,000	Islam	1134
Landawe	none	Landawe	1,500,000	Islam-Animist	948
Lara	none	Lara	nr	Animism	2964
Lemantang	not reported	Lemantang Malay	12,000	Animism	27
Lembak	BI	Lembak Malay	150,000	Islam	2933
Lemma	none	Lemma	50,000	Islam	953
Lemolang	none	Lemolang	nr	Syncretic Christian	952
Lengkayap	not reported	Lengkayap	2,000	Islam	354
Liambata	none	Liambata	40,000	Islam	954
Lima	none	Lima	nr	Animism	955
Limboto	none	Limboto	nr	Animism	956
Limera	none	Limera	nr	Animism	957
Lintang	not reported	Lintang	nr	Animism	1282
Lisabata	none	Lisabata	70,000	Islam	959
Lisela	none	Lisela	nr	Animism	960
Loho Loho	none	Kolaka	nr	Animism	137
Lola	none	Lola	10,000	Animism	961
Lolaki	none	Lalaki	nr	Animism	807
Lonchong	not reported	Lonchong	125,000	Animism	359
Long Bleh	none	Long Bleh	nr	Unknown	963
Lore	none	Kaili(Unde,orBanawa Dial)	nr	Animism	2970
Lubu	none	Lubu	100,000	Islam	2971
Luhu	none	Luhu	1,000,000	Islam	964
Luwu	none	Luwu	nr	Animism	2972
Maba	none	Maba	500,000	Islam	966
Madurese	portions	Madurese	6,000	Islam	78
•Madurese in So. Sumatra	portions	Madurese	7,000,000	Islam	1349
Mairiri	none	Mairiri	12,000	Islam	969
Makasai	none	Makasai	nr	Animism	2976
Makassar	Bible	Makassar	70,000	Animism	968
Makian, East	none	Makian, East	1,500,000	Islam	970
Makian, West	none	Makian, West	20,000	Islam	2977
Malays of Kalimantan	Bible	Malay	750,000	Islam	472

GROUP NAME	SCRIPTURE	LANGUAGE	PRIMARY RELIGION	GROUP SIZE	ID
Mambai	none	Mambai	Animism	80,000	2979
Mamuju	none	Mamuju	Islam	95,000	973
Mandar	portions	Mandar	Islam	250,000	2980
• Manggarai Muslims	none	Manggarai	Islam	25,000	7029
Mangole	none	Mangole	Islam	6,000	976
Manipa	none	Manipa	Animism	nr	977
Mapur Kedelai	not reported	Mapur Kedelai	Animism	400	53
Mapute	none	Mapute	Animism	nr	978
Masenrempulu	none	Masenrempulu	Islam	150,000	2988
Matbrat	none	Matbrat	Animism	550	2989
Mauta	none	Mauta	Animism	nr	983
Mekongka	not reported	Mekongka	Animism	nr	984
Meyah	portions	Meyah	Animism	6,000	1033
Mimika	portions	Mimika	Syncretic Christian	8,000	1049
Minangkabau	New Testament	Minangkabau	Islam	6,000,000	212
Modang	none	Modang	Animism	nr	988
Mongondow	portions	Mongondow	Animism	400,000	2997
Mori	New Testament	Mori	Islam	18,000	3000
Moskona	portions	Moskona	Animism	nr	992
Muko-Muko	none	Muko-Muko	Islam	30,000	69
Munggui	none	Munggui	Animism	800	3003
Murut, Southern	none	Murut, Southern	Animism	nr	994
Musi	Bible	Malay, Sumatra	Islam	150,000	4087
• Nabire Townspeople	Bible,NT,OT	Indonesian	Islam	nr	897
Nage	none	Nage	Roman Catholic	nr	2948
Napu	none	Napu	Animism	4,000	995
Nedebang	none	Nedebang	Animism	nr	998
Ngalik, North	portions	Ngalik, North	Animism	35,000	3011
Ntau	none	Ntau	Animism	nr	1014
Nuaulu	none	Nuaulu	Animism	nr	1015
Nunially	none	Nunially	Animism	nr	1016
Nusa	none	Nusa	Animism	nr	1017
Obi	none	Obi	Animism	nr	1018
Ogan	Bible	Ogan	Islam	500,000	4085
Oikusi	none	Oikusi	Animism	nr	1019
Orang Laut	not reported	Sumatra Malay	Animism	5,000	228
Ot Danum	portions	Ot Danum	Animism	50,000	3021
Palembang	none	Palembang	Islam	400,000	3022

GROUP NAME	SCRIPTURE	LANGUAGE	GROUP SIZE	PRIMARY RELIGION	ID
Pantu	none	Pantu	9,000	Animism	3023
Pasemah	Bible,OT,NT,portions	Pasemah	500,000	Islam	23
Patani	none	Patani	9,000	Islam	1042
Pattae	none	Pattae	35,000	Islam	1050
Pattinjo	none	Pattinjo	50,000	Islam	1051
Pekal	not reported	Pekal	30,000	Islam	38
Penesak	not reported	Penesak	20,000	Islam	352
Punan	none	Punan	nr	Animism	1331
Rana	none	Rana	nr	Animism	1111
Ranau	not reported	Ranau	60,000	Islam	1090
Ratahan	none	Ratahan	150,000	Animism	3030
Rawas	Bible	Rawas	150,000	Islam	898
Rejang	none	Rejang	250,000	Islam	694
Riantana	none	Riantana	1,000	Animism	3031
Riau	Bible,NT,OT,portions	Indonesian	nr	Islam	19
Ritok	none	Ritok	nr	Animism	693
Riung	none	Riung	nr	Roman Catholic	699
Rungu	none	Rungu	nr	Animism	1123
•Sabu (Rural)	portions	Savunese	60,000	Animism	2916
Sakai	not reported	Kubu	nr	Animism	118
Saluan	none	Saluan	100,000	Animism	2969
Sampit	none	Sampit	nr	Animism	1192
Samsam	none	Samsam	nr	Animism	1240
Sangire	portions	Sangire	85,000	Islam	3036
Sapolewa	none	Sapolewa	nr	Animism	1242
Sarudu	none	Sarudu	4,000	Islam	1244
Sasak	portions	Sasak	1,400,000	Islam-Animist	1095
Sauri	none	Sauri	nr	Animism	1246
Sawai	portions	Sawai	4,000	Islam	1247
Seget	none	Seget	nr	Animism	1250
Seho	none	Seho	nr	Animism	1251
•Sekah Laut Fishermen in Bangka	not reported	Sekah Malay	1,000	Animism	52
Sekayu	Bible	Musi (Sekayu)	400,000	Islam	4090
Selayar	none	Selayar	90,000	Islam	1252
Semang,Lowland	none	Semang,Lowland	nr	Animism	1253
Sembakung	none	Sembakung(Tidung dialect)	nr	Animism	1254
Semendo	+Bible,OT,NT,portions	Pasemah/Semendo Malay	105,000	Islam	36

GROUP NAME	SCRIPTURE	LANGUAGE	PRIMARY RELIGION	GROUP SIZE	ID
Sempan	none	Sempan	Animism	2,000	3041
Serawai	portions	Serawai	Islam	150,000	1091
Seruawan	none	Seruawan	Animism	nr	1256
Seti	none	Seti	Animism	nr	1257
Silen	none	Silen	Christianity	nr	1327
Simalur	none	Simalur	Animism	nr	3034
Sindang Kelingi	not reported	Sindang Kelingi Malay	Islam	50,000	356
Siromi	none	Siromi	Animism	nr	1259
Solorese, Eastern	none	Solor	Islam	60,000	1261
Solorese, Western	none	Solor	Animism	71,000	3049
Soow Huhelia	none	Soow Huhelia	Animism	nr	1271
Suku Batin	none	Melayu Jambi	Islam	70,000	6
Sula	none	Sula	Islam	20,000	1263
Sulamata	none	Sulamata	Animism	nr	1264
Sumbawa	none	Sumbawa	Islam	114,000	3052
Sundanese	Bible	Sundanese	Islam-Animist	25,000,000	273
•Sundanese Migrants/Kalimantan	Bible,NT	Sundanese	Islam	800	436
•Sundanese Refugees-Galunggung	OT,NT,Bible	Sundanese	Islam-Animist	35,000	344
•Sundanese in So. Sumatra	NT,Bible	Sundanese	Islam	900,000	1348
Suwawa	none	Suwawa	Animism	nr	1266
Tabenu	none	Tabenu	Animism	nr	1267
Tala	none	Tala	Islam-Animist	90,000	4089
Tamnim	none	Tamnim	Animism	nr	1273
Tara	none	Tara	Animism	125,000	3059
Tausug	NT,portions	Tausug	Animism	52,000	1279
Tengger	Bible,NT,OT,portions	Tenggerese	Hinduism	500,000	296
Tidorese	none	Tidore	Islam-Animist	43,000	3065
Tidung	none	Tidung	Animism	nr	1285
Tihoru	none	Tihoru	Animism	nr	1286
Tilamuta	none	Tilamuta	Animism	nr	1287
Tiro	none	Tiro	Animism	75,000	3067
Toala	none	Toala	Islam	30,000	3068
Tolitoli	none	Tolitoli	Animism	19,000	1291
Tomini	none	Tomini	Islam	68,000	3070
Topoiyo	none	Topoiyo	Islam	1,000	1294
•Tramps in Malang	portions,Bible,NT,OT	Javanese	Islam	4,500	128

Trangan	none		Animism	1295
•Transmigrants	+Bible,NT,OT	10,000,000	Islam	1346
Tukangbesi	none	nr	Animism	1297
Uhei Kachlakin	none	nr	Animism	1300
Ujir	none	nr	Animism	1299
•Univ.Students in Malang, Java	+Bible,OT,NT,portions	3,900	Islam	31
Uruangnirin	none	250	Animism	3081
Vaikino	none	14,000	Animism	3082
Waelulu	none	nr	Animism	1903
Waesama	none	nr	Animism	1304
Wahai	none	nr	Christianity	1305
Wamar	none	nr	Animism	1309
Warembori	none	400	Animism	3088
Warilau	none	nr	Animism	1312
Warkay-Bipim	none	nr	Animism	3090
Weda	none	300	Animism	3092
Welemur	none	2,200	Islam	1314
Wewewa	portions	nr	Animism	3093
Wolani	New Testament	55,000	Animism	3094
Wolio	none	4,000	Animism	3096
Workai	none	25,000	Islam-Animist	1317
Wotu	none	nr	Animism	1318
Yeretuar	none	5,000	Islam	3104
•Young Urban Sundanese-Bandung	OT,NT,Bible	150,000	Islam-Animist	346

Iran

Afshars	portions	290,000	Islam	2035
Ahl-i-Haqq	portions	500,000	Islam	1237
•Arab-Jabbari (Kamesh)	not reported	13,000	Islam	2044
•Arab-Shaibani (Kamesh)	not reported	16,000	Islam	2045
•Arabs of Khuzestan	Bible	520,000	Islam	2034
•Azerbaijani Turks	Bible	6,000,000	Islam	2026
•Bahais in Teheran	+Bible	45,000	Bahaism	5037

-254-

•Baharlu (Kamesh)	not reported	Turkish	8,000	Islam	2046
Bakhtiaris	portions	Bakhtiaris	590,000	Islam	2031
Baluchi	portions	Baluchi	1,100,000	Islam	2030
Barbaris	none	Barbari	nr	Islam	2066
Bayats	none	Bayat	nr	Islam	2067
Bovir-Ahmadi	portions	Lori	110,000	Islam	2040
Galeshis	none	Galeshi	2,000	Islam	2057
Gilakis	none	Gilaki	1,950,000	Islam	2027
Goudari	none	Goudari	2,000	Islam	2059
Gypsies	none	Not Known	30,000	Unknown	2049
Hezareh	none	Hezara'i	nr	Islam	2068
Inallu	not reported	Afshari	5,000	Islam	2048
•Iraqi Kurd Refugees	+New Testament	Kurmanji	300,000	Islam	9028
Jamshidis	none	Jamshidi	1,000	Islam	2063
•Jews	Bible	Farsi	93,000	Judaism	2042
Kazakhs	New Testament	Kazakhi	3,000	Islam	2055
Khalaj	none	Khalaj	20,000	Islam	2535
Kurds	New Testament	Kurdish Dialects	5,000,000	Islam	2036
Lors	none	Luri	600,000	Islam	2028
Mamasani	portions	Luri	110,000	Islam	2039
Mazandaranis	portions	Mazandarani	1,620,000	Islam	2029
Moqaddam	none	Moqaddam	1,000	Islam	2069
Nafar	not reported	Turkish	4,000	Islam	2047
Palanis	none	Palani	nr	Islam	2070
Pashtuns	Bible	Pashtu	3,000	Islam	2054
Persians	Bible	Persian	2,000,000	Islam	4010
Pishagchi	none	Pishagchi	1,000	Islam	2064
Qadikolahis	none	Qadikolahi	nr	Islam	2071
Qajars	not reported	Qajar	3,000	Islam	2056
Qara'i	not reported	Qara'i	2,000	Islam	2058
Qaragozlu	not reported	Qaragozlu	2,000	Islam	2060
Qashqa'i	none	Qashqa'i	350,000	Islam	2038
Sasanis	none	Sasani	1,000	Islam	2072
Shahsavans	none	Azerbaijani (Shahsavani)	180,000	Islam	2043
Tajik	portions	Dari	15,000	Islam	2053
Takestani	none	Takestani	220,000	Islam	2536

GROUP NAME	LANGUAGE	SCRIPTURE	GROUP SIZE	PRIMARY RELIGION	ID
Talish	Talish	none	20,000	Islam	2050
Tats	Tat	none	2,000	Unknown	2061
Teimuri	Teimuri	none	10,000	Islam	2051
Teimurtash	Teimurtash	none	7,000	Islam	2052
•Tertiary Level Youth	Persian	Bible	nr	Islam	4074
Turkomans	Turkomani	portions	550,000	Islam	2032
Zargaris	Zargaris	portions	nr	Unknown	2073

Iraq

GROUP NAME	LANGUAGE	SCRIPTURE	GROUP SIZE	PRIMARY RELIGION	ID
Adygey	Adygey	New Testament	8,500	Islam	7067
•Azerbaijani Turks	Azerbaijani	Bible,NT	900,000	Islam	7069
Chaldean	Chaldean	portions	47,000	Unknown	7070
Gypsys	Romany, Middle Eastern	not reported	84,000	Unknown	7074
Iranians	Farsi (Persian)	Bible,NT	190,000	Islam	7071
Iraqis	Arabic	Bible	12,397,000	Islam	7068
Kurds	Kurdi	portions	2,355,000	Islam	7072
Kurmanji	Kurmanji	NT,portions	100,000	Islam	7073
Suryoyo	Suryoyo	none	nr	Unknown	7075
Yahudic	Yahudic	none	4,300	Unknown	7076
Yezidi	Kirmanji Kurdish	NT,OT,portions	50,000	Other	79

Israel

GROUP NAME	LANGUAGE	SCRIPTURE	GROUP SIZE	PRIMARY RELIGION	ID
Arabs	Arabic	NT,OT,Bible	1,300,000	Islam	2080
•Aramaic Jews	Aramaic	none	7,300	Judaism	4848
•Bokharan Jews	Bukharic	New Testament	3,500	Judaism	4850
•Circassians	Adygey (Circassian)		2,000	Islam	4846
•Druzes	Arabic	Bible	33,000	Folk Religion	1230
•Gypsies in Jerusalem	Romany Dialect	+Bible	300	Islam	5042
•Israel Kibbutznicks	Hebrew	OT,NT,Bible	150,000	Judaism	307
•Jewish Imgrnts.-American	Hebrew	Bible	30,000	Judaism	327
•Jewish Imgrnts.-Argentine	Hebrew	Bible	20,000	Judaism	323
•Jewish Imgrnts.-Australia	Hebrew	Bible	1,000	Judaism	322
•Jewish Imgrnts.-Brazilian	Hebrew	Bible	4,000	Judaism	325
•Jewish Imgrnts.-Mexican	Hebrew	Bible	1,000	Judaism	326
•Jewish Imgrnts.-Uruguayan	Hebrew	Bible	3,000	Judaism	324
•Jewish Immigrants, Other	Hebrew	Bible	6,000	Judaism	321

GROUP NAME	SCRIPTURE	LANGUAGE	GROUP SIZE	PRIMARY RELIGION	ID
• Jewish Refugees from USSR	+Bible	Yiddish	170,000	Secularism	9013
• Targumic-speaking Jews	none	Targumic	5,000	Judaism	2537
Italy					
• Jews in Venice	+Bible	Italian	700	Judaism	5046
• Moroccan Peddlers in Naples	BI	Arabic	100,000	Islam	279
Ivory Coast					
Bambara	Bible	Bambara	11,700	Islam-Animist	2282
Birifor	portions	Birifor	2,000	Animism	2279
Dan	portions	Dan	436,000	Animism	4126
Dioula	OT,NT	Dioula	153,100	Islam	350
Fulbe	portions	Jula	45,500	Islam	2277
Gagu	portions	Gagou	42,275	Animism	480
Hwela-Numu	none	Hwela-Numu	50,000	Islam-Animist	2291
Kulango	New Testament	Kulango	132,600	Animism	481
Kulele	none	Kulele	15,000	Islam-Animist	2294
Ligbi	none	Ligbi	66,400	Islam	482
Lobi	New Testament	Lobi	58,600	Animism	483
Manding	New Testament	Malinke	523,500	Islam	4051
Maou	none	Maou	89,100	Islam-Animist	2295
Mo	none	Mo	800	Islam-Animist	2296
Mona	portions	Muan	9,200	Islam-Animist	2297
Moru	none	Moru	10,000	Islam-Animist	2298
Neyo	none	Nevo	7,600	Animism	1131
Ngain	portions	Ngen	11,700	Animism	698
Palara	none	Palara	10,000	Islam-Animist	2302
• Prostitutes in Abidjan	portions,Bible	Dioula	3,000	Unknown	8588
Senoufo, Niarafolo-Niafolo	none	Senoufo, Niarafolo-Niafol	12,700	Islam-Animist	8590
Senoufo, Palaka	none	Senoufo, Palaka	12,800	Islam-Animist	8591
Senoufo, Tagwana	New Testament	Senoufo, Tagwana	60,000	Islam-Animist	2304
Senoufu, Djimini	portions	Senoufu, Djimini	53,800	Islam-Animist	8589
Senoufo, Cebaara	New Testament	Senari	576,900	Animism	181
• Workers from Burkina Faso	Bible	Dioula	1,000,000	Animism	8593

GROUP NAME	SCRIPTURE	LANGUAGE	GROUP SIZE	PRIMARY RELIGION	ID
Jamaica					
•Jamaican Elite	Bible	Jamaican Patois	800,000	Secularism	4117
•Rastafarians	Bible	Jamaican Patois	100,000	Syncretic Christian	8630
Japan					
•Barbers in Tokyo	+Bible	Japanese	220,000	Buddhism	5009
•Boat People	+Bible	Vietnamese	1,800	Ancestor Worship	9036
•Chinese	Bible	Mandarin	50,000	Traditional Chinese	738
•Danchi Dwellers in Tokyo	+Bible	Japanese	2,500,000	Secularism	5005
•Deaf Japanese	portions	Japanese Sign	400,000	Secularism	281
•Dentists, Fukuoka	+Bible	Japanese	4,500	Secularism	4808
•Farmers of the Tsugaru	+Bible	Tsugaru Ben	275,000	Buddhist-Animist	810
•Geishas in Osaka	+Bible	Japanese	nr	Secularism	5025
•Inland Sea Island Peoples	Bible	Japanese	1,000,000	Traditional Japanese	708
•Soka Gakkai Believers	Bible	Japanese	6,500,000	Buddhism	20
•University Students	+Bible	Japanese	2,000,000	Traditional Japanese	2125
Jordan					
Arabs	Bible,OT,NT	Arabic	3,500,000	Islam	4852
Chechen	portions	Chechen	500	Christianity	4855
Circassians	New Testament	Circassian (Adygey)	20,000	Islam	4851
•Muslims	Bible	Circassian	2,430,000	Islam	220
•Palestinian Refugees	Bible,OT,NT	Arabic	1,100,000	Islam	1087
Samaritans	Bible,NT	Aramaic	300	Unknown	4853
Kampuchea, Democratic					
Brao	none	Brao	5,000	Animism	8579
Cham Malay	none	Cham	40,000	Islam	91
Chong	none	Chong	2,500	Animism	8580
Khmer	Bible	Khmer, Central	4,200,000	Buddhism	8581
Kuoy	none	Kuoy	40,000	Animism	8582
Stieng	none	Stieng	24,000	Animism	8583

GROUP NAME	SCRIPTURE	LANGUAGE	GROUP SIZE	PRIMARY RELIGION	ID
Kenya					
Arab	Bible	Swahili	81,760	Islam	8603
Arabs	Bible	Arabic	30,000	Islam	5236
• Asian Businessmen in Mombasa	Bl,portions,NT,OT	Hindustani	20,000	Islam	276
• Asians in Nairobi	Bible	Tamil	39,000	Hinduism	8692
Boni of Lamu	none	Boni	2,500	Islam-Animist	4803
Boran	New Testament	Borana	68,900	Islam-Animist	4077
Dasenech	portions	Dasenech	2,500	Animism	8595
Digo	portions	Digo	150,000	Islam	4050
Dorobo	portions	Nandi	22,000	Animism	151
El Molo	none	Samburu	1,000	Animism	533
Gabbra	New Testament	Galla	30,500	Folk Religion	715
Giryama	Bible	Giryama	350,000	Animism	534
Korokoro	none	Korokoro	5,000	Islam	8596
Mukogodo	New Testament	Maasai	10,000	Unknown	8597
Ndorobo/Okiek	Bible	Kalenjin	40,000	Unknown	8598
Njemps	+NT,portions	Njemps Maasai	10,000	Animism	8501
Orma	none	Orma	20,000	Islam	8599
Sebei	not reported	Sebei	3,000	Unknown	74
Somali, Ajuran	Bible	Somali (Ajuran)	25,000	Islam	467
Somali, Degodia	New Testament	Somali	70,000	Islam	464
Somali, Gurreh	New Testament	Somali	54,000	Islam	465
Somali, Ogadenya	Bible	Somali	100,000	Islam	466
Turkana	portions,NT	Turkana	224,000	Animism	219
• Turkana Fishing Community	portions	Turkana	20,000	Animism	475
Korea, Republic of					
Apartment Residents-Seoul	Bible	Korean	4,000,000	Folk Religion	301
• Bus Drivers	Bible	Korean	26,000	Unknown	1195
• Bus Girls in Seoul	+Bible	Korean	50,000	Secularism	5023
Chinese	Bible	Mandarin	20,000	Secularism	298
• Hwa-Jeon-Min in Sinrim	NT,OT	Korean	3,000	Buddhist-Animist	178
• Indust.Workers Yongdungpo	Bible	Korean	140,000	Folk Religion	387
Japanese	Bible	Japanese	5,000	Traditional Japanese	710
• Kae Sung People in Seoul	+Bible	Korean	20,000	Buddhism	5015

-259-

GROUP NAME	SCRIPTURE	LANGUAGE	GROUP SIZE	PRIMARY RELIGION	ID
•Korean Army Personnel	Bible,NT,OT	Korean	600,000	Protestant	804
•Prisoners	Bible	Korean	45,000	Secularism	300
•Vietnamese Refugees	+Bible	Vietnamese	500	Buddhism	9045

Kuwait

GROUP NAME	SCRIPTURE	LANGUAGE	GROUP SIZE	PRIMARY RELIGION	ID
Arabs	Bible	Arabic	1,165,000	Islam	4856
Kurds	+OT,NT,portions	Kurdish	145,000	Islam	4136
Mahri	OT,portions	Mahri	4,000	Islam	4857

Laos

GROUP NAME	SCRIPTURE	LANGUAGE	GROUP SIZE	PRIMARY RELIGION	ID
Akha	New Testament	Akha	10,000	Unknown	673
Alak	+none	Alak	107,500	Animism	112
Bit	not reported	Bit	200	Unknown	754
Blue Hmong	NT,portions	Hmong Njua (Meo)	128,000	Animism	443
Bo	none	Bo	nr	Unknown	1360
Brao	not reported	Brao	24,000	Animism	108
Chinese	Bible	Mandarin	25,000	Traditional Chinese	101
Galler	New Testament	Bru	67,000	Animism	111
Halang	portions	Halang	3,200	Animism	1361
Halang Doan	not reported	Halang Doan	1,725	Unknown	1363
Hani	none	Hani	200	Animism	674
Ir	none	Ir	nr	Unknown	1364
Jeh	portions	Jeh	nr	Unknown	1359
Jeng	not reported	Jeng	2,150	Animism	110
•Kampuchean Refugees	Bible	Khmer	10,400	Buddhist-Animist	9049
Kang	none	Kang	nr	Animism	793
Kantu	none	Kantu, Pilu/Tangpril-Tluy	nr	Unknown	1365
Kasseng	none	Kasseng	107,000	Animism	109
Kataang	none	Kataang	6,400	Unknown	1366
Katu	New Testament	Katu	33,600	Animism	1367
Kha Broa	none	Kha Broa	10,700	Unknown	1369
Kha Hog	none	Kha Hog	nr	Unknown	1370
Kha Pong	none	Kha Pong	nr	Unknown	1371
Kha Punoi	portions	Kha Punoi	16,000	Unknown	1372
Khmu	none	Khouen	200,000	Animism	785
Khouen	New Testament	Khmu	nr	Unknown	1373
Kui		Kui	nr	Buddhist-Animist	1374

GROUP NAME	SCRIPTURE	LANGUAGE	GROUP SIZE	PRIMARY RELIGION	ID
La-ven	none	La-ven	nr	Unknown	1375
Lamet	none	Lamet	6,400	Animism	617
Lao	Bible	Lao	1,910,000	Buddhism	121
Lao Soung	portions	Song	329,000	Animism	620
Leun	none	Leun	nr	Unknown	1376
Lor	none	Lor	nr	Unknown	1380
Loven	none	Loven	8,600	Buddhist-Animist	107
Lu	New Testament	Lu	27,600	Buddhist-Animist	722
Mien	New Testament	Mien (Yao)	70,000	Animism	778
Mrabri	-none	Mrabri	300	Animism	760
Mun	none	Mun	2,000	Buddhist-Animist	684
Ngeq	portions	Ngeq	50,300	Animism	105
Nung (Thai)	portions	Thai Nung	300	Animism	795
Nyaheun	not reported	Nyaheun	20,000	Animism	103
Oi	none	Oi	13,450	Animism	104
Pacoh	portions	Pacoh	20,000	Animism	1377
Phana	none	Phana	200	Unknown	685
Phu Thai	portions	Phu Thai	109,500	Buddhist-Animist	102
Phuan	none	Phuan	nr	Animism	762
Phunoi	rot reported	Phunoi	nr	Unknown	745
Pu Ko	none	Pu Ko	nr	Animism	800
Rien	none	Rien	nr	Animism	801
Saek	none	Saek	3,000	Animism	764
Sapuan	none	Sapuan	1,600	Unknown	1379
Soh	portions	Soh	15,350	Animism	98
Sok	none	Sok	600	Unknown	1381
Sou	none	Sou	1,375	Unknown	1382
T'in	none	T'in	6,300	Animism	776
Ta-Oih	none	Ta-Oih	134,000	Animism	99
Tai Phong	none	Tai Phong	nr	Animism	788
Tai, Black	portions	Tai, Black	307,000	Animism	773
Tai, Long	none	Tai, Long	nr	Animism	786
Tai, Muei	none	Tai, Muei	nr	Animism	787
Tai, Northern	Bible,portions	Tai, Northern	6,900	Animism	769
Tai, Red	none	Red Tai	25,000	Animism	792
Tai, White	portions	White Tai	100,000	Animism	791
Talieng	none	Talieng	nr	Unknown	1383
The	none	The	2,600	Unknown	1384
Tong	none	Tong	nr	Unknown	1385

GROUP NAME	SCRIPTURE	LANGUAGE	GROUP SIZE	PRIMARY RELIGION	ID
Vietnamese	Bible	Vietnamese	20,000	Buddhism	100
White Hmong	NT,portions	Meo (Hmong)	100,000	Animism	456
Yoy	portions	Yoy	900	Animism	782
Lebanon					
Arabs	Bible	Arabic	2,418,000	Islam	4858
Kurds	+Bible	Kurmanji	76,000	Islam	76
Ladinos	Bible	Ladino	10,000	Judaism	2538
•Palestinian Refugees	+portions	Arabic	240,000	Islam	9016
Samaritans	Bible	Arabic	18,900	Orthodox	4859
Lesotho					
•South African Refugee Students	+Bible	English	2,000	Christianity	9014
Liberia					
Bandi	+portions	Bandi	38,500	Islam	555
Dan	portions	Dan	94,000	Islam-Animist	5359
Gio	New Testament	Dan (Yacouba)	92,000	Animism	190
Gola	portions	Gola	47,000	Islam-Animist	5360
Kissi	+NT,portions	Kissi	40,000	Animism	691
Kpelle	New Testament	Kpelle	220,000	Animism	556
Mandingo (Manya)	portions	Mandingo(Manya kan)	60,000	Islam	622
Mano	portions	Mano	65,000	Animism	602
Mende	Bible	Mende	5,000	Animism	5363
Vai	portions	Vai	30,000	Islam	688
Libya					
Arab Bedouins (Abedette)	none	Arabic	nr	Islam	166
Libyans	Bible	Arabic	2,300,000	Islam	675
Teda	none	Teda	16,000	Islam	5364
Zaghawa	none	Zaghawa	nr	Islam	5365

GROUP NAME	GROUP SIZE	PRIMARY RELIGION	LANGUAGE	SCRIPTURE	I
Macau					
•Burmese Speaking Chinese	15,000	Traditional Chinese	Burmese	Bible	8688
•Chinese Refugees	100,000	Traditional Chinese	Cantonese	Bible	129
Madagascar					
•Prisoners in Antananarivo	10,000	Folk Religion	Malagasy	+Bible	5012
Tsimihety	700,000	Animism	Tsimihety	not reported	343
Malawi					
Asians	17,000	Islam	Nyanja	Bible	8657
Yao	850,000	Islam-Animist	Chiyao	Bible	1006
Malaysia					
Abai Sungai	550	Animism	Abai Sungai	none	4861
Arabs	nr	Islam	Malay	Bible	4176
Bajau, Land	90,000	Islam-Animist	Bajaus	none	4091
Baluchi	38,000	Islam	Baluchi, Western	none	4884
Bateq	500	Animism	Bateq	none	4114
Beketan	600	Animism	Beketan	none	5627
Besisi (Mah Meri)	1,525	Animism	Besisi	New Testament	4109
Biduanda	4,000	Animism	Biduanda	none	4098
Bisaya	3,000	Animism	Bisaya	portions	7022
Bruneis	25,000	Animism	Bruneis	none	4092
Chewong	350	Animism	Chewong	none	4862
•Chinese Babas	57,000	Traditional Chinese	Baba Malay	Bible	4164
•Chinese Fishermen	4,000	Traditional Chinese	Hokkien	not reported	4142
•Chinese Muslims	8,500	Islam	Chinese Dialects	Bible	4177
•Chinese in Sabah	180,000	Traditional Chinese	Cantonese	Bible	740
•Chinese in Sarawak	330,000	Traditional Chinese	Mandarin and dialects	Bible	737
•Chinese, Cantonese	789,100	Traditional Chinese	Cantonese	Bible,NT	8561
•Chinese, Hainanese	160,000	Traditional Chinese	Hainanese	Bible,NT	8575
•Chinese, Hakka	900,000	Traditional Chinese	Hakka	Bible,NT	8564
•Chinese, Hokchia	7,400	Traditional Chinese	Hokchia	Bible	8610
•Chinese, Hokchiu (Foochow)	78,325	Traditional Chinese	Hokchiu	Bible	4193

GROUP NAME	SCRIPTURE	LANGUAGE	GROUP SIZE	PRIMARY RELIGION	ID
•Chinese, Hokkien	Bible,NT	Hokkien	1,500,000	Traditional Chinese	8558
•Chinese, Kwongsai	Bible	Kwongsai	93,225	Traditional Chinese	757
•Chinese, Teochew	Bible	Teochew	510,000	Traditional Chinese	408
•Chinese, Henghua	Bible	Henghua	13,650	Traditional Chinese	4163
Chitty Melaka	Bible	Malay	200	Hinduism	4189
Embaloh	none	Embaloh	300	Animism	6053
•Eurasians	Bible	Malay	14,500	Christianity	4192
Ida'an	portions	Ida'an	2,500	Islam	4865
Illanun	none	Illanun	5,500	Islam	4869
Indian Ethnic Population	Bible	Indian Dialects	33,000	Hinduism	4190
•Indian Muslim Bus./Prof.Class	Bible	Malayalam	30,000	Islam	4165
•Indian Muslim Laborers,Vendors	Bible	Malay	20,000	Islam	4166
•Indian Muslim Merchants	Bible	Urdu	10,000	Islam	4167
•Indian Punjabi Farmer/Cowherds	Bible	Punjabi	1,000	Hinduism	4182
•Indian Tamil Plantation Wkrs	Bible	Tamil	140,000	Hinduism	1109
•Indian Tamil School Teachers	Bible	Tamil	3,000	Hinduism	4180
•Indian Tamil Urban Squatters	Bible	Tamil	200,000	Hinduism	4
•Indian, Chettyar Proprieters	Bible	Malay	7,000	Hinduism	4188
•Indian, Malayali Hindus	Bible,OT,NT	Malayalam	20,000	Hinduism	4178
•Indian, Punjabi Sikhs	Bible	Punjabi	32,684	Sikhism	4179
•Indian, Telegu Estate Workers	Bible	Telegu	20,000	Hinduism	4186
•Indian, Telegu Municipal Wkrs.	Bible	Telegu	6,100	Hinduism	4187
•Indian,Punjabi Hindu Urban Wkr	Bible	Punjabi	3,000	Hinduism	4181
Indonesian, Acehnese	Bible	Aceh	nr	Islam	4174
Indonesian, Banjarese	BI	Malay	84,000	Islam	4170
Indonesian, Boyanese	Bible	Malay	12,000	Islam	4171
Indonesian, Buginese	Bible	Bugis	16,700	Islam	4172
Indonesian, Javanese	Bible	Malay	200,000	Islam	4168

GROUP NAME	SCRIPTURE	LANGUAGE	GROUP SIZE	RELIGION	ID
Indonesian, Kerinchi	Bible	Kerinchi	5,800	Islam	4173
Indonesian, Mandailing	Bible	Mandailing	nr	Islam	4175
Indonesian, Minangkabau	Bible	Minangkabau	24,000	Islam	4169
Jahai	none	Jahai	800	Animism	4112
Kayan	NT,OT	Kayan	12,000	Animism	4102
Kedayanas	New Testament	Kedayanas	25,000	Animism	4094
Kelabit	portions	Kelabit	17,000	Animism	7025
Kemok	none	Kemok	400	Animism	4115
Kensiu	none	Kensiu	130	Animism	4863
Kenyah	New Testament	Kenyah	12,500	Animism	5610
Kintak	none	Kintak	130	Animism	4864
Kolod	none	Kolod	2,135	Animism	4875
Lanoh	none	Lanoh	400	Animism	4111
Linkabau	none	Linkabau	3,275	Animism	4876
Lundayeh	Bible	Lundayeh	14,800	Animism	4877
•Malay Business & Professional	Bible	Malay	nr	Islam	6090
•Malay Fishermen	Bible	Malay	nr	Islam	7065
•Malay Government Officials	Bible	Malay	nr	Islam	5964
•Malay Imam & Mosque Officials	Bible	Malay	nr	Islam	6035
•Malay Immigrants from Thailand	Bible	Malay	nr	Islam	8515
•Malay Political Elite	Bible	Malay	5,000	Islam	5899
•Malay Rural Poor	Bible	Malay	3,367,000	Islam	5898
•Malay University Students	Bible	Malay	nr	Islam	7030
•Malay Urban Laborer Class	Bible	Malay	nr	Islam	7062
•Malay Urban Middle Class	NT,Bible	Malay	nr	Islam	50
•Malay Villagers and Farmers	Bible	Malay	1,125,000	Islam	5897
Mantera	none	Mantera	4,000	Animism	4097
Melanau of Sarawak	none	Melanau	45,000	Animism	2122
Mendriq	none	Mendriq	130	Animism	4113
Mintil	none	Mintil	50	Animism	4867
Orang Kanaq	none	Proto Malay	4,000	Animism	4100
Orang Laut	none	Proto Malay	4,000	Animism	4101
Orang Ulu	none	Proto Malay	4,000	Animism	4099

GROUP NAME	SCRIPTURE	LANGUAGE	GROUP SIZE	PRIMARY RELIGION	ID
Paluan of Sabah	none	Paluan, Sabah	7,000	Animism	4878
Punan	none	Punan	7,000	Animism	4106
Sekapan	none	Sekapan	1,000	Animism	338
Selakau of Sarawak	none	Selakau	5,000	Animism	2124
Semai	portions	Semai	22,250	Animism	4868
Semang	none	Semang	2,500	Animism	4870
Semaq Beri	none	Semaq Beri	1,900	Animism	4872
Semelai	none	Semelai	3,000	Animism	4110
Sinhalese	Bible	Sinhalese	3,080	Buddhism	4185
• Sri Lankan Tamil Clerk & Prof.	Bible	Tamil	8,700	Hinduism	4184
• Sri Lankan Tamil Rail Workers	Bible	Tamil	8,700	Hinduism	4183
Sugut	Bible	Dusun	10,000	Animism	2118
Tausug	NT,portions	Tausug	110,000	Islam	4881
Temiar	none	Temiar	12,100	Animism	4108
Temuan	none	Temuan	14,000	Animism	4873
Thai	Bible	Thai	31,000	Buddhist-Animist	4191
Tidung	none	Tidung	10,000	Animism	4882

Maldives

Divehi	not reported	Maldivian	200,000	Islam	4005

Mali

Bambara	Bible	Bambara	2,336,000	Islam	604
Bobo Fing	New Testament	Bobo Fing	160,000	Animism	5373
Bobo Wule	New Testament	Bwamu	366,000	Animism	5374
Bozo	none	Bozo	87,000	Islam	5375
Fulbe (Macina)	BI,NT,OT	Fula, Macina	875,000	Animism	5376
Kagoro	Bible	Bambara	58,400	Animism	552
Khasonke	none	Khasonke	109,500	Islam	5378
Malinke	none	Malinke	445,300	Islam	8605
Mandinka	none	Mandinka	200,000	Islam	415
Maure	none	Arabic, Hassaniya	78,000	Islam-Animism	5379
Mossi	Bible	Moore	29,200	Animism	8606
Samogho	none	Dunn	46,100	Animism	5381
Senoufo, Suppire	portions	Senoufo, Supnire	300,000	Animism	

GROUP NAME	SCRIPTURE	LANGUAGE	GROUP SIZE	PRIMARY RELIGION	ID
Songhai	New Testament	Songhai	452,000	Animism	5382
Soninke	none	Soninke	560,000	Islam	5383
Toucouleur	portions	Toucouleur	39,800	Islam	8607
Tuareg	New Testament	Tamashek	365,000	Islam	416
Wolof	portions	Wolof	14,600	Islam	8609
Mauritania					
Bambara	Bible	Bambara	10,000	Islam	148
Fulbe	portions	Fufulde	100,000	Islam	138
Moors, Black	BI	Arabic, Hassaniya	700,000	Islam	4043
Moors, White	BI	Arabic, Hassaniya	80,000	Islam	6570
Soninke	none	Soninke	180,000	Islam	5386
Toucouleur	portions	Toucouleur	10,000	Islam	136
Wolof	portions	Wolof	16,000	Islam	135
Zenaga	none	Zenaga		Islam	5387
Mauritius					
Chinese	Bible	Hakka	30,000	Buddhist-Animist	4811
Mexico					
Chamula	+New Testament	Tzotzil (Chamula)	50,000	Syncretic Christian	162
• English speakers, Guadalajara	+Bible	English	25,000	Secularism	4816
• Guatemalan Refugees	+Bible	Spanish	70,000	Syncretic Christian	9057
Huave	New Testament	Huave	18,000	Syncretic Christian	113
Huichol	portions,NT	Huichol	8,000	Syncretic Christian	8043
• Koreans in Tijuana	+portions,NT,OT	Spanish	900	Secularism	1342
Mazahua	New Testament	Mazahua	150,000	Syncretic Christian	377
• Middle Class-Mexico City	+Bible	Spanish	nr	Roman Catholic	5014
Mixes	New Testament	Mixe	60,000	Syncretic Christian	1005
• Oaxaca Migrants in Baja	+Bible	Zapoteco	20,000	Syncretic Christian	426
Tepehuan, Northern	New Testament	Tepehuan, Northern	5,000	Syncretic Christian	5089
• University Students - Mexicali	+Bible,NT,OT,portions	Spanish	16,724	Secularism	664
Zinacantecos	+New Testament	Tzotzil, Zinacanteco	12,000	Syncretic Christian	95

GROUP NAME	LANGUAGE	SCRIPTURE	GROUP SIZE	PRIMARY RELIGION	ID
Mongolia					
Khalkha Mongols	Khalkha Mongol	portions	1,300,000	Secularism	2825
Morocco					
Arabs	Arabic dialect	portions	5,250,000	Islam	4029
Shilha	Shilha	not reported	3,000,000	Islam-Animist	5388
Shluh Berbers	Tashilhait	none	2,000,000	Islam-Animist	4028
Tamazight	Tamazight	portions	1,800,000	Islam-Animist	5389
Mozambique					
•Civil Servants	African languages	Bible	nr	Christianity	805
Lomwe	Lomwe	New Testament	1,000,000	Animism	565
Mvani	Mwani	not reported	100,000	Islam	8678
Nyungwe	Nyungwe	portions	700,000	Animism	5393
Podzo	Podzo	portions	45,000	Animism	5394
Tonga	Tonga	NT,portions	10,000	Animism	5397
Tsonga	Tsonga	Bible	1,600,000	Christianity	8674
Yao	Yao	Bible	220,000	Islam	143
•Zimbabwean Refugees	Tribal Languages	+not reported	170,000	Animism	9032
Namibia					
Bushmen (San)	San	none	32,000	Animism	562
Himba	OtJu Herero	NT,portions	17,000	Animism	303
Zu	Xun	portions	2,200	Animism	5406
Nepal					
Awadhi	Awadhi	portions	452,366	Hindu-Buddhist	6501
Baragaunle	Baragaunle	none	nr	Unknown	2309
Bhojpuri	Bhojpuri	portions	1,184,000	Hinduism	670
Bodo	Bodo	Bible,NT	1,700	Unknown	2201
Bote-Majhi	Bote-Majhi	none	6,300	Buddhist-Animist	6502
Byangsi	Byangsi	none	2,100	Buddhist-Animist	6503

GROUP NAME	SCRIPTURE	LANGUAGE	GROUP SIZE	PRIMARY RELIGION	ID
Chaudangsi	none	Chaudangsi	2,000	Buddhist-Animist	6504
Chepang	portions	Chepang	17,700	Buddhist-Animist	6505
Chhathar	none	Chhathar	nr	Unknown	2206
Damai	BI,NT	Nepali	nr	Hindu-Animist	2212
Darai	portions	Darai	4,000	Buddhist-Animist	6506
Darmiya	none	Darmiya	2,200	Buddhist-Animist	6507
Dhimal	none	Dhimal	14,800	Buddhist-Animist	6508
Dolpo	none	Dolpo	nr	Unknown	2286
Dzongkha	none	Dzongkha	10,500	Unknown	2308
Ghale Gurung	portions	Ghale Gurung	18,000	Buddhist-Animist	6509
Gharti	none	Gharti	nr	Unknown	2310
Gurung	New Testament	Gurung	250,000	Hinduism	1208
Janggali	none	Janggali	16,500	Buddhist-Animist	6510
Jirel	portions	Jirel	4,100	Buddhist-Animist	6511
Kaike	ncne	Kaike	nr	Unknown	2332
Kham	New Testament	Kham	54,500	Buddhist-Animist	6512
Khasiya	not reported	Khasiya Pahari	2,000,000	Hindu-Animist	2983
Kumauni	Bible,portions	Kumauni	nr	Hindu-Animist	2367
Kumhali	none	Kumhali	214,442	Unknown	2383
Kusanda	none	Kusanda	nr	Unknown	2396
Lepcha	portions	Lepcha	2,300	Unknown	2401
Lhomi	portions	Lhomi	13,600	Buddhist-Animist	6513
Limbu	none	Limbu	247,345	Buddhist-Animist	2283
Lo-Ba	none	Tibetan	8,000	Buddhist-Animist	186
Lohorong	none	Lohorong	2,000	Unknown	2284
Magar	portions	Magar	412,000	Hindu-Animist	395
Maithili	portions	Maithili	1,895,000	Hindu-Animist	398
Majhi	none	Majhi	6,000	Buddhist-Animist	6514
Manang	none	Manangba	nr	Unknown	2410
Mundari	Bible,portions	Mundari	nr	Unknown	2411
Musasa	none	Musasa	nr	Unknown	2426
•Nepali in Kathmandu	Bible,NT	Nepali	8,400,000	Hinduism	668
•Newar in Kathmandu	,Bible,NT +portions	Nepali (Pahari)	250,000	Hinduism	2222
Newari	portions	Newari	400,000	Buddhism	5030
Palpa	New Testament	Palpa	5,430	Hindu-Buddhist	660
Rai	none	Rai	270,000	Buddhist-Animist	6515
Rai				Hindu-Buddhist	663
Rai, Danuwar	portions	Danuwar Rai	14,500	Hindu-Animist	661

GROUP NAME	SCRIPTURE	LANGUAGE	GROUP SIZE	PRIMARY RELIGION	ID
Rai, Khaling	portions	Rai, Khaling	13,300	Buddhist-Animist	6516
Rai, Kulung	portions	Rai, Kulung	13,300	Buddhist-Animist	6524
Rai, Thulunge	none	Rai, Thulunge	25,000	Buddhist-Animist	6517
Rajbansi	none	Rajbansi	78,700	Hindu-Animist	659
Raji	none	Raji	166,196	Unknown	2929
Rangkas	none	Rangkas	750	Buddhist-Animist	6518
Santali	Bible,NT	Santhali	29,500	Animism	669
Shemba	OT,NT,Bible	Tibetan	nr	Buddhism	185
Sherpa	portions	Sherpa	20,000	Buddhism	671
Sunwar	portions	Sunwar	30,000	Buddhist-Animist	6519
Syuwa	portions	Syuwa	5,400	Buddhist-Animist	6520
Tamang	+NT,portions	Tamang	519,000	Hindu-Buddhist	666
Thakali	none	Thakali	7,500	Buddhist-Animist	6521
Thami	none	Thami	16,400	Buddhist-Animist	6522
Tharu	portions	Tharu	800,000	Hinduism	1064
Tibetans	Bible,OT,NT	Bhotia (Tibetan)	80,000	Other	2299
Tsaurasya	none	Tsaurasya	nr	Unknown	2919
Tseku	none	Tseku	nr	Unknown	2909
Vayu	none	Vayu	nr	Unknown	2908
Yakha	none	Yakha	1,450	Buddhist-Animist	6523
Yanphu	none	Yanphu	nr	Unknown	2869

Netherlands

GROUP NAME	SCRIPTURE	LANGUAGE	GROUP SIZE	PRIMARY RELIGION	ID
• Amsterdam Boat Dwellers	Bible	Dutch	8,000	Secularism	4159
• Dead-End Kids - Amsterdam	+Bible	Dutch	30,000	Secularism	5034
• Muslims in Holland	BI	Arabic	170,000	Islam	285

Niger

GROUP NAME	SCRIPTURE	LANGUAGE	GROUP SIZE	PRIMARY RELIGION	ID
Dendi	none	Dendi	36,400	Islam	8611
Dyerma	New Testament	Dyerma	884,500	Islam-Animist	4014
Fulbe (Bororo)	none	Fulfulde, Bororo	200,000	Islam	196
Fulbe, Sokoto	New Testament	Fulfulde, Sokoto	452,700	Animism	241
Gourma	NT,portions	Gourma	36,600	Animism	8612
Hausa	OT,NT	Hausa	2,659,600	Islam	256
Kanembu	none	Kanembu	2,000	Islam-Animist	5407

GROUP NAME	SCRIPTURE	PRIMARY RELIGION	GROUP SIZE	LANGUAGE	ID
Kanuri	portions	Islam	335,500	Kanuri	8613
Kurfei	none	Animism	50,000	Hausa	561
Manga	portions	Islam	95,900	Manga	193
Mauri	none	Animism	100,000	Hausa	560
Mober	none	Islam	48,800	Mober	8614
Songhai	New Testament	Islam-Animist	335,500	Songhai	5408
Teda	none	Islam-Animist	120,000	Teda	5409
Tuareg	+New Testament	Islam	547,800	Tamachek	46

Nigeria

GROUP NAME	SCRIPTURE	PRIMARY RELIGION	GROUP SIZE	LANGUAGE	ID
Afawa	none	Animism	10,000	Afanci	559
Afo	none	Animism	25,000	Eloyi	558
Alago	none	Animism	35,000	Alago	1058
Ankwe	portions	Animism	10,000	Ankwai	557
Arawa	Bible	Islam	200,000	Hausa	644
Ayu	none	Islam	4,000	Ayu	2324
Babur Thali	New Testament	Animism	75,000	Bura (Babur)	1057
Bada	none	Animism	10,000	Bada	2326
Bade	none	Islam	100,000	Bade	2327
Bali	none	Islam-Animist	1,000	Bali	2328
Bambuka	none	Islam	10,000	Bambuka	2329
Banga	none	Islam	8,000	Banga	2331
Bariba	portions	Islam-Animist	55,000	Bariba	7041
Bata	none	Islam-Animist	30,000	Bata	2334
Baushi	none	Islam	3,000	Baushi	2336
Binawa	none	Islam	2,000	Binawa	2341
Boghom	portions	Animism	50,000	Boghom	2343
Buduma	none	Islam	80,000	Buduma	2346
Burak	none	Islam	2,000	Burak	2347
Busa	portions	Islam	50,000	Busa (Bokobarn Akiba)	1055
Butawa	none	Islam	20,000	Buta	548
• Chadian Refugees	+portions	Islam	3,000	Arabic	9043
Chip	none	Animism	6,000	Chip	2351
Chokobo	none	Animism	400	Chokobo	2352
Dadiya	none	Islam	2,000	Dadiya	2353
Dass	none	Islam-Animist	9,000	Dass	2354

GROUP NAME	LANGUAGE	SCRIPTURE	GROUP SIZE	PRIMARY RELIGION	ID
Degema	Degeme	none	10,000	Animism	2355
Deno	Deno	none	10,000	Islam	2356
Dghwede	Zighvana(Dghwede)	portions	13,000	Animism	1179
Dirim	Dirim	none	11,000	Islam-Animist	2358
Dirya	Dirya	none	4,000	Islam	2359
Duguir	Duguri	none	12,000	Islam	2360
Duguza	Duguza	none	2,000	Islam	2361
Duka	Dukanci	none	10,000	Animism	1054
Dyerma	Dyerma	New Testament	50,000	Islam	2362
Fakai	Faka	none	15,000	Animism	1053
Fali	Fali	none	25,000	Animism	1052
Fulbe, Igboro	Fulfulde, Adamawa	+Bible	450,000	Islam-Animist	216
Fyer	Fyer	none	3,000	Animism	2380
Galambi	Galambi	none	1,000	Islam	2382
Geji	Geji	none	3,000	Islam	2385
Gera	Gera	none	13,000	Islam	2386
Geruma	Geruma	none	5,000	Islam	2387
Glavda	Glavda	not reported	19,000	Animism	1174
Goemai	Goemai	none	80,000	Animism	2389
Gudu	Gudu	none	1,000	Animism	2392
Guduf	Guduf	portions	21,000	Animism	2393
Gure-Kahugu	Gure-Kahugu	none	5,000	Islam	2394
Guruntum-Mbaaru	Guruntum-Mbaaru	none	10,000	Islam	2395
Gwandara	Gwandara	none	25,000	Animism	1113
• Hausa in Birni	Hausa	OT,NT,Bible	1,000,000	Islam	809
Higi	Higi	New Testament	150,000	Animism	1118
Hwana	Hwana	none	20,000	Islam	7043
Hyam	Hyam	portions	60,000	Islam	2398
Ikulu	Ikulu	none	6,000	Islam	2409
Ikwere	Ikwere	none	200,000	Animism	7045
Isekiri	Isekiri	none	33,000	Animism	2412
Jara	Jara	none	40,000	Islam	2418
Jibu	Jibu, Jibanci	portions	20,000	Animism	1172
Jimbin	Jimbin	none	2,000	Islam	2420
Kagoma	Kagoma	none	6,000	Islam	2421
Kamantan	Kadara	none	5,000	Animism	537
Kamo	Kamo	none	3,000	Islam	2424
Kamuku	Kamuku	none	20,000	Animism	536
Kanuri	Kanuri Dialects	portions	2,500,000	Islam	4007

GROUP NAME	SCRIPTURE	LANGUAGE	GROUP SIZE	PRIMARY RELIGION	ID
Karekare	none	Karekare	39,000	Islam	2427
Kariya	none	Kariya	2,000	Islam	2428
Kirifi	none	Krifi	14,000	Islam	2431
Kofyar	none	Kofyar	40,000	Animism	2433
Kono	nore	Kono	2,000	Islam	2436
Koro	New Testament	Koro	35,000	Animism	572
Kuda-Chamo	none	Kuda-Chamo	4,000	Islam	2438
Kushi	none	Kushi	4,000	Islam	2443
Kuzamani	none	Kuzamani	1,000	Islam	2446
Kyibaku	none	Kyibaku	20,000	Islam	2448
Laamang	none	Laamang	40,000	Islam	2449
Lakka	ncne	Lakka	500	Islam	2450
Lungu	none	Lungu	10,000	Animism	571
Mandara	portions	Mandara	20,000	Islam	2459
Matakam	New Testament	Matakam	2,000	Islam	2461
Mbembe (Tigong)	none	Mbembe	3,000	Animism	2463
Miya	none	Miya	5,000	Animism	1175
Mober	none	Mober	45,000	Islam	2468
Mumuye	Bible	Mumuye	200,000	Animism	570
Ngizim	none	Ngizim	40,000	Islam	2475
Ninzam	none	Ninzam	35,000	Islam	2477
Numana-Nunku-Gwantu	none	Numana-Nunku-Gwantu	15,000	Islam	2479
Nupe	Bible	Nupe	600,000	Islam	17
Nzanyi	none	Nzanyi	14,000	Islam	2481
Piti	none	Piti	2,000	Islam	2495
Puku-Geeri-Keri-Wipsi	none	Puku-Geeri-Keri-Wipsi	15,000	Islam	2499
Reshe	none	Reshe	30,000	Animism	2500
Rumaya	none	Rumaya	2,000	Islam	2503
Ruruma	none	Ruruma	2,000	Islam	2504
Sanga	none	Sanga	5,000	Islam	2505
Shuwa Arabic	none	Shuwa Arabic	100,000	Islam	2509
Sukur	none	Sukur	10,000	Islam	2511
Surubu	none	Surubu	2,000	Islam	2513
Tula	portions	Tula	19,000	Islam	2519
Utugwang	none	Utugwang	12,000	Animism	2525
Waja	portions	Waja	30,000	Islam	2529
Warjawa	none	Warji	70,000	Animism	595
Yandang	none	Yandang	10,000	Islam-Animist	2531
Yeskwa	none	Yeskwa	13,000	Islam	2532

GROUP NAME	SCRIPTURE	LANGUAGE	GROUP SIZE	PRIMARY RELIGION	ID
Yungur	none	Yungur	44,000	Islam	2533
Zaranda Hill Peoples	not reported	local languages	10,000	Animism	1178
Zari	none	Zari	4,000	Islam	2534
Oman					
Arabs	Bible	Arabic	1,085,000	Islam	4883
Iranians	Bible,NT	Kumzai	28,500	Islam	4885
Mahra	portions	Mahri	50,000	Animism	2539
Pakistanis	Bible	Urdu	18,000	Islam	4886
Pakistan					
• Afghan Refugees (NWFP)	+Bible	Dari	1,835,000	Islam	9004
• Afghan Turkic Refugees	not reported	Urdu	65,000	Islam	432
Ahmadis in Lahore	+Bible	Panjabi	60,000	Islam	5016
Bagri	none	Bagri	20,000	Hinduism	268
Bajania	none	Gujarati Dialect	20,000	Hinduism	263
Balmiki	not reported	Hindustani	20,000	Hinduism	254
Balti	none	Balti	80,000	Islam	4802
Bhil	portions	Marwari	800,000	Hinduism	35
Brahui	portions	Brahui	745,000	Islam	4049
Chitralis	none	Khuwar	120,000	Islam	1234
Gagre	New Testament	Punjabi	40,000	Animism	264
Hunzakut	+portions	Burushaski	40,000	Islam	1236
• Iranian Bahai Refugees	+Bible	Farsi	5,000	Bahaism	9024
Kafirs	none	Kafiristani (Bashgali)	3,000	Animism	1233
Kalash	+none	Kalasha	3,000	Animism	155
Kohli, Kutchi	portions	Gujarati, Koli	50,000	Hinduism	258
Kohli, Parkari	portions	Gujarati, Koli	100,000	Hinduism	261
Kohli, Tharadari	none	Gujarati, Koli	40,000	Hinduism	259
Kohli, Wadiara	portions	Gujarati Dialect	40,000	Hindu-Animist	260
Lohar	none	Marwari	nr	Hinduism	266
Meghwar	none	Odki	100,000	Hinduism	262
Od	Bible	Punjabi	40,000	Hinduism	265
Punjabis	none	Pushtun	49,000,000	Islam	4021
Pushtun, Babuzi	none	Shina	nr	Islam	2636
Shina	portions		100,000	Islam	2102
• Sindhi Muslims in Karachi	+Bible	Sindhi	350,000	Islam-Animist	5036

-274-

GROUP NAME	SCRIPTURE	LANGUAGE	GROUP SIZE	PRIMARY RELIGION	ID
Sindhis	Bible	Sindhi	11,500,000	Islam	8640
Sochi	not reported	Sindhi	nr	Hinduism	255
Swatis	none	Swati	600,000	Islam	1232
• USSR Kirghiz Refugee Shepherds	+nct reported	Turkic	1,200	Islam	9042
Vagari	none	Gujarati Dialect	30,000	Hinduism	267
Panama					
Chinese	Bible	Spanish	25,000	Traditional Chinese	4140
Papua New Guinea					
Ankave	none	Ankave	2,000	Animism	5928
Arafundi	none	Arafundi	1,000	Animism	5931
Bo	none	Bo	175	Animism	320
Bosavi	none	Bosavi	400	Animism	5989
Chenapian	none	Chenapian	200	Animism	6006
Kara	none	Kara	2,000	Animism	6117
Mari	none	Mari	300	Animism	6208
Musan	none	Musan	150	Animism	329
Pay	none	Pay	600	Animism	6300
Rao	none	Rao	3,000	Animism	6312
Rocky Peak	none	Rocky Peak	275	Animism	328
Sumau	none	Sumau	800	Animism	6364
Paraguay					
Guayaki	none	Guayaki	400	Animism	5124
Peru					
Achual	NT,portions	Achual	5,000	Animism	3162
Aguaruna	New Testament	Aguaruna	22,000	Animism	3163
Amahuaca	portions	Amahuaca	2,000	Animism	2203
Amarakaeri	portions	Amarakaeri	500	Animism	3164
Candoshi	portions	Candoshi	3,000	Animism	3167
Capanahua	NT,portions	Capanahua	500	Animism	2205
Cashibo	NT,portions	Cashibo	2,000	Animism	3168

GROUP NAME	SCRIPTURE	LANGUAGE	GROUP SIZE	PRIMARY RELIGION	ID
•Chinese in Lima	Bible	Cantonese	30,000	Traditional Chinese	9187
Cocama	portions	Cocama	18,000	Animism	3170
Cujareno	none	Cujareno	100	Animism	3171
Huachipaire	none	Huachipaire	200	Animism	3172
Huambisa	New Testament	Huambisa	5,000	Animism	3173
Manu Park Panoan	none	Manu Park Panoan	200	Animism	3179
Mayoruna	portions	Mayoruna	1,000	Animism	3180
Morunahua	none	Morunahua	200	Animism	3181
Quechua, Huanca	none	Huanca Quechua		Roman Catholic	175
•Upper Class of Lima	+Bible,portions,OT,NT	Spanish	30,000	Syncretic Christian	1345
Urarina	portions	Urarina	100,000	Animism	3187
Yagua	portions	Yagua	4,000	Animism	3188

Philippines

GROUP NAME	SCRIPTURE	LANGUAGE	GROUP SIZE	PRIMARY RELIGION	ID
Abaknon	none	Abaknon	10,000	Syncretic Christian	3239
Adasen	portions	Itneg, Adasen	4,000	Animism	204
•Aeta	none	Aeta	500	Syncretic Christian	3240
Ati	Bible	English	2,000	Islam	2101
Badjao	not reported	Ati	2,000	Syncretic Christian	3243
•Baguio Area Miners	Bible	Badjao	4,900	Islam	4832
Balangao	portions	Ilocano	40,000	Roman Catholic	7004
Batak, Palawan	portions	Balangao	5,000	Syncretic Christian	633
Blind, Philippines	+NT,portions	Batak, Palawan	400	Syncretic Christian	3245
Bontoc, Central	+portions	Kapampangan,Pangasinan	1,236,000	Roman Catholic	623
Bontoc, Eastern	portions	Bontoc, Central	20,000	Animism	632
Bontoc, Southern	portions	Bontoc, Eastern	5,700	Protestant	5235
Bukidnon	portions	Southern Bontoc	5,700	Syncretic Christian	1060
Cabuloan Dumagat	portions	Manobo, Binukid	100,300	Animism	1063
Casiguranin	none	Cabuloan Dumagat	10,000	Islam-Animist	5354
•Cebu, Middle-Class	Bible	Casiguranin	500,000	Roman Catholic	4055
Dumagat, Casiguran	portions	Cebuano	1,000	Syncretic Christian	1079
•Factory Workers in Manila	+Bible	Dumagat	5,000,000	Animism	2
Hanonoo	portions	Tagalog	6,000	Roman Catholic	553
•Hotel Workers in Manila	Bible	Hanonoo	11,000	Syncretic Christian	3253
Ibatan	none	Pilipino	500	Roman Catholic	7036
Ifugao (Kalangoya)	portions,NT	Ibatan	35,000	Syncretic Christian	4056
Ifugao in Cababuyan	New Testament	Kalangoya	4,000	Animism	697
		Ifugao		Animism	2104

-276-

GROUP NAME	SCRIPTURE	LANGUAGE	GROUP SIZE	PRIMARY RELIGION	ID
Ifugao, Amganad	portions	Ifugao, Amganad	15,000	Animism	3255
Ifugao, Antipolo	New Testament	Keley-i	5,000	Animism	1047
Ifugao, Kiangan	portions	Ifugao, Kiangan	25,000	Animism	3256
Igorot	portions	Igorot	20,000	Animism	3247
Ilanon	not reported	Ilanun	12,041	Islam	4833
Ilongot	portions	Ilongot	8,000	Animism	3257
Iraya	portions	Iraya	6,000	Syncretic Christian	3259
Isnag	portions	Isnag	12,000	Roman Catholic	1201
Isneg, Dibagat-Kabugao	portions	Isneg, Dibagat-Kabugao	10,000	Animism	3260
Isneg, Karagawan	New Testament	Isneg, Karagawan	8,000	Animism	3261
Itawit	none	Itawit	15,000	Syncretic Christian	3262
Itneg, Adasen	none	Itneg, Adasen	4,000	Syncretic Christian	3263
Itneg, Binongan	portions	Itneg, Binongan	7,000	Syncretic Christian	3264
Itneg, Masadiit	none	Itneg, Masadiit	8,000	Syncretic Christian	3265
•Jeepney Drivers in Manila	+Bible,NT,OT,portions	Tagalog	20,000	Roman Catholic	7018
•Jeepney Drivers, Cebu City	+Bible	Cebuano	1,000	Roman Catholic	235
Kadaklan-Barlig Bontoc	none	Kadaklan-Barlig Bontoc	4,000	Animism	3248
Kalagan, Kaagan	portions	Kaagan	6,000	Syncretic Christian	3266
Kalagan, Tagakaolu	portions	Kalagan	19,000	Animism	630
Kalinga, Kalagua	none	Kalinga, Kalagua	4,000	Animism	3268
Kalinga, Limos	portions	Kalinga, Limos	20,000	Syncretic Christian	3269
Kalinga, Quinaang	portions	Kalinga, Quinaang	41,000	Animism	3267
Kalinga, Southern	portions	Kalinga,Sumadel-Tinglayan	12,000	Animism	1147
Kalinga, Tanudan	none	Kalinga	8,000	Roman Catholic	4054
Kalinga,Northern	none	Kalinga	20,000	Syncretic Christian	1146
Kankanay, Central	portions	Kankanay	40,000	Animism	1200
Kankanay, Northern	portions	Northern Kankanay	40,000	Animism	4057
Maguindanaon	portions,NT,OT,tracts	Maguindanaon	800,000	Islam	629
Mamanua	portions	Minamanua	1,000	Syncretic Christian	628
Mandaya, Mansaka	New Testament	Mandaya, Mansaka	40,000	Animism	3271
Manobo, Agusan	portions	Manobo, Agusan	40,000	Animism	3272
Manobo, Atao	portions	Manobo	20,000	Animism	627
Manobo, Cotabato	portions,NT	Cebuano	10,000	Animism	626
Manobo, Dibabawon	New Testament	Manobo, Dibabawon	10,000	Animism	3275
Manobo, Ilianen	portions	Ilianen Manobo	5,000	Animism	625
Manobo, Kinamiguin	not reported	Manobo, Kinamiguin	nr	Unknown	1171
Manobo, Matig Salug	Bible	Manobo, Matig Salug	22,000	Animism	639
Manobo, Obo	portions	Manobo, Obo	4,000	Animism	3276

GROUP NAME	SCRIPTURE	LANGUAGE	GROUP SIZE	PRIMARY RELIGION	ID
Manobo, Sarangani	New Testament	Manobo, Sarangani	30,000	Unknown	3274
Manobo, Tagabawa	portions	Manobo, Tagabawa	10,000	Animism	3278
Manobo, Tigwa	portions	Visayan	4,000	Animism	640
Manobo, Western Bukidnon	NT,portions	Manobo, Binokid	15,000	Animism	618
Mansaka	portions,NT	Mansaka	40,000	Animism	1035
Maranao	NT,portions,stories	Maranao	500,000	Islam	638
Maranao, Lanao	NT,portions	Maranao, Lanao	500,000	Islam-Animist	3279
Metro Manila Poor	Bible,OT,NT	Tagalog	1,500,000	Syncretic Christian	806
Molbog	portions	Molbog	5,000	Islam-Animist	1039
Northern Cagayan Negrito	portions	Northern Cagayan Negrito	1,000	Syncretic Christian	3292
Pala'wan	New Testament	Pala'wan	50,000	Animism	4162
Palanan Dumagat	portions	Paranan	10,000	Animism	5626
Palawano, Quezon	New Testament	Palawano, Central	3,000	Animism	3281
Palawano, Southwest	none	Palawano	3,000	Animism	3280
Paranan	none	Paranan	8,000	Roman Catholic	3282
Prisoners in Manila	Bible	Tagalog	nr	Syncretic Christian	802
Sama Bangingi	portions	Sinama Bangini	60,000	Islam-Animist	1148
Sama Pangutaran	portions	Sama Pangutaran	15,000	Islam	1150
Sama, Mapun	portions,OT	Sama, Mapun	15,000	Islam-Animist	3284
Sama, Siasi	portions	Sama, Siasi	100,000	Islam-Animist	3285
Sama, Sibuku	none	Sama, Sibuku	11,000	Islam-Animist	3286
Sama-Badjaw	portions	Samal Moro	60,000	Islam-Animist	389
Sangil	none	Sangil	8,000	Islam	637
Subanen (Tuboy)	portions	Subanen, Tuboy	20,000	Animism	51
Subanun, Sindangan	portions	Subanun	80,000	Animism	1062
Subanun,Lapuyan	New Testament	Subanun, Lapuyan	25,000	Islam-Animist	3287
T'boli	+portions,NT	Tboli	100,000	Animism	624
Tadyawan	none	Tadyawan	1,000	Animism	3288
Tagbanwa, Aborlan	portions	Tagbanwa	8,000	Animism	1153
Tagbanwa, Kalamian	+portions	Tagbanwa, Kalamian	5,000	Syncretic Christian	636
Tala-Andig	+not reported	Tala-Andig	3,000	Animism	370
Tausug	portions,NT	Tausug	250,000	Islam	635
Tiruray	New Testament	Tiruray	40,000	Christianity	3290
Umiray Dumagat	NT,portions	Dumagat (Umiray)	5,000	Animism	369
University Students	Bible	Tagalog (Umiray)	1,000,000	Roman Catholic	803
Western Subanon	portions	Sinubanon	10,000	Animism	5353
Yakan	portions,NT	Yakan	60,000	Islam-Animist	25

GROUP NAME	ID	PRIMARY RELIGION	GROUP SIZE	LANGUAGE	SCRIPTURE

Qatar

GROUP NAME	SCRIPTURE	LANGUAGE	GROUP SIZE	PRIMARY RELIGION	ID
Arabs	Bible	Arabic	125,000	Islam	4887
Iranians	Bible,NT	Farsi	27,000	Islam	4888
Pakistanis	Bible	Urdu	18,200	Islam	4889

Reunion

GROUP NAME	SCRIPTURE	LANGUAGE	GROUP SIZE	PRIMARY RELIGION	ID
Swahili	portions	Creole, Reunion-Seychelle	16,000	Islam	8636

Saudi Arabia

GROUP NAME	SCRIPTURE	LANGUAGE	GROUP SIZE	PRIMARY RELIGION	ID
•Africans in Jiddah	Bible	Local Dialects	nr	Islam	6593
Bedouin	Bible	Arabic	nr	Islam	6585
Chinese	Bible	Arabic	20,000	Islam	4135
Egyptians of Medina	Bible	Arabic	nr	Islam	6590
•Expatriates in Riyadh	+Bible	English	nr	Secularism	5024
•Filipino Migrant Workers	+Bible	Tagalog	132,000	Roman Catholic	4815
•Hadrami in Jiddah	Bible	Arabic	nr	Islam	6592
•Hijazi Merchants	Bible	Arabic	nr	Islam	6581
•Indians of Mecca	Bible	Local Dialects	nr	Islam	6586
•Indonesians of Mecca	Bible	Indonesian	nr	Islam	6587
•Najdi Bureaucrats	Bible	Arabic	nr	Islam	6577
•Najdi Technocrats	Bible	Arabic	nr	Islam	6578
•New Urban Middle Class	Bible	Arabic	nr	Islam	6580
•Persians of Jiddah	Bible	Persian	nr	Islam	6591
•Saudi Tribespeople	Bible	Arabic	nr	Islam	6584
•Saudi Ulama in Najd	Bible	Arabic	nr	Islam	6576
•Shia Agriculturalists	Bible	Arabic	nr	Islam	6583
•Shia Oil Industry Workers	Bible	Arabic	nr	Islam	6582
•Syrians of Medina	Bible	Arabic	nr	Islam	6589
•Turks of Medina	Bible	Turkish	nr	Islam	6888
•University Students	Bible	Arabic	nr	Islam	6579

Senegal

GROUP NAME	SCRIPTURE	LANGUAGE	GROUP SIZE	PRIMARY RELIGION	ID
Badyara	none	Badyara	1,200	Islam-Animist	8617
Balanta	portions	Balanta	63,700	Animism	1142
•Balanta Refugees	+portions	Balanta	60,000	Animism	9030

-279-

GROUP NAME	LANGUAGE	SCRIPTURE	PRIMARY RELIGION	GROUP SIZE	ID
Bambara	Bambara	Bible	Animism	40,000	8618
Banyum	Banyum	none	Islam-Animist	17,000	5421
Bassari	Bassari	+none	Animism	12,000	5422
Bayot	Bayot	none	Islam-Animist	1,800	5423
Bedik	Bedik	none	Animism	2,000	5566
Diola	Diola	portions	Islam-Animist	320,000	434
Fulbe (Cunda)	Fufulde, Cunda	none	Islam	930,900	2262
Fuuta Jalon	Fuuta Jalon	portions	Islam	100,000	8619
Mandinka	Malinke, Senegalese	portions	Islam-Animist	298,900	1138
Manjack	Mandjak	none	Roman Catholic	67,100	1140
Mankanya	Mankanya	none	Islam-Animist	54,900	5425
Maure	Arabic, Hassinya	none	Islam	73,200	723
Sarakole	Soninke	none	Islam	91,100	1139
Tandanke	Tandanke	none	Animism	1,000	1145
*Tidjiane Muslims	Wolof	not reported	Islam	1,100,000	412
*Toucouleur	Toucouleur	portions	Islam	602,700	1137
*University Students in Dakar	French	+Bible,NT,OT	Islam	20,000	250
Wolof	Wolof	NT,portions	Islam-Animist	2,100,300	96

Sierra Leone

GROUP NAME	LANGUAGE	SCRIPTURE	PRIMARY RELIGION	GROUP SIZE	ID
Bullom, Northern	Bullom, Northern	portions	Islam-Animist	167,000	5428
Bullom, Southern	Bullom, Southern	portions	Islam-Animist	40,000	5429
Fula	Fula	portions	Islam	250,000	4035
Gola	Mende	portions	Islam-Animist	1,000	5430
Kissi	Kissi, Southern	not reported	Animism	60,000	271
Kono	Kono	portions,stories,tracts	Animism	130,000	203
Koranko	Kuranko (Maninka)	NT,portions	Islam-Animist	100,000	201
Krim	Mende	none	Islam-Animist	3,000	5432
Loko	Loko	portions	Animism	80,000	586
Maninka	Maninka	portions,NT	Islam-Animist	64,000	5434
Mende	Mende	Bible	Islam	1,100,000	585
Susu	Susu	portions	Islam-Animist	90,000	5435
Temne	Temne	New Testament	Animism	1,000,000	123
Vai	Vai	portions	Islam-Animist	3,000	5436
Yalunka	Yalunka	+NT,tracts	Islam-Animist	25,000	455

GROUP NAME	SCRIPTURE	LANGUAGE	GROUP SIZE	PRIMARY RELIGION	ID
Sikkim					
Lepcha	New Testament	Lepcha	18,000	Hindu-Buddhist	2127
Singapore					
•Elderly Cantonese Spkg Chinese	Bible	Cantonese	100,000	Traditional Chinese	8668
•English Speaking Community	+Bible,OT,NT	English	200,000	Secularism	4842
•Handicapped	+Bible	Chinese Dialects	10,000	Traditional Chinese	8638
•Hindu	Bible	Tamil	15,000	Hinduism	8669
Merchants-Serangoon Ar					
•Industrial Workers	Bible	English	250,000	Buddhism	8667
•Malay Construction Workers	+New Testament	Malay	8,300	Islam	221
Malays	New Testament	Hokkien	300,000	Islam	120
•Prostitutes	Bible	Hokkien	nr	Unknown	8672
•Secret Society Members	+Bible	Hokkien	10,000	Traditional Chinese	218
•Tamil Muslims	Bible	Tamil	nr	Islam	8670
•Tamils	Bible,NT	Tamil	204,000	Hinduism	4841
•Teen-age School Dropouts	Bible	Hokkien	nr	Unknown	2117
•Thai Construction Workers	Bible	Thai	20,000	Buddhism	8671
Somalia					
•Ethiopian Refugees	+Bible	Oromo	700,000	Islam	9027
Somalis	Bible,NT	Somali	3,400,000	Islam	418
South Africa					
•Cape Malays	+Bible	Afrikaans	185,000	Islam	5006
•Indian Hindus	+Bible	Telegu	535,000	Hinduism	11
•Indian Muslims	Bible	Urdu	170,000	Islam	8690
Ndebele in Kwandebele	+NT,OT,portions	Sindebele (N.Sotho)	40,000	Other Christian	66

GROUP NAME	SCRIPTURE	LANGUAGE	GROUP SIZE	PRIMARY RELIGION	ID
• Zanzibari Muslims, Chatsworth	OT,portions	Makua	1,000	Islam	8682
Spain					
• Gypsies	Bible	Romany	200,000	Folk Religion	393
• Lao Refugees	+Bible	Lao	1,000	Buddhist-Animist	9056
• Pension Students-Madrid	+Bible	Italian	2,000	Secularism	5032
Sri Lanka					
• Indian Tamils - Colombo	+Bible	Tamil	nr	Hindu-Animist	5004
Malays	Bible	Malay	42,000	Islam	1423
Moors	Bible	Tamil	1,000,000	Islam	309
Sinhalese, Kandyan	Bible	Sinhalese	4,231,000	Buddhism	1420
Sinhalese, Low Country	Bible	Sinhala	6,890,000	Buddhism	286
• Slum Dwellers in Colombo	Bible,NT	Tamil	351,000	Buddhism	1421
Veddahs	not reported	Veddah	1,000	Unknown	1424
Sudan					
Afitti	none	Afitti	3,000	Islam	5439
Aja	none	Aja	1,000	Islam	5440
Anuak	New Testament	Anuak	30,000	Animism	584
Atuot	none	Atuot	8,000	Islam	5441
Bai	none	Bai	3,000	Islam	5443
Baka	portions	Baka	23,000	Animism	5329
Beja, Bisharin	portions	Beja	15,000	Islam	5446
Beja, Hadendoa	portions	Beja	60,000	Islam	399
Binga	none	Binga	1,000	Islam	5450
Burun	none	Burun	5,000	Islam	5452
• Chadian Refugees	Bible	Tribal Languages	100,000	Islam	459
Dair	none	Dair	200	Islam	5454
Daju,Darfur	none	Daju	12,000	Animism	5455
Daju,West Kordofan	none	Daju	6,000	Islam	5456
Dar Hamid	Bible	Arabic	160,000	Islam	5458
Didinga	portions	Didinga	58,000	Animism	583
Dinka	+New Testament	Dinka	1,940,000	Animism	582
• Eritrean Refugees	+not reported	Galla	150,000	Islam	9007

GROUP NAME	LANGUAGE	SCRIPTURE	GROUP SIZE	PRIMARY RELIGION	ID
•Eritrean Refugees (Rural)	Tigre	+New Testament	300,000	Islam	9008
Fulbe	Fulfulde, Bagirmi	none	90,000	Islam	705
Fungor	Fungor	none	5,000	Animism	5472
Fur	Fur	none	380,000	Islam	706
Gberi	Gberi	none	600	Islam	5473
Ghulfan	Ghulfan	none	3,000	Islam	5474
Golo	Golo	none	3,000	Unknown	5447
Gumuz	Gumuz	none	40,000	Islam	5475
Ingassana	Tabi	none	35,000	Animism	581
Inyimang	Inyimang	portions	70,000	Islam	5448
Kababish	Arabic	Bible	nr	Islam	402
Kadugli	Kadugli	none	47,000	Islam	5477
Kanga	Kanga	none	6,000	Islam	5479
Karko	Karko	none	2,000	Islam	5480
Katla	Katla	none	22,000	Islam	5482
Keiga	Keiga	none	6,000	Islam	5483
Keiga Jirru	Keiga Jirru	none	1,000	Islam	5484
Kenuzi-Dongola	Kenuzi-Dongola	portions	170,000	Islam	5459
Koma, Central	Koma, Central	none	3,000	Islam	5489
Kresh	Kresh	portions	16,000	Islam	5485
Krongo	Krongo	portions	15,000	Animism	579
Lafofa	Lafofa	NT,portions	2,000	Islam	5494
Lapit	Lopit	not reported	20,000	Syncretic Christian	8621
Laro	Laro	+none	4,000	Islam	5495
Maba	Maba	none	9,000	Islam	5498
Mararit	Mararit	none	42,000	Islam	5487
Masakin	Masakin	none	38,000	Islam	5501
Masalit	Arabic	none	115,000	Islam	5502
Meidob	Midob	none	2,000	Islam	5503
Miri	Miri	none	8,000	Islam	5504
Moro Hills	Moro Hills	none	3,800	Unknown	5488
Morokodo	Morokodo	none	4,600	Unknown	5490
Murle	Murle	portions	60,000	Animism	577
Njalgulgule	Njalgulgule	none	900	Islam	5513
Nuer	Nuer	New Testament	844,000	Animism	576
Qimant	Qimant	Bible	17,000	Unknown	5521
Shatt	Shatt	none	4,000	Islam	5516
Shilluk	Shilluk	+NT,portions	175,000	Animism	5517
•Sudanese Repatriates	Tribal Languages	+portions	1,000,000	Animism	9009

GROUP NAME	SCRIPTURE	LANGUAGE	GROUP SIZE	PRIMARY RELIGION	ID
Sungor	none	Sungor	9,000	Islam	5520
Tagoi	none	Tagoi	13,000	Islam	5508
Talodi	none	Talodi	1,000	Islam	5522
Tama	none	Tama	60,000	Islam	5507
Tegali	none	Tegali	80,000	Islam	5523
Temein	none	Temein	2,300	Islam	5524
Tenext	+portions	Murle	2,000	Animism	8639
Thuri	none	Thuri	154,000	Islam	5525
Tira	none	Tira	40,000	Islam	5526
Tulishi	none	Tulishi	9,000	Islam	5528
Tumma	none	Tumma	5,000	Islam	5529
Tumtum	none	Tumtum	7,000	Islam	5530
•Ugandan Refugees	+Bible	Swahili	100,000	Animism	9048
Yulu	portions	Yulu	2,000	Islam	5531
Zaghawa	none	Arabic	105,000	Islam	5532
Zande	Bible	Zande	350,000	Animism	5461

Surinam

GROUP NAME	SCRIPTURE	LANGUAGE	GROUP SIZE	PRIMARY RELIGION	ID
Javanese	Bible,NT	Javanese	60,000	Islam-Animist	12
Matawari	none	Matawari	1,000	Animism	5130
Wayana	portions	Wayana	600	Animism	5133

Switzerland

GROUP NAME	SCRIPTURE	LANGUAGE	GROUP SIZE	PRIMARY RELIGION	ID
•Americans in Geneva	Bible	English	45,000	Secularism	4118
•Auberge Crowd in Geneva	+Bible	Arabic	200	Secularism	5002
•Tibetan Refugees	+Bible	Tibetan	1,000	Buddhism	9015
•Turks in Basel	+Bible	Kurdish	3,000	Islam	5011

-284-

GROUP NAME	SCRIPTURE	LANGUAGE	GROUP SIZE	PRIMARY RELIGION	ID
Syria					
Alawites	Bible	Arabic	600,000	Islam	1104
Yezidi	OT,NT,portions	Kirmanji Kurdish	10,000	Other	80
Taiwan					
Chinese Hakka	Bible	Hakka	3,500,000	Traditional Chinese	746
Chinese Mainlanders	Bible	Mandarin	2,000,000	Traditional Chinese	85
•Chinese Muslims	Bible	Mandarin	45,000	Islam	7019
•Deviant Youth in Taipei	+Bible	Chinese, Min-Nan	80,000	Folk Religion	5044
Fishing Village People	Bible	Amoy	150,000	Traditional Chinese	2107
Industrial Workers	+Bible	Taiwanese (Hoklo)	3,500,000	Animism	4121
•Taiwan-Chinese Un. Stud.	not reported	Mandarin	310,000	Secularism	7038
Tsou	none	Tsou	4,000	Animism	7035
•Women Laborers	Bible	Amoy	1,200,000	Traditional Chinese	2115
Tanzania					
Arusha	New Testament	Arusha	110,000	Christianity	142
Barabaig	none	Tatoga	49,000	Animism	573
Baraguyu	+NT,portions	Maa	30,000	Animism	8632
•Burundian Hutu Refugees	+Bible	Kirundi	120,000	Animism	9006
Burungi	none	Burungi	20,000	Animism	493
Dhaiso	Bible	Dhaiso	19,000	Christianity	5538
Digo	none	Digo	48,000	Islam	5539
Dorobo	none	Hadza	3,000	Animism	490
Iraqw	portions	Iraqw.	218,000	Animism	492
Kisankasa	none	Kisankasa	6,000	Christianity	5561
Maasai	Bible,OT,NT	Maasai	116,000	Animism	477
Makonde	not reported	Makonde	550,000	Islam	144
Makua	portions,OT	Makua	3,000,000	Islam	8686
Malila	none	Malila	24,800	Christianity	5570
Ndengereko	none	Ndengereko	89,000	Christianity	5583
Ndomde	none	Ndomde	20,000	Christianity	5584
Ngasa	none	Ngasa	1,670	Christianity	5585
Ruihi	none	Ruihi	119,000	Christianity	5599
Safwa	New Testament	Safwa	100,000	Animism	486
Sonjo	none	Sonjo	7,000	Animism	217

GROUP NAME	SCRIPTURE	LANGUAGE	GROUP SIZE	PRIMARY RELIGION	ID
Wasi	none	Wasi	20,000	Christianity	5616
Yao	Bible	Yao	205,000	Islam	8689
Zaramo	portions	Zaramo	300,000	Islam	147
Zigwa	portions	Zigwa	187,000	Christianity	5619
Zinza	none	Kizinza	2,000	Animism	1210

Thailand

GROUP NAME	SCRIPTURE	LANGUAGE	GROUP SIZE	PRIMARY RELIGION	ID
Akha	NT,portions	Lahu	16,000	Ancestor Worship	609
Bisu	none	Bisu	400	Buddhist-Animist	292
•Blind Persons	portions	Northeast Thai	100,000	Buddhist-Animist	4810
Blue Hmong	NT,portions	Meo	28,000	Animism	610
Cambodians	portions	Northern Kamer	1,000,000	Buddhist-Animist	606
Central Thailand Farmers	Bible	Chinese (Teochu)	5,000,000	Buddhist-Animist	645
Chinese	Bible	Hakka	3,600,000	Traditional Chinese	749
Chong	none	Chong	1,500	Animism	438
•Government officials	Bible	Thai	100,000	Buddhism	59
•Hmong Refugee Women, Ban Vinai	+Bible	Miao	12,000	Buddhist-Animist	9003
Indians	not reported	Tamil	nr	Hinduism	460
Kalerng	portions	Kalerng (Phu Tai)	nr	Animism	783
Karen, Pwo	portions	Pwo Karen	40,000	Animism	30
Kensiu-Senoi	none	Kensiu	300	Animism	766
Khamu	portions	Khamu	6,000	Animism	2087
•Khmer Refugees	Bible	Cambodia	30,000	Buddhist-Animist	2094
•Khmer Refugees, Unaccd. Minors	not reported	Khmer	3,000	Buddhist-Animist	9050
Khmer, Northern	portions	Khmer, Northern	1,000,000	Buddhist-Animist	470
Khun	portions,NT	Khun Shan	20,000	Buddhism	471
Kui	New Testament	Kui	160,000	Buddhist-Animist	607
Lahu,Black	Bible	Lahu	10,000	Animism	2088
•Lao Refugees	+portions	Lao	20,000	Buddhist-Animist	2090
Lao Song	New Testament	Lao-Song	20,000	Buddhist-Animist	75
Lawa, Eastern	New Testament	Tibeto-Burman Dialect	4,000	Buddhist-Animist	7039
Lawa, Mountain	New Testament	Lawa	7,650	Buddhist-Animist	612
•Lepers of Cen. Thailand	Bible	Thai	20,000	Buddhist-Animist	7003
•Lepers of N.E. Thailand	Bible	Northeast Thai	200,000	Buddhism	236
Lu	New Testament	Lu	53,000	Animism	2815
Mien	portions	Mien (Yao)	31,150	Animism	611

GROUP NAME	SCRIPTURE	LANGUAGE	PRIMARY RELIGION	GROUP SIZE	ID
Moken	none	Local dialects	Animism	6,400	2092
Moklen	none	Moklen	Animism	1,900	726
Mon	Bible	Mon	Animism	106,000	727
Mpi	none	Mpi (Bisu)	Animism	600	728
Mrabri	none	Mrabri	Animism	2,000	729
Nyaw	Bible	Nyaw	Animism	32,500	730
•Pattaya Hotel Workers	+Bible,OT,NT	Thai	Buddhist-Animist	5,000	40
Phu Thai	none	Phu Thai	Buddhist-Animist	53,000	4809
•Ramkamhaeng Un. Students	Bible	Thai	Buddhism	200,000	4053
Saek	none	Saek	Animism	300	763
Shan	NT,OT,Bible	Shan	Buddhist-Animist	32,000	2086
•Slum Dwellers of Bangkok	Bible	Thai	Buddhism	45,000	4052
Soh	portions	Soh	Animism	21,000	2091
T'in	NT	T'in	Animism	25,000	81
T'in Pray (Thung Chan)	portions	T'in Pray	Animism	4,000	767
•Tai, Black, Refugees	portions	Tai, Black	nr	nr	772
Tai, Central(Siamese)	Bible,portions	Tai, Standard	Animism	31,750,000	770
Tai, Isan (Laotian)	Bible,portions	Laotian	Animism	15,900,000	774
Tai, Khorat	none	Tai, Khorat	Animism	415,000	775
Tai, Northern	Bible	Tai, Northern	Animism	6,350,000	768
Tai, Southern	none	Tai, Southern	Animism	4,232,000	771
•Thai Islam (Malay)	portions,NT	Malay, Pattani	Islam-Animist	1,000,000	39
•Thai Islam (Thai)	none	Thai, Southern	Islam-Animist	600,000	2093
•Thai University Students	Bible	Thai	Buddhism	105,000	7015
•Vietnamese Refugees	not reported	Vietnamese	Buddhism	140,000	2083
White Hmong	NT,OT	Meo, Hmong Daw	Buddhist-Animist	25,000	440
•Yao Refugees from Laos	none	Yao	Animism	7,000	2097
Yoy	portions	Yoy	Animism	900	781

Togo

GROUP NAME	SCRIPTURE	LANGUAGE	PRIMARY RELIGION	GROUP SIZE	ID
Basari	New Testament	Ntcham	Animism	50,400	599
Chakossi	none	Chakossi	Animism	42,000	598
Fulbe	portions	Fulfulde, Benin-Togo	Islam	41,500	8623
Gangam	none	Gangam	Animism	19,711	5628
Gourma	NT,portions	Gourma	Animism	20,611	8624
Hausa	Bible	Hausa	Islam	8,400	8625
Konkomba	not reported	Kom Komba	Animism	61,600	253
Lamba	-New Testament	Lamba	Animism	92,400	425

GROUP NAME	SCRIPTURE	LANGUAGE	GROUP SIZE	PRIMARY RELIGION	ID
Moba	portions	Bimoba	140,000	Animism	597
Tem	none	Tem (Kotokoli, Krachi)	150,000	Islam	596
Watchi	Bible	Ge	279,500	Animism	424

Turkey

GROUP NAME	SCRIPTURE	LANGUAGE	GROUP SIZE	PRIMARY RELIGION	ID
Abazin	none	Abazin	30,000	Islam	1209
Abkhaz	portions	Abkhaz	15,000	Islam	2540
Albanian, Tosk	New Testament	Albanian, Tosk	61,000	Islam	5551
Arabs	New Testament	Turkish	810,000	Islam	5640
Azerbaijani	Bible,NT	Azerbaijani	530,000	Islam	5885
Circassian	portions	Turkish	137,000	Islam	2541
Crimean Tatar	New Testament	Turkish	325,000	Islam	5887
Georgian	Bible,NT	Georgian	91,000	Islam	5888
•Greeks in Istanbul	Bible,NT	Greek	8,000	Orthodox	5889
Gypsy	none	Romany	22,000	Folk Religion	2542
Kabardian	New Testament	Kabardian	nr	Islam	5890
•Kazakh Afghan Refugees	Bible,OT,NT	Kazakh	611	Islam	2108
•Kazakhs in Kayseri	Bible,NT,OT	Kazakh	8,360	Islam	433
•Kirghiz Afghan Refugees	+portions,OT,NT	Kirghiz	1,400	Islam	9060
Kurds	portions,NT	Turkish	5,500,000	Islam	180
Ladino	Bible	Turkish	20,000	Judaism	5891
Laz	Bible,NT	Laz	92,000	Islam	5892
Osetin	portions,NT	Osetin	nr	Orthodox	5893
Pomak	Bible,NT	Bulgarian, Pomak	76,500	Islam	5886
Serbo-Croatian	Bible,NT	Serbo-Croatian	61,000	Islam	5894
Shikaki	none	Shikaki	nr	Islam	5895
Tatar	portions	Tatar	7,000	Islam	5896
•Turkmen Afghan Refugees	Bible,OT,NT	Turkmen	858	Islam	2138
Turks, Anatolian	Bible	Turkish, Osmanli	44,500,000	Islam	4022
•Turks,Anatolian in Istanbul	+Bible	Turkish, Osmanli	2,500,000	Islam	5041
Uighur	Bible,OT,NT	Uighur	2,000	Islam	2167
•Uzbek Afghan Refugees	Bible,OT,NT	Uzbek	1,905	Islam	2110
•Uzbek in Istanbul	Bible,OT,NT	Uzbek	nr	Islam	2109
Yazidi Kurds	Bible,NT	Kirmanji	nr	Other	2190
Yoruk	Bible	Turkish (Danubian)	9,000	Islam	4048

GROUP NAME	LANGUAGE	SCRIPTURE	GROUP SIZE	PRIMARY RELIGION	ID
USSR (Soviet Union)					
Abazin	Abazin	none	25,000	Islam	5821
Adygei	Adygei	not reported	100,000	Islam	5811
Agul	Agul	none	9,000	Islam	5823
Akhavakh	Akhavakh	none	5,000	Unknown	5824
Alutor	Alutor	none	2,000	Unknown	5825
Andi	Andi	none	9,000	Unknown	5826
Archin	Archin	none	900	Unknown	5827
Balkars	Balkar	not reported	60,000	Islam	5813
Bashkir	Tatar	portions	1,200,000	Islam	4001
Batsi	Batsi	none	3,000	Unknown	5828
Botlikh	Botlikh	none	4,000	Unknown	5829
Budug	Budug	none	2,000	Unknown	5830
Buriat	Buriat	portions	315,000	Buddhist-Animist	5831
Chamalin	Chamalin	none	6,000	Unknown	5832
Chechen	Chechen	portions	756,000	Islam	8641
Cherkess	Cherkess	not reported	40,000	Islam	5814
Chukot	Chukot	none	14,000	Unknown	5833
Dargin	Dargin	portions	231,000	Islam	5834
Didoi	Didoi	none	7,000	Unknown	5835
Dungan	Dungan	none	39,000	Islam	5836
Evenks	Evenk	none	25,000	Buddhist-Animist	5837
Gilyak	Gilyak	none	4,000	Unknown	5839
Ingushes	Ingush	none	158,000	Islam	5840
Kabardinian	Kabardinian	not reported	368,000	Islam	8643
Kalmytz	Kalmytz	NT,portions	137,000	Buddhism	5844
Kapuchin	Kapuchin	none	3,000	Unknown	5845
Karachay	Karachay-Balkan	New Testament	173,000	Islam-Animist	4042
Karagas	Karagas	none	600	Unknown	5846
Karaim	Karaim	none	1,000	Unknown	5847
Karakalpak	Karakalpak	not reported	277,000	Islam	4011
Karatin	Karatin	none	6,000	Unknown	5849
Kazakhs	Kazakh	NT,portions	6,900,000	Islam	5630
Ket	Ket	none	1,200	Animism	5850
Khanti	Khanti	portions	21,000	Unknown	5852
Khinalug	Khinalug	none	2,000	Unknown	5853
Khvarshin	Khvarshin	none	2,000	Unknown	5854
Kirgiz	Kirgiz	not reported	1,700,000	Islam-Animist	4016

GROUP NAME	SCRIPTURE	LANGUAGE	GROUP SIZE	PRIMARY RELIGION	ID
Koreans	+Bible,NT,OT,portions	Korean	600,000	Secularism	1339
Koryak	none	Koryak	8,000	Unknown	5857
Kryz	none	Kryz	6,000	Unknown	5858
Kumyk	not reported	Kumyk	220,000	Islam	8645
Kushan	none	Rushani(Rushan Valley)USSR	nr	Islam	2836
Kvanadin	none	Kvanadin	6,000	Unknown	5859
Lakians	not reported	Lakian	86,000	Islam	5812
Lezgin	not reported	Lezgin	383,000	Islam	8646
Mansi	portions	Mansi	8,000	Unknown	5861
Mingat	none	Mingat	4,000	Unknown	5863
Nanai	portions	Nanai	12,000	Unknown	5864
Nentsy	not reported	Nentsy	29,000	Unknown	5815
Nganasan	none	Nganasan	1,000	Unknown	5865
Oroch	none	Oroch	1,000	Unknown	5866
Orok	none	Orok	400	Unknown	5867
Rutul	none	Rutul	12,000	Islam	5868
Selkup	none	Selkup	4,000	Unknown	5869
Tabasaran	none	Tabasaran	55,000	Islam	5872
Tajik	portions	Persian (Tajiki)	2,500,000	Islam	4041
Tat	portions	Tat	17,000	Islam	5873
Tatars	Bible	Tatar dialects	6,000,000	Islam	4008
Tindin	none	Tat	5,000	Unknown	5874
Tsakhur	none	Tsakhur	11,000	Islam	5875
Tuvinian	none	Tuvin	139,000	Buddhist-Animist	5876
Udegeis	portions	Udegeis	1,400	Animism	5877
Udin	not reported	Udin	4,000	Unknown	5878
Ulchi	New Testament	Ulchi	2,000	Unknown	5818
Uzbeks	not reported	Uzbek	12,500,000	Islam	8647
Yagnobi	none	Yagnobi	2,000	Unknown	5881
Yazgulyam	not reported	Yazgulyam	2,000	Unknown	5882
Yukagirs	none	Yukagir	nr	Unknown	5820
Yurak	none	Yurak	29,000	Unknown	5883

Uganda

GROUP NAME	SCRIPTURE	LANGUAGE	GROUP SIZE	PRIMARY RELIGION	ID
Ik	-none	Ik	5,000	Animism	71
Jiye	none	Karamojong-Jie dialect	50,000	Animism	494
Kakwa	New Testament	Kakwa	73,000	Animism	5643
•Kenyi of Lake Kyoga	none	Kenyia	10,000	Animism	531

GROUP NAME	SCRIPTURE	LANGUAGE	PRIMARY RELIGION	GROUP SIZE	ID
Kumam	portions	Kumam	Animism	80,000	5644
Labwor	none	Labwor	Animism	nr	1067
Lendu	none	Lendu	Animism	25,000	5677
• Muslims (West Nile Dist.)	Bible	Lugbara	Islam	1,200,000	238
Napore	none	Napore	Animism	12,000	530
Napore-Nyangea	none	Napore-Nyangea	Animism	12,000	5328
Nyakwai	none	Nyakwai	Animism	12,000	5332
Okebo	none	Okebo	Animism	14,115	5686
Palwo	none	Palwo	Animism	18,500	714
Pokot	New Testament	Pokot	Animism	45,000	368
Teuso	none	Teuso	Animism	12,000	3233

United Arab Emirates

GROUP NAME	SCRIPTURE	LANGUAGE	PRIMARY RELIGION	GROUP SIZE	ID
• Indians in Dubai	+Bible	Malayalam	Hinduism	24,000	5047
• Muslims	Bible	Arabic	Islam	752,000	365
Shihu	none	Shihu	Islam	10,000	2543

United Kingdom

GROUP NAME	SCRIPTURE	LANGUAGE	PRIMARY RELIGION	GROUP SIZE	ID
Bengalis in London	+Bible	Bengali	Islam	15,000	5038
Chinese Students	Bible	Mandarin	Traditional Chinese	110,000	1225
Chinese Students Glasgow	Bible	Mandarin	Traditional Chinese	1,000	2078
Gujarati	Bible	Gujarati	Hinduism	300,000	1239
• Muslim Immigrants	not reported	Large Number of Asian	Islam	500,000	1099
Sylhetti	none	Sylhetti	Islam	150,000	6566
• Ugandan Refugees	+Bible	English	Islam	27,000	9021

United States of America

GROUP NAME	SCRIPTURE	LANGUAGE	PRIMARY RELIGION	GROUP SIZE	ID
• Arabs in New Orleans	+Bible	Arabic	Islam	1,000	5008
• Bengali, Los Angeles area	Bible	English	Islam	4,000	4818
• Cambodians in Long Beach	NT,OT	Cambodian Khmer	Buddhism	25,000	417
• Casual Laborers-Atlanta	+Bible	English	Secularism	3,000	5048
• Chicanos in Denver	+Bible	Spanish	Roman Catholic	121,000	5029
• Chinese in Boston	+Bible	Mandarin	Secularism	20,000	5019
• Chinese in Portland	OT,NT	Cantonese	Buddhism	20,000	42
• Ex-Mental Patients in NYC	+Bible	Spanish	Secularism	20,000	5007
• Gays in San Francisco	+Bible	English	Secularism	150,000	5010

GROUP NAME	SCRIPTURE	LANGUAGE	GROUP SIZE	PRIMARY RELIGION	ID
• Haitian Refugees	+Bible	Creole	40,000	Folk Religion	9044
• Hispanics in Paso Robles	Bible,OT,NT	Spanish	1,000	Roman Catholic	43
• Hmong Refugees	+Bible	Miao	35,000	Buddhist-Animist	9055
• Hmong, Twin Cities	+Bible	Miao	11,000	Roman Catholic	9034
• Homosexuals of W.Hollywood	+Bible,OT,NT,portions	English	40,000	Secularism	1344
• India Hindus in New York City	+portions,OT,NT	Hindi	150,000	Hinduism	117
• Japanese Students In USA	Bible	Japanese	nr	Secularism	54
• Japanese, New York City	+Bible	Japanese	20,400	Protestant	70
• K'anjobal of Los Angeles	portions	K'anjobal	5,000	Syncretic Christian	8500
• Koreans in So. California	NT,OT,Bible	Korean	200,000	Buddhism	349
• Lao Refugees, Los Angeles	not reported	English	5,000	Buddhism	174
• Marielito Refugees in Florida	Bible	Spanish	125,000	Secularism	6565
• Nurses in St. Louis	+Bible	English	3,000	Secularism	5031
• Pakistani Muslim, Los Angeles	OT,NT,Bible	Urdu	12,000	Islam	187
• Pro Hockey Players	+Bible	English	600	Secularism	5020
• Racetrack Residents	Bible	Spanish	50,000	Secularism	476
• Rajneeshees of Oregon	+Bible	English	1,000	New Eastern	4806
• Taiwanse in Los Angeles	portions,NT,OT	Taiwanese	60,000	Animism	427
• Thai Immigrants, Los Angeles	+Bible	Central Thai	60,000	Buddhism	4813
• Urban Elite Vietnamese	+Bible	Vietnamese	90,000	Ancestor Worship	9035
• Urban Street Women/Los Angeles	+Bible	Spanish	100	Secularism	4826
• Vietnamese Fishermen, Biloxi	+Bible	Vietnamese	1,300	Roman Catholic	4835
• Vietnamese Refugees	Bible	Vietnamese	2,700,000	Buddhism	1222
• Vietnamese, Refugees, Orange Cy	+Bible	English	70,000	Protestant	239
• Wandering Homeless	+Bible	English	15,000	Secularism	4804
• Zuni	portions	English	6,000	Animism	410

GROUP NAME	SCRIPTURE	LANGUAGE	GROUP SIZE	PRIMARY RELIGION	ID
Venezuela					
Yanomamo	portions	Shamatali	nr	Animism	2024
Yuana	none	Yuana	300	Animism	5146
Viet Nam					
Blue Hmong	NT,OT	Hmong Njua (Meo)	311,000	Animism	457
Cham	portions	Cham	45,000	Hindu-Animist	272
Lu	New Testament	Lu	1,150	Buddhist-Animist	717
Nung (Thai)	portions	Thai Nung	50,000	Animism	797
•Street Vendors in Saigon	+Bible	Vietnamese	nr	Buddhist-Animist	5035
Tai, Red	none	Red Tai	25,000	Animism	799
Tai, White	portions	White Tai	100,000	Animism	798
Yemen, Arab Republic					
•Akhdam Low Caste Tradesmen	Bible	Arabic	nr	Islam-Animist	4064
•Ethiopian Refugees, Yemen	+not reported	Tigre	480	not reported	9040
•Shafi Univ.Students at Zabid	Bible	Arabic	nr	Islam	6573
•Shafii Commercial Enterprisers	New Testament	Arabic (Eastern)	nr	Islam	1061
Somali	Bible,NT	Somali	nr	Islam	6594
•Tribal Chiefs	Bible	Arabic	nr	Islam	6575
•Tribal Villagers & Farmers	Bible	Arabic	nr	Islam	6574
•Zaydi Imams	Bible	Arabic	nr	Islam	6572

GROUP NAME	SCRIPTURE	LANGUAGE	GROUP SIZE	PRIMARY RELIGION	ID
• Zaydi-Sayyid Political Elite	Bible	Arabic	nr	Islam	4067

Yemen, Democratic

GROUP NAME	SCRIPTURE	LANGUAGE	GROUP SIZE	PRIMARY RELIGION	ID
• Adenese Merchant/Prof. Class	Bible	Arabic	nr	Islam	4894
• Adenese Shopkeepers & Laborers	Bible	Arabic	nr	Islam	4893
• Adenese Upper Class Merchants	Bible	Arabic	nr	Islam	4895
• Bedouin	Bible	Arabic	nr	Islam	4899
• Despised Caste Artisans	Bible	Arabic	nr	Islam	4897
• Mahrah	none	Local dialects	50,000	Islam	4066
• Mashaykh Tribal Leaders	Bible	Arabic	nr	Islam	4891
• Rural Artisan & Merchant Class	Bible	Arabic	nr	Islam	4892
• Rural Poor Farm Laborers	Bible	Arabic	nr	Islam	4898
• Rural Villagers and Farmers	Bible	Arabic	nr	Islam	4065
• Secularist Political Leaders	Bible	Arabic	nr	Islam	4896
• Shafii Sayyid Elite	Bible	Arabic	nr	Islam	4890
• Union of Yemeni Women	Bible	Arabic	nr	Islam	4900

Yugoslavia

GROUP NAME	SCRIPTURE	LANGUAGE	GROUP SIZE	PRIMARY RELIGION	ID
Albanians	portions	Albanian (Gheg)	1,500,000	Islam	4036
Bosnian	Bible	Serbo-Croation	1,740,000	Islam	4004
• Muslim Gypsies in Skoplje	+not reported	Romany Dialects	23,000	Islam	5026
• Slavic Muslims	Bible	Serbocroatian	1,300,000	Islam	282

GROUP NAME	SCRIPTURE	LANGUAGE	GROUP SIZE	PRIMARY RELIGION	ID
Zambia					
• Luvale Refugees from Angola	+Bible	Luvale	11,000	Animism	9061
Zimbabwe					
Bushmen (Hiechware)	none	Ndbele	2,000	Animism	588
Indians	Bible	Gujarati	10,000	Hinduism	182

LAUSANNE COMMITTEE FOR WORLD EVANGELIZATION

One outcome of the International Congress on World Evangelization held in Lausanne, Switzerland, in the summer of 1974, was a mandate from the more than 2400 participants to form an ongoing committee. The "spirit of Lausanne" was a powerful new thrust for completing the task of world evangelization. The Lausanne Committee for World Evangelization (LCWE) was born in a meeting in Mexico City in 1975. The Committee drew up a constitution, named 48 charter members, and elected Leighton Ford as president and Gottfried Osei-Mensah as executive secretary.

First major meeting of the Committee was in January, 1978. At that time it received a report from its Strategy Working Group on the concept of viewing the world as people groups. The Committee accepted the basic concept and determined that this should be the central focus of a Consultation on World Evangelization at Pattaya, Thailand, in 1980.

Six hundred participants and 230 consultants, observers and guests were present at Pattaya. As a result of that consultation, the decision was made to reaffirm the mandate of Lausanne and to continue the work of the movement.

At its 1984 meeting in Stuttgart, West Germany, LCWE announced its plans for a second International Congress for World Evangelization to be held in July, 1989.

A current listing of committee and working group members is as follows:

Lausanne Committee

Mr. Lucien Accad (Cyprus)
The Rev. Pierre Allard (Canada)
The Rt. Rev. Hakon Anderson (Norway)
Mr. Ramez Atallah (Egypt)
Dr. Saphir Athyal (India)
Mr. Menahem Benhayim (Israel)
The Rev. Wim Bouw (Netherlands)
Mrs. Vonette Bright (U.S.A.)
The Rev. Clive Calver (England)
The Rev. Brian Carrell (New Zealand)
Dr. Ruben Cavallero (Argentina)
Dr. Paul Cedar (U.S.A.)
The Rev. David Chan (Singapore)
The Rev. Jonathan Chiu (Taiwan)
Mr. Alain Choiquier (France)
The Rt. Rev. Sundar Clarke (India)
Dr. Wade Coggins (U.S.A.)
Dr. Robert Coleman (U.S.A.)
Mr. Charles Colson (U.S.A.)
The Rt. Rev. A. Jack Dain (Australia)
Mr. Gilberto da Silva (Brazil)
Mr. Ed Dayton (U.S.A.)
Miss Lancy Leigh DeMoss (U.S.A.)
Pastor Daidanso Ma Djongwe (Kenya)
Mr. Paul Eshleman (U.S.A.)
Mr. Ajith Fernando (Sri Lanka)
Dr. Leighton Ford (U.S.A.), Chairman
The Rev. Juan Gili (Spain)
The Rt. Rev. David Gitari (Kenya)
Mr. H. Richard Glaser (Brazil)
Dr. Michael Griffiths (England)
Dr. Michael Haynes (U.S.A.)

Daikon Fritz Hoffman (Germany)
Dr. Bill Hogue (U.S.A.)
Dr. Donald Hoke (U.S.A.)
Dr. George Hunter III (U.S.A.)
Mr. Kweku Hutchful (Ghana)
The Rev. Akira Izuta (Japan)
The Rt. Rev. Bashir Jiwan (Pakistan)
The Rev. James Katarikawe (Uganda)
Dr. Peter Kuzmic (Yugoslavia)
Mrs. Oknah Kim Lah (Korea)
Miss Ellie Lau (Hong Kong)
Dr. Lee Jong Yun (Korea)
Mr. Costas Macris (Greece)
The Rev. Fred Magbanua (Philippines)
Dr. Dirinda Marini-Bodho (Zaire)
The Rev. Horst Marquardt (Germany)
The Rev. John Matulessy (Indonesia)
The Rev. Jose Missena (Paraguay)
Miss Kirsti Mosvold (Norway)
The Rev. Inoke Nabulivou (Fiji)
The Rev. Makram Naguib (Egypt)
Dr. Claude Noel (Haiti)
Dr. Emilio Nunez (Guatemala)
Dr. Samuel Odunaike (Nigeria)
The Rev. Marcelino Ortiz (Mexico)
The Rev. Gottfried Osei-Mensah (England)
The Rev. Seikku Paunonen (Finland)
Miss Susan Perlman (U.S.A.)
The Rt. Rev. John Reid (Australia)
The Rev. D. John Richard (India)
The Rev. Eduardo Ruan (Venezuela)
The Rev. Jonathan Santos (Brazil)
Dekan Rolf Scheffbuch (Germany)
The Rev. Eliseu Semeao (Angola)
The Rev. Simon Sircar (Bangladesh)
The Rev. Alfredo Smith (Ecuador)
The Rev. Brian Stiller (Canada)

Mrs. Juliet Thomas (India)
Mr. John Tooke (South Africa)
Dr. C. Peter Wagner (U.S.A.)
The Rev. Thomas Wang (Hong Kong)
Miss Esther Waruiru (Kenya)
Dr. David Wells (U.S.A.)
Dr. Ursula Wiesemann (Cameroon)
Dr. Thomas Zimmerman (U.S.A.)

Honorary Life Member

Dr. Billy Graham (U.S.A.), Ex-Officio

Lausanne Committee Alternates

Dr. Tokunboh Adeyemo (Kenya)
Dr. Bukovsky Akos (Hungary)
The Rev. Luis Bush (U.S.A.)
The Rev. Jonathan Chao (Hong Kong)
The Rt. Rev. Luke Chhoa (Malaysia)
The REv. David Cohen (England)
Mr. Petru Dugulescu (Romania)
Mr. Eric Gay (Switzerland)
Dr. Robert Hamblin (U.S.A.)
Dr. Cyril Horak (Czechoslovakia)
Dr. Erwin Kolb, (U.S.A.)
Mrs. Iqbal K. Massey (Cyprus)
Mr. Caesar Molebatsi (South Africa)
Pastor Victor Musa (Nigeria)
The Rt. Rev. Michael Nazir-Ali (Pakistan)
Dr. John Olley (Australia)
The Rev. Samuel Olson (Venezuela)
The Rt. Rev. Shantu Kumar Parmar (India)
Mr. Hans-Gunther Sachse (Germany)
Mr. George Samuel (India)
The Rev. Viggo Sogaard (Denmark)
The Rev. Valdir Steuernagel (U.S.A.)

The Rev. Elon Svanell (Sweden)
The Rev. Carmelo Terranova (Puerto Rico)
The Rev. Tite Tienou (U.S.A.)
Dr. Jan Urban (Czechoslovakia)
The Rev. Jun Vencer (Philippines)
Dr. Warren Webster (U.S.A.)
Dr. Henryk Wieja (Poland)
Dr. Ravi Zacharias (U.S.A.)

Communications Advisory Group

Dr. Sigurd Aske (Norway)
The Rev. Horst Marquardt (Germany)
Dr. Viggo Sogaard (Denmark)

Intercession Advisory Group

Mrs. Vonette Bright (U.S.A.)
Mr. David Bryant (U.S.A.)
Miss Nancy Leigh DeMoss (U.S.A.)
Mr. Eric Gay (Switzerland)
Mr. Juan Gili (Spain)
Daikon Fritz Hoffman (Germany)
Mr. James Katarikawe (Uganda)
Mrs. Oknah Kim Lah (Korea)
Mr. D. John Richard (India)
The Rev. Jonathan Santos (Brazil)

Strategy Working Group

Dr. Ray Bakke (U.S.A.)
The Rev. David Chan (Singapore)
Mr. Ed Dayton (U.S.A.)
The Rev. Richard Glaser (Brazil)
Dr. Robert Hamblin (U.S.A.)
The Rev. Patrick Johnstone (England)
Mr. Fred Magbanua (Philippines)

The Rev. Don McCurry (U.S.A.)
The Rev. Samuel Olson (Venezuela)
Miss Susan Perlman (U.S.A.)
Dr. Viggo Sogaard (Denmark)
Miss Esther Waruiru (Kenya)

Theology Working Group

Dr. Saphir Athyal (India)
Dr. Tormod Engelsviken (Norway)
The Rev. Akira Izuta (Japan)
The Rev. Peter Kuzmic (Yugoslavia)
Dr. Agne Nordlander (Sweden)
Dr. Emilio Nunez (Guatemala)
The Rev. Gottfried Osei-Mensah (England)
The Rt. Rev. John Reid (Australia)
The Rev. Tite Tienou (U.S.A.)
Dr. David Wells (U.S.A.)

Lausanne Office

The Rev. Thomas Wang, International Director
    LCWE
    Fairview Plaza 3
    5950 Fairview Rd. Suite 202
    Charlotte, North Carolina, 29210, U.S.A.

MARC Office

Dr. Samuel Wilson, Director
    MARC
    919 W. Huntington Drive
    Monrovia, California, 91016, U.S.A.